BAZBALL

BAZBALL

The Inside Story of a Test Cricket Revolution

LAWRENCE BOOTH AND NICK HOULT

BLOOMSBURY PUBLISHING
LONDON · OXFORD · NEW YORK · NEW DELHI · SYDNEY

BLOOMSBURY PUBLISHING
Bloomsbury Publishing Plc
50 Bedford Square, London, WC1B 3DP, UK
29 Earlsfort Terrace, Dublin 2, Ireland

BLOOMSBURY, BLOOMSBURY PUBLISHING and the Diana logo are trademarks of
Bloomsbury Publishing Plc

First published in Great Britain 2023

All images supplied by Getty

A catalogue record for this book is available from the British Library

ISBN: HB: 978-1-5266-7208-7; eBook: 978-1-5266-7209-4; ePDF: 978-1-5266-7212-4

2 4 6 8 10 9 7 5 3 1

Typeset by Deanta Global Publishing Services, Chennai, India
Printed and bound in Great Britain by CPI Group (UK) Ltd, Croydon CR0 4YY

To find out more about our authors and books visit www.bloomsbury.com
and sign up for our newsletters

Contents

Introduction

Don't mention the B-word

On the first day of the fourth Test at Old Trafford in July 2023, jockey Clifford Lee rode to victory in the 2.30 at Bath. The horse in second – 'no match for winner', noted the *Racing Post* – finished two lengths back. And the winner itself? An Irish two-year-old, name of Bazball.

This was an unexpected answer to a question that cropped up regularly between the start of June 2022 and the end of the Ashes almost 14 months later: what is Bazball? Up in Manchester, England's batsmen spent the two days after Clifford Lee's triumph providing their own response by thrashing Australia for 592 at 5.49 an over. Zak Crawley hit 189 off 182 balls, and Jonny Bairstow 99 not out off 81, while four other members of the top seven passed 50, none sluggishly. Had rain not wiped out all but 30 overs of the last two days, England would have been well placed to square the Ashes series and set up a once-in-a-lifetime decider at The Oval.

Had a penny dropped for sceptical Australians? 'I get it now, this Bazball thing,' wrote Justin Langer, their former opening batsman and coach who is suspected of bleeding green and gold. 'We had heard about it, even been threatened by it. Now we have seen it with our own eyes, and I have to say, it was spectacular to watch.'

So spectacular, in fact, that – even before Langer's Eureka moment – Bazball had achieved what brand marketers call 'cut-through', transcending its normal sphere of influence. It wasn't just the 2.30 at Bath. On the Saturday of the Lord's Ashes Test, prime minister Rishi Sunak reckoned he had spotted similarities with his own captaincy of the Tories: 'You've got to give it to the team for what they've done, especially when they're essentially the same group of players with a different approach to playing and leadership,' he told *Test Match Special (TMS)*.

The *International Financing Review* suggested the Bank of England take a Bazball approach to interest rates to save the pound. A columnist for Christians in Sport drew biblical parallels with England's recapturing 'some of the joy that previously seemed lost'. He went on: 'Bazball may not be perfect. But it does offer us a fresh glimpse of how God designed both sport and his wider creation.' Less exaltedly, there was talk of Bazball cycling and Bazball tennis. In the week leading up to the fifth Test at The Oval, there were 339 mentions in the British press of 'Bazball' and its linguistic off-shoots. Could it be long before the *Oxford English Dictionary* paid attention?

The word seems to have been used first on a podcast for the ESPNcricinfo website on 24 May 2022, less than a fortnight after Brendon 'Baz' McCullum, once New Zealand's captain, had been confirmed as England's new coach. The first Test at Lord's against his compatriots was nine days away, and Andrew Miller – Cricinfo's UK editor – was telling listeners about the retention of Crawley and the promotion of Ollie Pope. 'Already you can sense there are mindset shifts going on,' he said. 'Obviously come the Headingley Test in late June it will be full-out total cricket and Bazball. Bring it on.' The podcast host, Alan Gardner, replied: 'Bazball sounds like it might be worth the entry fee.'

Miller later referred to the 2015 Lord's Test between England and New Zealand, when McCullum moved down a spot between innings from No 5 to No 6, to supervise a 'second wave of attack' as his team chased 345 on the last day. He had made the decision with New Zealand 12 for three. McCullum was bowled first ball by none other than Ben Stokes, but his golden duck was not the point. 'That was Bazball with New Zealand in mind,' said Miller, 'but it's probably going to be Bazball with England in mind now.'

The podcast episode was called 'Let's play... Baz-ball!' (No one uses the hyphen any more, while the second bit of punctuation was instantly redundant: Bazball has exclamation built into its fabric.) The word was picked up in the media and spread on Twitter. Soon, it was being used as a widely accepted code for aggressive batting, even if it lacked the precision of the only previous one-word description of an English Test strategy: Bodyline. This made Bazball open to abuse. To its supporters, it was everything the previous set-up, under Chris Silverwood and Joe Root, was not: vibrant, spontaneous, un-English. To its detractors, it was faddish and fraudulent, slogging dressed up in the emperor's new clothes. Test cricket needed reinvigorating, not reinventing. As one Pakistani journalist put it to Stokes in Karachi: 'Sixes are for one-dayers and T20. Aren't you ruining Test cricket?'

Miller says the phrase 'just came to me, obviously as a riff on baseball. I was in no doubt how McCullum's tenure would unfold: why else would he have got the job? The point is, it was clearly Bazball (not Benball), because he'd played Bazball himself as a player.'

In the second Test of that 2015 summer, New Zealand had travelled to Headingley and crashed 350 in 72.1 overs (McCullum 41 off 28 balls), then 454 for eight declared in 91, their overall run-rate a tick under five. They won by 199 runs, squaring the series. England had been Bazballed. But it was one thing for happy-go-lucky New Zealanders to express themselves, quite another for England, cricket's high priests of orthodoxy and self-anointed guardians of the game's spirit. No, an English Bazball was another matter altogether.

The idea for this book took seed on a sunny afternoon in Nottingham, where Jonny Bairstow went berserk during a run-chase against, inevitably, New Zealand. There was thrilling talk of 'running towards the danger', of casting aside thoughts of a draw – so often the height of English ambitions. As the world began to remove its Covid straitjacket, there was freedom in the air. Stokes had emerged from his own difficulties: a court case, the death of his father, exhaustion and injury. McCullum wanted to revivify Test cricket, a format under assault from the T20 franchises. And so the players were encouraged to think of themselves as entertainers, even rock stars – not as cricketers, with all the baggage that entails in a country obsessed with football. If Bazball sounded a bit theoretical, Bairstow's ferocious Trent Bridge hundred was the moment English cricket first put it into practice.

Plenty needed to happen to make the story worth telling, and plenty did. England whitewashed New Zealand, then the world Test champions. They knocked off a record target to stun India in the delayed fifth Test at Edgbaston. And they came from behind to beat South Africa, after the first wave of Bazball naysayers had cackled 'I told you so'. They went to

Pakistan, scored 506 for four from 75 overs on the first day, and did what no touring team had ever done, winning 3–0. For the first time, they won a pink-ball floodlit Test abroad, hammering New Zealand at Mount Maunganui. Even when they lost the next game, at Wellington, by one run – having enforced the follow-on rather than pragmatically bat again – they were box office.

Everyone had a view on Bazball. And not all of it was positive, despite the fact that victory over Ireland at Lord's in the build-up to the Ashes had left England with 11 wins out of 13, and a run-rate of 4.85. Perhaps critics had forgotten what had come before: one win out of 17, a run-rate of 2.89, a sense of atrophy and decay.

McCullum hated the phrase, partly because he felt it was a crude distillation of the strategy, partly because he resented a descriptor that placed him in the shop window. When he was asked by Sky's pundits after the home series against New Zealand what he thought Bazball was, he replied with a chortle: 'I don't know what Bazball is. You tell me.' Throughout his tenure, he has been a reluctant spokesman, preferring his players to do the talking, on and off the pitch. He also rejected the idea of copying Langer's Australians and allowing the Amazon Prime cameras into the dressing-room during the Ashes. Perhaps he regarded his philosophy as Walter Bagehot once regarded the monarchy: 'Its mystery is its life. We must not let in daylight upon magic.' The players, meanwhile, thought 'Bazball' reflected a media misunderstanding: they were not, they complained, sloggers. The media knew this, but relished the shorthand, which eased communication with the public.

An uneasy truce set in, though England eventually had to concede that the phrase had struck a chord with the people. And despite their emphasis on shutting out the noise, of which there was much, they also acknowledged the importance of turning heads. By the start of the 2023 season, Root – who had flourished in the 15 months since relinquishing the captaincy – explained Bazball's place in the dressing-room's affections. 'It is not a well-liked phrase,' he told us. 'But the great thing about it is that it has been more for the public. They are starting to see there might be another way of playing Test cricket.'

How not well liked was it really? Later that summer, the cricket photographer Philip Brown designed a badge, depicting McCullum in his ubiquitous shades wearing a grin and throwing a ball in the air above the words 'Let's Bazball'. Brown ordered 100 and slipped them to the players. Knowing McCullum's views on the matter, Root would grab a handful and leave them in McCullum's golf bag. Bazball had gone meta: a compliment used to irritate the man it was named after.

But what *was* Bazball? It meant freedom of expression, sure, but beyond that? Was it simply a group of talented cricketers applying a white-ball attitude to the red-ball arena? Was it a skilful con trick, persuading the players that none of it mattered, while suppressing the suspicion that, deep down, it really did? Perhaps it smacked of an amateur-era arrogance, the plaything of one of cricket's most privileged set-ups, a team that could *afford* not to fear failure? Was it a dereliction of duty, the easy way out, the pinnacle of 'this is how we play'? Was it more like a cult, with charismatic leaders selling snake oil to gullible disciples? Or was it, as someone once said of the Conservative Party, more an instinct than an idea, a term so indefinable as to mean whatever its practitioners chose?

While following the Test team around the UK and abroad, we asked the players themselves. In 18 Bazball Tests so far, 24 have been selected. Only Stokes, Root and Crawley have been ever-present, though Pope would no doubt have joined them had he not dislocated a shoulder during the Ashes. Almost every one of them agreed to reflect on their experiences, cheerfully sharing stories about golf in Scotland, Formula One in Abu Dhabi, sickness in Rawalpindi, sledging in the Ashes and sometimes even a bit of cricket.

England's Test team, long reluctant to shoot from the hip, began to fire a few bullets. Root, for one, was happy to tell us about the impact the new approach was having on opponents: 'People have said you won't be able to do that in the subcontinent, or against us. Well, let's see. South Africa said the same thing against their attack. A lot of people thought it would be impossible in Pakistan, because it spins. We managed to play good stuff in New Zealand against a top bowling side too. It will be interesting to see if it takes off with other teams.'

This last point encouraged the view that England were in danger of getting preachy, which hooked into an old stereotype, and may explain why some – particularly outside the UK – took against Bazball. When Australia arrived to defend the Ashes, an age-old rivalry came with a new twist: irritated that their opponents were attracting the headlines, Pat Cummins's team – who had just beaten India in the final of the World Test Championship at The Oval – set about restating the case for the Australian Way. A clash of cultures ensued: England made the running, Australia tried to trip them up. Thanks to a fittingly thrilling final day, it finished 2–2. This book includes the story of one of the most remarkable Ashes of all time, a series on a par with 1981 and 2005.

As with those two summers, 2023 grabbed the attention of cricket agnostics. Time and again, a group of players who had spent their entire England careers behind Sky's satellite paywall – Jimmy Anderson was the exception – said they felt more recognised in the streets, in greater demand for selfies and autographs. The ECB had thrown millions at The Hundred in the hope of attracting a new demographic to a sport always teetering on existential crisis. Yet here were the Test team doing the job for them.

When England won the third Test at Headingley, an average viewership of 965,000 tuned into Sky's coverage across the four days – which broke the channel's previous record, achieved during the first Test at Edgbaston. It was also 56 per cent up on the third Test of the 2019 Ashes, also at Headingley, where Stokes had turned water into wine. On the fourth day of the 2023 Headingley Test, where England completed a three-wicket win, Sky's audience peaked at 2.05 million, despite competing with the British Grand Prix and the men's final at Wimbledon. And when rain wiped out the last day in Manchester, *TMS* said they had five times as many listeners as the last day of the Open golf championship at Hoylake. With the women's Ashes taking place at the same time, and producing its own sequence of thrillers as England shared the series on points, a total of 17.8 million were said to have watched both series either live on Sky or via the BBC's highlights.

England were clearly doing something right. But, again: what *were* they doing? Of all the players we asked to define Bazball, the most succinct answer came from Stuart Broad. Wearing the blue bucket hat that became England's sartorial leitmotif, and was bought by nearly 10,000 fans, he says: 'It is a mentality to get the most freedom and attacking style of play out of you, while loving cricket as much as you can.'

Anderson, his new-ball compadre, expands on the theme. 'It is trying to remember why you started playing the game.

As a kid, you went down to your local club and wanted to hit fours and sixes and knock the stumps out of the ground. You wanted to take the diving catch. When you play international cricket there is pressure, and that can be stifling. Bazball is trying to encourage people to get back to that kid in you, and imagine back to when you started watching cricket and what you wanted to see. How you imagined the game would be played: exciting, fast and fun. That is what Bazball is to me.'

Chris Woakes was a latecomer, not playing under McCullum until Headingley against Australia. 'The best way to describe it, I suppose, is we try to play expansively, but try not to be reckless. Some people will see it as reckless, but we try to push the boundaries as close to reckless as possible. The entertainment side of it is a big thing – to make sure we're putting bums on seats.'

Moeen Ali retired from Test cricket in September 2021, but was so taken by what he had seen that he answered Stokes's SOS message when England's first-choice spinner, Jack Leach, injured his back after the Test against Ireland. 'When you speak to Baz and Stokesy, there is no Bazball,' he says. 'But I think it means a lot of things. It is about doing everything for the team – being selfless, then going out there and applying pressure when it needs applying, and soaking up pressure with the bat when it needs soaking up. Bowling-wise, it is about taking 20 wickets as quick as possible. And playing with a smile on your face. If you do that well, the results take care of themselves. You might not have a team of world beaters, but if you stick to those methods you will beat any team in the world. That is what it is to me.' After playing in four of the five Ashes Tests, Moeen retired again, even more fulfilled than he had been first time round.

Harry Brook struggles to articulate his answer, perhaps because Bazball comes so naturally to him as to preclude analysis. 'Good question,' he says. 'What does Bazball mean? The coach doesn't like the phrase. It's banned in the dressing-room. Nobody uses it. For me it means... ha ha... well... oh God, great question! If you asked people in the pub, they would say you smack it. But for us it is a bit different. As a batting group, when you get an opportunity to score you take it and don't hold back. You go hard at them. You're not out there to survive. Bazball is about the team, not yourself. And enjoying each other's success.'

What wasn't to like? Then again, we can't say we weren't warned. Back in early May 2022, no one had heard of Bazball. But Rob Key, the ECB's managing director of men's cricket, had just appointed McCullum, and knew change was coming. 'Time for us all to buckle up,' he said, 'and get ready for the ride.' He didn't know the half of it.

I

Different strokes

It was approaching 6.30 on a sunny Monday evening in late July when Stuart Broad ran in to bowl to Alex Carey at The Oval. One of the most memorable of all Test series was about to come to an end. A month earlier, on a dramatic final day of the second Test, north of the river at Lord's, Broad had taunted Carey, telling him he would only ever be remembered for the stumping of Jonny Bairstow, who had ducked under a bouncer from Cameron Green, wrongly assumed the ball was dead at the end of the over, and strolled off for a chat with his partner, Ben Stokes. A split second earlier, with the ball very much alive, Carey had rolled it towards the stumps, having noticed Bairstow's tendency to wander quickly from his crease. It was cricket's most famous underarm – though England preferred 'underhand' – since Greg Chappell instructed his brother Trevor to roll the last ball of a one-day international at Melbourne along the ground in February 1981, denying New Zealand's Brian McKechnie a shot at the six that would have secured a tie. If ever a scorecard entry failed to tell the whole story, 'Bairstow st Carey b Green 10' was surely it.

Yet as the two teams went their separate ideological ways – England invoking cricket's spirit, Australia citing its laws – the gap on the field began to narrow. England still went 2–0 down, a position from which Australia had never failed to win a series. But Stokes had given them an almighty fright with a furious innings of 155, adding 108 for the eighth wicket with a pumped-up Broad, who spent two hours causing mayhem and delivering lectures on sportsmanship, without irony, to anyone close enough to listen. After Australia won by 43 runs, Brendon McCullum said, with a smile that meant business: 'Three–two has a nice ring to it.'

At Headingley, England pulled one back, thanks to potent interventions from Chris Woakes and Mark Wood, both fresh to the series, and bowling with high skill in one case, high pace in the other; they would finish with 33 wickets between them at just 19 each. And at Old Trafford, England were on course to make it 2–2, only for rain to fall on their parade. The Australians had retained the urn but, after drawing in England four years earlier, and not won there at all since 2001, they still craved a series victory; their celebrations in Manchester were as muted as they were damp.

In English circles, meanwhile, talk was growing of the 'Moral Ashes', a tabloid concoction that nonetheless hooked into the national mood. For the Australians, already irritated by the Spirit of Cricket hoo-ha at Lord's, English sanctimony was getting out of control. But, by Moral Ashes logic, victory for England at The Oval would represent more than a sporting comeback: it would be a realignment of the cosmic order after the weather gods had come to Australia's aid. The urn might have passed England by for the fourth series in a row, but justice remained up for grabs. The Ashes seemed to be taking place on some higher plane, both cricketing and philosophical. Or had it become a self-parody, full of rabble-rousing and nonsense? No one could say for sure. Besides, they were all having too much fun.

The fortunes of Carey and Bairstow, too, had begun to diverge. In the first Test at Edgbaston, Bairstow had won points for a run-a-ball 78, then lost them for a creaking display behind the stumps; Carey had made 66, and kept neatly. When he exploited Bairstow's perambulation at Lord's, it seemed clear which of the wicketkeepers would end up on the winning side. But the plummy boos and catcalls led by MCC members unwilling to respect the laws written by their own club seemed to play on Carey's mind. Broad's sledge added to the sense he was a marked man. Australia's captain Pat Cummins spent the press conference after Lord's, and those both before and after Headingley, fending off suggestions he ought to have recalled Bairstow. A charming man, he began to look strained; polite engagement gave way to tetchy monosyllables; and, no, he said, the momentum after the third Test was not with England.

Lost in translation across the cultural divide was the fact that almost all cricket in England below Test level, and almost no cricket in Australia at any level, is played according to some notion of the game's spirit. The two teams might as well have been speaking a different language, encouraging each side's fans to brandish old stereotypes as if they were new, wounding witticisms: it was no longer England v Australia but Whingeing Poms v Cheating Aussies. And yet it was England, nursing grievance while Australia battled bemusement, who emerged from the farrago with a greater sense of purpose.

At Headingley, Carey was bumped on the helmet by Wood, and twice fell cheaply. In one of the more bizarre pieces of instant Ashes folklore, he was even wrongly accused by

Alastair Cook on *Test Match Special* of failing to pay £30 for a haircut in Leeds city centre. Bairstow remained flaky with the gloves, but was all bristle, waiting for his chance to do what he does best, and prove a point. At Old Trafford, the chance came. After holding a one-handed blinder to dismiss Mitchell Marsh, he smashed 99 not out as England came close to 600. Then came The Oval, where Carey dropped Harry Brook five runs into his eventual 85, and Bairstow made 78. Finally, on the last day, as Australia began to stumble in a daunting chase of 384, he flung himself to his right to take a smart catch off Marsh's inside edge and pad.

With the Australians nine down and 50 short of victory, Carey faced Broad, who 48 hours earlier had announced the Test would be his 167th and last, and was gearing up for a Hollywood ending. In his previous over, Carey had edged towards second slip, where Zak Crawley's right hand couldn't grasp a tough, low chance. Now, Broad drew Carey forward, kissing the outside edge, which was easily pocketed by Bairstow. Such a narrative-filled Ashes had seemed to demand not only that Broad should claim the decisive wicket, but that Carey would provide it and Bairstow confirm it.

As The Oval erupted, comparisons with 2005, aired even before the first ball at Edgbaston, went into overdrive. Back then, an England draw had confirmed a series win; this time, a win had rescued a draw. The comparisons – and cricket does like a comparison – were understandable. If 2005 had been the last Ashes to take place on free-to-air TV, uniting a nation that didn't always love the sport but lapped up the pleasure of a long-awaited victory over Australia, 2023 was England's highest-profile series since Sky's money changed the landscape. And if, man for man, Michael Vaughan's class of '05 had the edge, Ben Stokes's team were trying to change the way Test cricket was played. This series also had four close games to 2005's three. Before 2023, only 28 of the previous 356 Tests between the countries had been decided by margins of 50 runs or fewer, or three wickets or fewer. In 2023, it was four out of five. The only one-sided game was the one that didn't produce a result – a typical piece of illogic in a series full of it.

The Oval had shaped up as a kind of referendum not just on Bazball itself, but on the competing merits of Australia's more traditional approach, which five days before Edgbaston had earned them the title of world Test champions. Ashes cricket had always been competitive. At stake this time, it seemed, were more than runs, wickets and Anglo-Aussie bragging rights, but the future of Test cricket – how to play it, nurture it and leave it in good health for the next generation.

This wasn't simply English vainglory: nations outside the so-called Big Three of India, England and Australia were fast losing interest in Tests, preferring to set up T20 franchise tournaments. And while the Big Three's administrators were not helping matters by arranging marquee series among themselves, largely to the exclusion of everyone else, the players could at least make a point of their own. The English players, that is. Australia could not have adopted Bazball even if they had wanted to: a top four containing Usman Khawaja, Marnus Labuschagne and Steve Smith was geared towards a different tempo. David Warner once had the game to score freely but was faltering towards the end of a long career. Travis Head, the lone Australian batsman whose aggression made Stokes wary, couldn't do it all by himself. Marsh scored a run-a-ball hundred, but only after sitting out the first two Tests.

England wanted to inspire the kids by exploring a new way. Australia, a country where cricket has rarely faced the same existential angst, were content to consolidate the old.

As the show headed for The Oval, there seemed no middle ground, little scope for compromise. Channelling the Ashes' foundation story, one Australian website idly wondered: 'Will Bazball die at The Oval like English cricket did in 1882?'

Yet while England focused on their own game, it was Australia who adapted theirs – and from the word go, starting with a deep point for the first ball at Edgbaston. No matter: Crawley thrashed Cummins for four, setting the tone not only for a series in which he finally repaid the faith of his captain and coach, but in which England never relented. By the end of the Oval Test, they had scored at 4.74 an over – their fastest-ever Ashes – and Australia at 3.35, the biggest gap in any series between the countries. It amounted to a difference of 125 runs across a notional 90-over day, not that either side were troubled by anything so trivial as over-rates: both were later docked World Test Championship points for falling miles behind.

Even with Australia generally batting against fields designed to take wickets, and England generally batting against fields designed to stop fours, it was England who found the boundary more regularly: Australia hit 339 fours at a rate of one every 15 balls, England 304 at a rate of one every 12. The statistical analysts CricViz, who are also responsible for the WinViz predictor that aims to keep viewers abreast of a game's undulations, calculated that England had fared better than Australia while playing defensively. According to their number-crunchers, Australia lost a wicket every 48 balls to defensive strokes, which produced a batting average of 7, and England every 67 balls, with an average of 13. This wasn't a huge surprise to those who had read Bazball's fine print, with its emphasis on absorbing pressure when necessary, but it seemed counter-intuitive all the same.

Meanwhile, Australia's tactics – with three, four or more men regularly patrolling the fence – also gave England the chance to work the ball around, and they took advantage, scoring 1,009 singles, at a rate of 1.55 an over. England's tactics, with more men close in more often, limited Australia to 770 singles, at 0.85 an over. The numbers challenged the assumption that Bazball couldn't survive without fours and sixes (though on the second measure, England outhit Australia by 43 to 31).

Less surprising was the number of deliveries from which both sides failed to score: England 2,389, Australia 4,097. In other words, Australia faced nearly 285 overs more of dot-balls, or the equivalent of nine-and-a-half 30-over sessions. Their bowlers sent down a grand total of 34 maidens, comfortably a new low for a five-Test series. Yet while records were being broken, the 2–2 scoreline seemed to confirm one of the series' most frequently heard clichés – that there is more than one way to skin a cat. True enough, though one team was having more fun skinning it than the other.

The starkest contrast came at the top of the order, where Crawley and Khawaja were Aesop's hare and tortoise. Crawley finished with 480 runs at 53 and a strike-rate of 88, Khawaja with 496 at 49 and a strike-rate of 39. While scoring only 16 more runs than Crawley, Khawaja had faced 722 more balls, the equivalent of 120 overs. Among top-seven batsmen on either side, Crawley was the fastest, Khawaja the slowest. Yet they reached roughly the same destination via diametrically opposed routes – Crawley speeding down the new toll road, Khawaja stopping to smell the flowers along the coast. Crawley played the series' most thrilling innings, 189 off 182 balls at Old Trafford; Khawaja kept reeling off its most pleasing shot, the on-drive, with gentle timing and an easy break of the wrist. Each offered an exaggerated version of his team's predilections; neither finished on the winning side. The discrepancy captured the ideological battle.

At the end of the series, Cummins dismissed the idea that a bowler's run-rate was worth losing sleep over. Again, he could point to his side's retention of the urn. But if you lined up the bowlers in order of economy-rate, starting with the most expensive, the top nine were Australian. No Australian who bowled more than a single over went at a rate below four, no Englishman at more than 3.67.

Across a five-match series, this would normally mean only one winner. Without Manchester's monsoon, England knew that winner would probably have been them. But in the two Tests the Australians won, they did the basics better – unlike England, they held their catches, and didn't take wickets with no-balls. They also seized the moment. At Edgbaston, they needed 54 with two wickets left, and got over the line; at Lord's, they reacted to Nathan Lyon's series-ending injury by bowling bouncers, a trap into which England readily fell. Australia could also argue that Stokes's counter-attack merely massaged the margin of England's inevitable defeat.

So why did their 2–0 lead – a deficit from which England had salvaged a draw only once, under Len Hutton in the Caribbean in 1953–54 – feel so fragile? England told themselves they had made all the running at Edgbaston, and in a sense they were right. They declared at 393 for eight on the first evening, a decision whose significance was overplayed, mainly in hindsight; and they scored so quickly that bad weather on the third day did not preclude a result. Australia grabbed on to their coat-tails and pinched the game late on – the act of a savvy, battle-hardened side delighted to dampen Bazball's spirits. Then, at Lord's, England got into a muddle against the short ball, and left themselves with too much to do.

They refreshed their attack with Wood and Woakes for Headingley, and vowed to play more smartly, not that they would admit it in public, with Stokes giving short shrift to press-conference questions offering an alternative view. Even at Headingley, though, Australia looked set for a 3–0 lead when England went into lunch on the second day at 142 for seven in reply to 236. But Wood smacked 24 off eight balls on the resumption, and Stokes dragged his side close to Australia's total with five sixes off Todd Murphy, Lyon's young replacement. From there until the end of the series, they mainly kept control, despite Australia's brave chase at The Oval.

To the last, there were squabbles, each heightened by what had gone before. On the fourth afternoon of the fifth Test, with Australia's openers progressing smoothly, umpires Joel Wilson and Kumar Dharmasena changed the ball because it had gone out of shape after Wood hit Khawaja on the helmet. Rain fell soon after, which meant the behaviour of its replacement could not be fully gauged until the morning. To Australia's chagrin, Woakes made it sing, quickly removing Warner and Khawaja; Wood added Labuschagne. It was true that the new ball looked redder and shinier than its predecessor, but while Ricky Ponting fulminated in the commentary box, and demanded an investigation, Smith and Head moved calmly to 264 for three: far from unplayable, then. Not until Moeen Ali and Woakes teamed up did Australia crumble.

An hour after England completed victory, McCullum – the New Zealander who had once lacked skin in the Ashes game – sat before the media in The Oval's cavernous indoor school, and answered the inevitable question: was his team's comeback vindication of their approach? 'Look, we have a certain style we try and exhibit every time we play,' he said. 'Obviously early in the series, Australia were good enough to stand up in their own way against us, and be successful. From our point of view, the most pleasing aspect is, when we were under the most pressure at 2–0 down, we stayed true to that and were able to manufacture some results that allowed us to walk away at 2–2. I think, for us, that is our best chance of winning. The skipper and I firmly believe that, and some of the performances we've seen from some of the guys is testament to that.'

McCullum also confronted an issue that had simmered throughout his tenure, but only become pertinent after they lost the first two Tests – the idea that England cared more about entertaining than winning. For many fans, this had been just about tolerable after the one-run defeat by New Zealand at Wellington a few months earlier. But against Australia? Some of the messaging, it's true, could have been clearer. Ollie Robinson's claim, for instance, that England felt as if they had won at Edgbaston made them look deluded. At 2–0 down in the Ashes, the last thing fans wanted to hear was that their team cared more about the process than the outcome.

And there had also been scepticism over the recall of Moeen, who had long retired from Test cricket, and bowled only seven overs on the decisive last day at Edgbaston because of a blister. This was all cannon fodder for the Australians, who already thought England's approach slightly barmy. Now they were talking like madmen too. That Moeen smeared Manuka honey on his damaged finger, before being granted his request to bat at No 3, a position he had last occupied five years earlier, summed up the other-worldliness of these Ashes.

England, though, wanted to win very much: after Edgbaston, where Stokes had so nearly caught Lyon,

Australia's No 10, with 37 still needed for victory, he said he was 'gutted' – and looked it too, as you would expect from one of the most competitive cricketers ever to play the game. That miss remained his only moment of regret of the series, or at least the only one he would share. But England had long realised that the pursuit of entertainment would produce positive cricket. And with the players at their disposal, this meant a greater chance of victory. The desire to put bums on seats was genuine in its own right, as was England's concern for Test cricket's future. But, despite their repeated insistence that they were not a 'results-driven side', they also knew entertainment gave them the best chance of victory.

As McCullum put it: 'Look, you're always trying to win, right? You just don't want to be bogged down in key moments by the result. What we are trying to do is allow ourselves to get in a space in our own minds where your talent can come out. If you're weighed down by fear of failure or by external noise, all you're doing is suffocating that talent. So it's as simple as that. For us, entertainment is a big part of it. But, for sure, we want to win. Sometimes we'll get the balance wrong with the style we play. But I think we refined it slightly as the series wore on.'

This last point was central to England's fightback, just as Eoin Morgan had finessed the all-out aggression of his white-ball sides. Brook, for instance, shelved the pulling and hooking that had caused his downfall at Lord's, and shepherded England to victory at Headingley. And Stokes reinforced the example of when to attack and when to defend. At Lord's, he declined to get sucked into Australia's bouncer tactics, only to fall to Mitchell Starc's second ball the following morning. But he knew exactly when to press the trigger: at the fall of England's sixth wicket in the second innings of that game, because Broad was as high as No 8; and at the fall of the eighth at Headingley, where he thrashed 52 of the 60 added for the last two wickets.

Stokes faced criticism for his first-evening declaration at Edgbaston, but was the more proactive leader, and didn't endure a meltdown of the kind suffered by Cummins at Manchester, where England unleashed the full force of their batting arsenal; for one painful afternoon, it seemed impossible to be both captain and fast bowler at the same time. In fact, England didn't once suffer the kind of horror collapse that had pockmarked their 2021–22 Ashes campaign. Their lowest total in nine innings was 237, which would have been their fourth-highest 18 months earlier. On five occasions in 2023, they passed 300, having not done so at all in 2021–22. If anything, their most disappointing passages of play came with the ball, allowing Australia's lower order off the hook at Edgbaston, then bowling poorly in helpful conditions on the first day at Lord's, where Australia at one stage reached 316 for three. And if Stokes had any kind of blind spot, it was his repeated faith in Jimmy Anderson, who managed five wickets all series at 85 each and looked nearer than Broad to the end of a magnificent career.

England had won the toss at Lord's, as they did in each of the first four Tests, persuading some to argue they enjoyed the better of conditions. At times, they did, not least when they delivered a decisive spell with the ball under glowering skies on the third afternoon at Headingley. But Australia had their luck too, removing Crawley and Ben Duckett in near-apocalyptic darkness on the third afternoon at Edgbaston, then seeing their prayers for rain answered in spectacular fashion in Manchester. The overwrought reactions to these slings and arrows told of a mutual parochialism which seemed pettier than in previous series. In *The Times*, Gideon Haigh – the English-born Australian writer with a foot in both camps – suggested 'this England feels a coarser, meaner, nastier place than even four years ago'. The Australian team, for their part, could be quick to take offence, apparently forgetting the treatment doled out to visiting teams by their own fans.

Overall, Stokes ended the series by giving Bazball a clean bill of health. 'If you look at the success over the amount of games we've played, the style obviously works,' he said. 'We've been very successful. Criticism is part and parcel of everything you do, but the most important views and opinions are the ones around me.'

If the dismissal of external viewpoints seemed slightly at odds with England's desire for connection, then his diagnosis of Bazball felt valid. In the 18 Tests since it began, England had won 13 and drawn only in rainy Manchester. Of their four defeats, one had been by a run, another by two wickets, a third by 43 runs. The last two had come against the world champions.

The Ashes remained with Australia, but Stokes was not despondent. 'I think 2–2 is genuinely a fair reflection of two very, very good teams going at it over a five-match series. Being 2–0 down is a very hard task to come back from, so to be able to say we've levelled the series… The game in Manchester was obviously affected by the rain, but it is what it is. Coming here and playing the way we did, I couldn't be any more proud of the team. We continued everything in the style of play we have over the last 15 months, and it's been everything I could have asked for – minus getting the urn back.'

Then there was the bigger picture. 'Over the last seven weeks in particular, we've managed to drag a new audience towards Test cricket,' he said. 'This series is genuinely what

Test cricket needed. Two high-quality teams going at it toe-to-toe, and the cricket has been something you couldn't take your eyes off. Every session has been its own game. We've been in control, then Australia have been in control. Everyone who's bought a ticket has really enjoyed their days of cricket. I really hope we've inspired a new generation. I look back to 2005 and what that series did for me as a young person, and I really hope there's someone who's the age I was then and says: "That's what I want to be doing when I'm 21 or 22."'

Partly, England were relieved that 2–0 hadn't turned into something worse, including question marks about Bazball's validity. But there was disappointment too that they had been denied the chance to become only the second team, after Don Bradman's 1936–37 Australians, to win a Test series from two down. Back then, Bradman had masterminded the recovery himself, in successive Tests scoring 270 from No 7 after reversing the batting order on a sticky dog at Melbourne, followed by 212 and 169. But with the exception of Walter Hammond and Hedley Verity, his English opponents lacked star quality. Stokes's team faced an Australian side who began the series with the top three in the ICC's batting rankings – Labuschagne, Smith and Head – and the world's best seam attack, supplemented by Lyon, one of the game's greatest off-spinners. Most of the pre-series predictions from Australian pundits made bad reading for England. A plethora of 3–2 predictions among their English counterparts felt like hopeful retaliation.

'We look at the growth of the team in the last 14 to 15 months as being quite significant,' said McCullum. 'You look back when the skipper took over: would we be able to take on a great Australian team – and they are a great Australian team – and go toe-to-toe with them? I think the answer is yes, and that's a tremendous confidence booster for the group, but also testament to the investment in all the guys who have really gone quids in with their belief in this side and the direction the skipper wants it to head. I think both sides have stayed true to their styles and that's what makes a great heavyweight fight. It's two different styles – and total conviction in them.'

McCullum had annoyed Australia after Lord's, suggesting his players wouldn't be sharing a beer with them any time soon because of the Bairstow stumping. After The Oval, he was asked if that had changed. With a sheepish grin, he said it had, though that didn't stop the Australian media later claiming England had snubbed their attempts to have that drink. In fact, England were simply finishing off their dressing-room presentations. By the time they sent a delegation to sort out the beer, the Australians had returned to their hotel. Well after 4 a.m., Stokes clarified the situation on Twitter: the two teams had reconvened in a Soho nightclub.

Not for the first time, England and Australia had taken different routes to the same destination.

Us against the world

Waterloo Street in South Dunedin, on New Zealand's South Island, is perfect for a game of cricket between two competitive brothers. The road has a camber, but it's barely noticeable, so the bounce is true. And it is wide enough for kids to play without worrying too much about denting a car when they swing a bat. Hitting straight brings the greatest reward, which could be why Brendon McCullum became so strong smacking sixes down the ground. Perhaps Bazball started right here, on a suburban street built on reclaimed land called the 'Flat', comprising what Wikipedia calls 'lower-quality residential properties', and nestled below the posh houses up on the hills, with their commanding views of the beaches and out towards the Southern Ocean. The neat, detached, corrugated-roofed clapboard houses, with their postage-stamp front gardens, some boasting small driveways, huddle together against the southerly wind that whips off St Clair Beach, one of the area's best surfing spots, across Forbury Park race track, and up the gently rising Waterloo Street.

The area was formed from part of old Forbury Park, a trots racetrack where a young McCullum would bunk over the fence and fell in love with horses and betting. The streets are named after battles involving Britain – Trafalgar, Nile, Corunna, Alma, Montreal. McCullum lived on Waterloo. It was here, in this working-class neighbourhood in the late 1980s, when there were fewer parked cars than there are today, that Brendon and his brother Nathan – another future international cricketer – would play with a hard ball, at least when the Scottish mist allowed. In fact, they would play anywhere. From the age of four, Brendon would go down to Logan Park in the city centre, play with his mum and friends, before heading for Culling Park to watch his dad, Stuart, turn out for Albion Cricket Club. Then it would be back home, where he would repeat the matches in the front of the house.

More than 30 years later, Colleen Beaumont, a long-term resident of Waterloo Street, can still picture the scene. 'Oh, yeah, I remember them. There were these two little boys playing in the street with real bats and balls, and it was so funny because my next-door neighbour at the time used to freak out. He had a huge front window, and he used to say: "Colleen, I'm surprised we have not lost our windows. Have you seen the ball those little boys are hitting around the street?" Little Brendon would hit the ball hard, and it would make such a crack, but do you know what? He never broke a single window.

'When Brendon played for New Zealand, I would say to the girls at work: "Look, I live on a famous street." But Brendon always says he is a boy from South Dunedin. It is lovely to hear him say that. It is a big reality check. You can come from anywhere and do really well. He is just an ordinary lad from an ordinary street.'

McCullum has always talked proudly of his blue-collar roots, and of how his family made do with what they had, which wasn't much. The boys even supplemented their pocket money by doing odd jobs for neighbours. 'Their dad brought the two boys over one day and said if I needed someone to mow the lawn, they would do it for me,' says Colleen. 'They were so shy, barely looking up at me and saying: "Oh, Dad."' McCullum remembers his dad, who played for Otago, as a willing twelfth man, since he liked being around the boys. He lived for a 'pint, a bet and a durry [cigarette]'.

Stuart was frequently away with work as a salesman. Brendon's mother, Jan, did not work due to a repetitive strain injury, and shouldered the responsibility of bringing up the boys. Nathan was often ill as a child – he was nicknamed 'mattress', because of the time he spent in bed – and Brendon talks of resenting the attention he would receive from their mother. But the boys were close and, had Brendon visited Waterloo Street all these decades later, and walked into the house in which he grew up, he might have smiled at the sight of two brothers, around the same age as he and Nathan when they lived there, playing in the back garden.

The current owner of No 11 knew vaguely of its link to the McCullums, and with his boys gave a tour of the house. Standing in McCullum's boyhood bedroom, the one he shared with Nathan, feels slightly like stalking his past, but by walking the ground you understand your subject better. And it is illuminating to make the short journey from Waterloo Street to Albion CC, where he first made his mark on the field. 'It really was quite tight-knit,' says Richard Boock, who also grew up in South Dunedin, before becoming a cricket journalist, then the head of corporate affairs for New Zealand Cricket. 'It was us against the rest of the world. Everyone knows each other really well.'

It is a 15-minute stroll past the local ice-skating rink, along the beachside road to Culling Park where Albion have played for more than 150 years. The club is famous throughout New Zealand, and there is a boy standing next to the Albion CC sign on Royal Crescent posing for a photograph for his dad. Albion fourths are playing a T20 game; cricketers, girlfriends and mates are sprawled on the grass, while Phil Morris chats about coaching the nine-year-old McCullum and attempts to grab glimpses of his son, Chris, out in the middle. Chris scores 101, and wins the game shortly after his dad leaves.

Phil played to a decent standard himself, reaching first-class level for Otago, and was an Albion teammate of Stuart McCullum. Stuart now lives in Christchurch and is remembered fondly at Albion for his love of a good time and being great company in the small clubhouse after play, as well as an attacking batsman who taught his boys the game. He was a good wicketkeeper, as was his brother Grant. Keeping is in the McCullums' DNA.

'When I was playing senior cricket here, the kids would be outside hitting balls and playing cricket,' says Phil. 'We always made sure the seniors joined up with the kids and had a good wee bash for an hour with them. They would talk to you by first name, and it was a real family feel. We always felt the kids would improve playing with us, the men's first team.'

It is a childhood experience McCullum shares with Ben Stokes. He too grew up in a sporting family: his father, Ged, coached professional rugby league sides. McCullum and Stokes were immersed in dressing-room life and culture from childhood, so progressing through the age grades was less daunting. Playing alongside men as a child may break a lot of health and safety rules now, but back then it was part of the process of improving a junior player's understanding of the game – the young boys learning off the seniors. The *Otago Times* snapped what would become a famous photograph of the McCullum boys leading Albion off the field, with Stuart in his wicketkeeping pads and gloves looking on proudly after his sons had helped win a game. Rifling through a few photo albums strewn around the clubhouse, Morris finds the one he wants.

'Brendon played the odd senior game when we were short. He would only have been ten or 12, but he was just a magic wicketkeeper. I remember one game, a President's XI match. The first ball went way out wide, zinging down the leg side. The batsman tried to get hold of it and put it in the bowling green next door but missed it altogether, and next thing there was a rattle of the stumps and Brendon had taken a stumping first ball. I remember the look of disbelief on the batsman's face as he walked back with a duck quacking in his head. It was one of the funniest things to happen in the five years I coached.

'Brendon was a keeper, but a casual sort of batsman then. When he changed from being keeper to batter he really had to work on it because it was not as strong as his keeping. He was brave, all right. If he could, he would stand up to stumps. He was fearless. He made the bowlers look good. Stuart would always make Brendon play with a light bat because he wanted him to play his strokes. And he has never looked back, playing with that attacking intent. His dad did all the background work on his character. I did not need to coach Brendon much. He probably coached me because it was the start of my coaching career and I had a lot to learn. He moved on to the Metro Dunedin team very early, from the age of ten or so, and played with older boys. He was always ahead of the game.'

Albion is the oldest continuous cricket club in Australasia, its history stretching back to 1862. It does not have a flash, ornate clubhouse, its modesty in keeping with the roots of the area. The pavilion is small, the carpet worn and the walls covered with clippings, old bats and photographs. It is a welcoming place, the hub of the community. There are meat pies in a glass cabinet in the corner, and a crate of beers in an Esky waiting for the players to finish their game.

Every inch is covered in memorabilia, and the club counts among its alumni five New Zealand captains, which is why the McCullums have only a small corner dedicated to their achievements. Ken Rutherford, Bert Sutcliffe, Glenn Turner and Andrew Jones are all Albion old boys, and their pads, blazers and kit are everywhere, nailed to posts, stuck on doorways, leaning against the wall. Piles of photo albums and scrapbooks of newspaper clippings going back decades are piled high on bookshelves.

'A few years ago, the sponsors of the Black Caps gave an award for the man of the match,' says Tony Buchanan, the club's secretary. 'I think it was about $500, and Brendon said: "Give it to Albion." The next week, West Indies won the game and whoever the player was thought for a minute and said: "Give it to the Albion Cricket Club in Dunedin," because Brendon had given them the word. He used to come around the end of the season and give his kit to the boys, but the problem was he is so bloody small, and our guys are pretty big. He was always a very aggressive player. It was in his nature, in his personality. He is full bore.'

Albion, another step on the road for Bazball.

A couple of blocks north of Waterloo Street is King's High School, where there is now a McCullum Family High Performance Cricket Centre, marking the contribution made by the school's most famous sporting old boys. King's lacked the facilities of Otago Boys School up the hill, but when McCullum joined as a 13-year-old, the geography teacher and cricket coach, John Cushen, spotted talent – as well as a personality that would need a guiding hand. Cushen, who had a long career as a fast bowler for Otago and Auckland, once dismissing Geoffrey Boycott, misread the young Brendon early on.

'I tell you what, the key reason he has done so well and played cricket the way he has is because he didn't listen to me,' he says. 'I got him into the first XI at the end of the third form. I had to go and see his parents to get permission, because no kid that age had played for the first XI. The first game, we were playing against Southland Boys, which is a hate match: it is like the War of the Roses for schools. We were nine down, playing in Invercargill with two umpires who loved Southland, and needed 14 runs to win with about an over and a half to go. Brendon, just 13, says: "I think I can get this, sir." I said: "Listen, no you don't. You get out, and I will kick your arse all the way back to Dunedin." I was senior master, so he had to do as he was told, and he went out and put a dirty block on and we drew. Imagine telling him that now: don't go for the runs, play for the draw. So the key thing is he didn't listen to me: I was just an into-the-wind dribbler. He was a star.

'He was a competitive bugger. But the other thing was he had a great ability to lift players around him. Even when he was not captain, he would give people belief and motivate them, he gave out energy. There is no blueprint for that. When I've been captain, I've had a serious team talk before the game and a few drinks after. Brendon would probably have the team talk with a few drinks, and then a few more drinks afterwards.'

It sounds familiar. McCullum's love of a beer and a laugh with his mates is the simple recipe for his man-management of players from junior grade to international cricket. New

Zealand players talk freely of his ability to motivate in the hardest of circumstances, and England's Test team – which has traditionally played conservative cricket – embraced a simpler approach because McCullum has made it OK to fail. He puts the emphasis on having fun; otherwise, what is the point? Those lessons learned at King's and Albion are now being played out in the England dressing-room. McCullum recognises that modern players are pulled in many directions, so he has created an environment that leaves them wanting more. They are desperate to be a part of it, this gang they never want to leave.

'He just had a positive belief right from the start,' says Cushen. 'You see it now. He had a degree of confidence too. I got interviewed when he retired. People asked me if he was cocky. I have never seen him be cocky. He remembers every rung in the ladder that helped him get to the top. He had attributes that made it easy to earn the respect of those around him.'

McCullum moved out of the family house, just after his 18th birthday. He was suspended from King's for holding parties, hiring out halls and DJs with his friend, and selling tickets to fellow students. But as captain of the first XI at rugby and cricket, he was forgiven, and made a prefect. He left school briefly to work in a supermarket but returned for his higher education.

'How do I put this? He was mature for his age,' says Cushen. 'I was the social principal, and if there was an issue with Brendon they would send me to sort him out. He went flatting [living away from parents] for one year. No kid at school goes flatting. Straight away you know what boys are like. They enjoy a beer. Where do you go? Ah, to Brendon's place. There were a couple of times where he was pushing the boundaries a bit. He never had an excuse. He was, "Hey I've been caught, take the chop." He was not evil. It was just under-age drinking, that's all. But it attracted some other kids that may not have been great company for him and needed a bit of readjustment on the road of life. But look at the positive side: he learned from it. Ben Stokes has had a couple of issues and overcome that. I don't know what the English dressing-room culture is like, but there will be respect for Brendon and Ben because of the black clouds in their past. It makes them human.'

Mike Hesson first saw McCullum play as a six-year-old. Hesson, then 13, was practising in Dunedin when Brendon, his brother and father were hitting balls in an indoor cricket centre in Otago. Hesson is the straight man to McCullum's flamboyance. Years after that first encounter, their careers would become entwined with New Zealand, when Hesson was made coach. But he always felt McCullum never left Dunedin behind.

'South Dunedin is where you grow that humility and those social skills to interact with people of all ages and backgrounds. That is one trait Brendon has. He has the ability to connect with everybody in the group. Very few people have that quality. He was around cricket, and exposed to older people, from a young age, playing and being part of teams with people from all sorts of socio-economic backgrounds and finding a way to build a relationship and having fun. I guess it is clear his background played a part in it.'

Nothing, though – not even the streets of South Dunedin – can prepare a player for what happened on 18 April 2008. It was a day that changed McCullum's life, at least financially – and changed cricket itself. His innings at the Chinnaswamy Stadium in Bangalore on the opening night of the Indian Premier League (IPL) was one of the most pivotal ever played.

A few weeks earlier, McCullum had been eating pizza and sipping beers with his New Zealand team-mates at the Shoreline Motel in Napier, recovering from an extraordinary tied ODI against England. Instead of watching highlights of the game and wondering where they might have nicked that extra run, the players were studying their laptops and the first-ever IPL auction, in Mumbai. McCullum's gambler instinct would serve him well. Players had a choice between putting themselves forward for a guaranteed maximum of $200,000 over three years – way more than he earned in New Zealand – or take a risk on the auction at a lower base price of $175,000. McCullum went for the risk.

As the numbers rolled in, and the auctioneer prepared to call some of the names of the Kiwi contingent – McCullum, Jacob Oram, Daniel Vettori and Scott Styris – the motel Wi-Fi dropped out. There was no WhatsApp to fall back on in 2008, no 4G. Instead, Vettori phoned his agent in Mumbai, who talked the players through the sale. Vettori was bought by the Delhi Daredevils (now the Delhi Capitals) for $625,000 – an unheard-of sum for a New Zealand cricketer. Oram went for $675,000 to the Chennai Super Kings, McCullum for $700,000 to the Kolkata Knight Riders. He phoned his wife, Lis, in a daze. 'It looked like freedom to me,' he said. Freedom from worrying about injuries, from losing his NZ contract, from being a washed-up ex-cricketer.

But such sums also come with pressure and, while McCullum had spent a career trying to justify his talent, he now had a different challenge: to prove he was worth this show of faith by the team's owners. What happened next would have echoes years later for the England team.

McCullum arrived in India out of form, low on confidence. He was hitting the ball terribly in the nets, worrying for the first time about whether he might not be as good as the price tag suggested. Matthew Mott, now in charge of England's white-ball teams, was just starting out as a coach, and had landed a gig with KKR as assistant to his fellow Australian John Buchanan, a scholarly figure who sweated the details and was not necessarily on McCullum's wavelength. They would later have a distant relationship when Buchanan joined New Zealand Cricket as head of performance.

McCullum's form in the nets was so poor that Mott took him for a one-to-one session with the bowling machine, but it only made matters worse. Instead, Mott intuitively knew how to lift his confidence: they retired to the bar of Kolkata ITC Towers for beer and cricket chat. 'That session helped turn a corner,' said McCullum. He made 40 and 50 in the next two warm-up games. His chat with Mott stayed with him. This laid-back approach works well with super-gifted cricketers like McCullum; perhaps something else is needed for the less talented. But nobody will ever forget the result.

After a three-hour opening ceremony that confirmed the IPL's scope and ambition, he opened the batting with Sourav Ganguly against Praveen Kumar, a clever swing bowler, difficult to get away, and India's attack leader, Zaheer Khan. At first it seemed the uncertainty had returned: McCullum failed to score from his first six balls. But his next four from Zaheer lit the spark. Go for it or get out: four, four, six, four. He slowed when Ganguly was dismissed and Ricky Ponting joined him, but went on the charge when the spinners came on, allowing him to exploit Bangalore's small boundaries. The Chinnaswamy is a quick pitch by Indian standards, the metal roof amplifies the noise in the stadium and the fans are right on top of the action, behind high-wired fences. It is arguably the best atmosphere in the country, which may be why Lalit

Modi, the IPL's flamboyant architect, chose it for his opening night. As McCullum laced boundaries, the fans were making more noise than he had ever heard on a cricket field.

He reached his fifty off 32 balls, and his second half-century required just 21. McCullum smashed 39 off his last 11, and his eventual 158 not out (from 73 balls, with 10 fours and 13 sixes) has since been bettered only once in IPL history. His KKR team-mates managed just 47 runs from 47 balls, before Royal Challengers Bangalore were skittled for 82; no one else in the game passed 20. 'What I did that night was something I didn't think I was capable of achieving,' he said years later. 'It was just a surreal moment in time where you just look back and say, "How lucky was I?"'

How could he live up to that night? It was impossible. McCullum scored only one more century in his next 108 IPL games, but enjoyed 11 years' employment, making more than £4 million and securing his future: he owns a stud farm and racehorses, and can pick and choose his jobs. Foregoing the extra $25,000 to gamble on the auction seems obvious now, but it was new territory in those days. The innings is regularly ranked as the best ever in the IPL, even if Chris Gayle surpassed it with an unbeaten 175 in 2013. Given the significance of the evening, it will never be forgotten.

In fact, McCullum was an inspiration to the England team long before he became head coach. Eoin Morgan always credited McCullum's New Zealand side as a role model for his World Cup-winning team. Despite that, McCullum's 101 Test matches confirm Hesson's view that the long format was always his favourite, regardless of his white-ball achievements. An average of 38 might have been better had he played more conservatively, but that would have blunted his edge. He will be more proud of the fact he ended his career in his last match with the fastest Test hundred of all time – 54 balls against Australia in Christchurch – and more sixes, 107, than anyone else, at least until Stokes went past his tally.

He endured some tough times. In 2015, he gave evidence against his former friend and cricketing idol Chris Cairns in a crown court case in London, after Cairns was accused of perjury. When the jury believed Cairns, it was a blow to McCullum's credibility. He was overlooked for the Test captaincy until a bloody removal of Ross Taylor from the job in 2012 divided New Zealand; McCullum later described the row as a 'blot' on the game. John Parker, a former Test cricketer, wrote a letter leaked to the media claiming McCullum knew all along that Taylor would be sacked, and he would be made his replacement. Parker later withdrew the allegation under the threat of legal action. Martin Crowe, the country's greatest ever batsman, burned his New Zealand blazer in anger at the treatment of Taylor, and the rancour over McCullum's appointment clouded his first tour, of South Africa. Things would only get worse when the cricket started: New Zealand were bowled out for 45 inside 20 overs in his first Test as captain, at Cape Town. But McCullum now showed the streak of fortitude, the street-fighting skills honed in South Dunedin. In a management meeting after the match, he drew a line. 'It could not get much worse after that,' he said. 'But it allowed us to strip things back. We just had to be honest and brutal with ourselves, and the perception we had of ourselves. We had to realign those and be honest that we had no soul about our team. We were not purposeful in the time we had as cricketers and needed to make some changes.'

New Zealand became a more aggressive side. McCullum would set attacking fields and an example to his team-mates, chasing down every ball to the rope. To them, this was not unusual: just another example of Bazball before it was given a name. 'New Zealanders can be quite conservative, probably similar to Englishmen,' says Hesson. 'That conservatism can drive us: we worry in case we get it wrong. But that was never a factor in the way Brendon thought. That was from under-14 age. It is how he has lived his life. His career was based around trying to create special memories. It was not about being consistent. It was about accepting that when you have your day, make it a special day.

'In South Africa we were at rock bottom, so let's do it our way. He was of the view that if you are going to do the job, do it the way you want it to be done, and not worry about consequences. That brought the best out of Brendon. The players always wanted to follow him. He had this aura. He would not ask others to do things he would not do himself. He was willing to back up his messaging with actions as well, and back players trying to do the right thing: this is the way we want to play, we will give you plenty of rope as long as you play the way the team wants you to play.'

McCullum drew up a players' charter, banned sledging and decided it was time to have fun while working. He wrote in his autobiography, *Declared*, that personalities had to adapt. 'The environment had not changed, where some of the senior players acted like w******, egotistical and unwelcoming, like some kind of boarding-school hierarchy where the seventh-formers lorded it over the third-formers.' Ultimately, he embraced a famous All Blacks' policy: 'no dickheads'.

'Brendon is authentic,' says Hesson. 'He does not hide who he is, what his values are, and doesn't force those on others. He is very comfortable in his own skin. One of the things we did well in New Zealand is we want people to be themselves. We have 15 different people in our squad, and that is great.

He knew he needed senior players working for him. He is strong when he needs to be, but he is happy to listen to other views. With Tim Southee and Trent Boult, as they started to grow and become more experienced players, Brendon would give them a lot more rope. Even if he did not agree with the field they wanted, he would 100 per cent back them. If they had faith in it, then there was a chance of [it] working. Those guys grew in confidence because the captain backed them during some challenging times. He played a huge part in their development.'

Southee made a beeline for McCullum when he showed up to England's warm-up game on their tour of New Zealand in February 2023, spending hours chatting in a corner of the ground in Hamilton. He knew what to expect from Bazball when the teams met in the series that followed. He had lived it, and his side were more aggressive than they had been under his predecessor, Kane Williamson, adopting a little of England's edge. McCullum took on the role of tour guide, as much as head coach, showing off his home country to the England players, organising golf, jaunts to the races and a barbeque at his farm, on the North Island. But the old South Dunedin boy came out too. Occasionally he would leave the team hotel, pull his cap down, hoick his collar up and head to the local TAB bar, where he would have a pint and a bet on the horses, and mind his own business, as if he were back home again, where it all started. 'He is a normal person,' says Colleen Beaumont. 'I don't think he thinks he is someone.' Then she heads back to her gardening on Waterloo Street.

3

'Everyone has got a story...'

The Radisson Hotel in Grenada sits on the white sands of Grand Anse Beach. On a clear day, you are guaranteed a sunset to lift any mood. A small white picket fence separates the hotel pool from the beach, allowing easy access to wander the three-kilometre stretch of sand, or grab a drink at one of the wooden shacks and gather your thoughts. For two days at the end of England's tour of the Caribbean in March 2022, you did not have to linger long to bump into players still reeling from their ten-wicket defeat in the third Test, a result that gave West Indies a 1–0 series win.

The man with most on his mind was Joe Root. A 15-month spell he had said would define his captaincy was at an end. His team had won one Test in their last 17 and flopped in both India and Australia. In 2021 alone, they had lost nine times, equalling the record for a calendar year, set by Bangladesh in 2003. Now, they had collapsed under the first hint of pressure from a moderate but motivated West Indies.

Chris Silverwood and Ashley Giles had already lost their jobs as head coach and managing director, sacked after the 4–0 Ashes defeat. Assistant batting coach Graham Thorpe had been axed, too – mainly for the failure of the players to make big scores. It didn't help his cause when, on the last night in Australia, police were called to the team hotel in Hobart because he had refused to extinguish a cigar. Everything was going up in smoke.

Like a batsman watching from the other end as his partners are picked off, Root had survived the carnage. Arguably, and paradoxically, his position as captain had been strengthened as his team headed for the West Indies. He had been placed in charge of a 'red-ball reset' by interim managing director Andrew Strauss, who had led the review of the Ashes tour, and said of Root: 'At the moment, he is 100 per cent the right person to take the team forward.'

To assist him, Strauss dropped James Anderson and Stuart Broad. It was never said explicitly, but it gave Root a chance to establish his authority without two commanding figures prepared to question his decisions. Broad responded angrily, even though he could sense it coming, while Anderson was upset and stunned. 'I was low, he was low,' says Broad. 'We FaceTimed a lot the day we found out because we were both taken aback. We booked a golf trip to Scotland that night. We needed a lift. What is going to cheer us up? Let's go and play the Old Course at St Andrews. We had a brilliant time and felt refreshed for the season.'

Without the two old campaigners, Root's voice may have been louder in the dressing-room, but his options were more limited on the field: the new ball was now in the hands of Chris Woakes, whose overseas record was poor, and the inexperienced Craig Overton. England lost because they panicked in the final Test when West Indies reopened wounds not yet healed from the Ashes. Earlier in the series, England had lacked the guile and skill to finish off their opponents on dead pitches. The absence of Broad and Anderson was supposed to allow Root to spread his wings. Instead, they were badly – and terminally – clipped.

Root must have known what was coming when he talked to the media on the outfield while the DJ at the Grenada National Stadium ramped up the volume, and the West Indies team enjoyed a lap of honour. 'We have definitely made big improvements,' he said, unconvincingly. 'I'm passionate about taking the team forward. I feel like the group are behind me.'

On that score, at least, he was right. 'Sometimes it amazes me that he gets questioned, because of how it feels within the dressing-room,' said Paul Collingwood, who had stepped in temporarily after Silverwood's sacking. 'It's the first time as a head coach I've experienced him, and you can see the passion, the drive. There's a hunger to get it right. These aren't just words coming out of his mouth.' The attitude was better-the-devil-you-know. Root was popular, and nobody in the group wanted to criticise him in public. But this was the end – and everyone knew it.

Even during this dark time, he never lost his cheerfulness, remaining polite and approachable. Moments after his final press conference, he rifled through his kit bag in the Devon Smith Pavilion and dug out a pair of batting gloves. He signed them and handed them to one of the press photographers who earlier in the tour had asked for a gift for a friend's cricket-mad son. Root's decency never wavered.

Collingwood had done his best to lift the team, concentrating on hard work with rigid fitness drills and fielding exercises. But England's premature defeat meant two nights would now be spent in the hotel bar, letting off steam and contemplating the future. Caribbean tours are popular with fans, and there were plenty at the Radisson.

One evening, Root politely listened as a well-oiled England supporter showed him how to play a cover-drive with a Carib beer bottle. 'Think you need more wrists, mate,' said Root, as the fan insisted his technique had served him well in Surrey club cricket. Ben Stokes remained as loyal as ever, jokingly threatening any journalist who considered writing anything nasty about 'my mate Joe'. Even while he knew change was inevitable, he was doing his best to cheer Root up.

Stokes's loyalty was understandable. During Root's 64 Tests in charge, he had won 27, more than any England captain, but he had never claimed the Ashes – and his 26 defeats were a national record too. Collingwood's comments confirmed the suspicion that the set-up had become too cosy. England needed shaking up, preferably by an outsider. Root was too nice to be captain, and lacked the courage of his convictions, never settling on a strategy. His batting was outstanding in the final 18 months of his captaincy, and in 2021 he had scored 1,708 Test runs, the third-highest tally in a calendar year. His mental strength was not in doubt. But he had to go.

Three weeks later came the inevitable announcement – accompanied by a mixture of disappointment and relief. 'I came back from the West Indies and I remember being at home for that first week,' Root tells us more than a year later. 'I was home – and I wasn't home. I was thinking about other things. I just looked at my kids, Alfie and Isabella, and my wife, Carrie, and I thought: *I am just not here, and it is not fair on you guys any more.* I had done it for such a long period of time. I took the job on a few weeks after Alf was born, so he had not known anything else.

'It is probably one of the best decisions I have made in my career, for me personally and for the team. I am really pleased I did it. I spoke to a few people, and they said I should have a think about it for a few days to see if I feel the same. I made that call and spoke to [ECB chief executive] Tom Harrison and Keysy, who had just been appointed. They were very good with it. It would not have been fair to carry on from a family perspective. It is a job that needs full attention and all the energy you possess, and I didn't have that any more. It would not be fair on the team either. It is not how you win at cricket.'

Root, Silverwood and Giles, it's true, had been dealt an impossible hand by Covid. England played 23 Tests during the pandemic – more than any other team. Almost half were overseas, and those in England in 2020 took place in stifling conditions, with players confined to rooms and forced to eat dinner wearing latex gloves. There was almost a national outcry when Jofra Archer was discovered to have nipped home to Hove to see his dogs. Giles argued his breach of bubble protocol could have cost English cricket 'tens of millions of pounds'. Everyone was walking on eggshells. The cricket had to proceed because of TV deals, but at what cost to the players?

Ollie Pope was grateful just to be playing at all in the summer of 2020, but he struggled on the field, and the confines off it meant no escape, with all England's Test matches at either the Ageas Bowl or Old Trafford, which both had hotels on site. 'When things didn't go to plan, I really felt it,' he said. 'Against West Indies, I got out towards the end of a day, and half an hour later I was sat in my room overlooking the pitch. Closing the curtains was the only way to switch off. Cricket is one of those sports where you have as many average days as you do good days. When it did go badly, I would wake up and hear the lawnmower going outside as the groundsman went around the outfield. You had to find ways of coping.'

At the start of 2021, England were greeted by airport staff in Sri Lanka wearing hazmat suits. Moeen Ali tested positive for Covid and had to isolate for ten days along with Woakes, who had shared a taxi with him to Birmingham airport. Almost a year later, in Australia, Silverwood missed the Sydney Test after he and his family tested positive; stuck in Melbourne, with his job on the line, he was unable to influence the result. Both cities had been overwhelmed by cases of the virus's Omicron strain, and the cricketers had to undergo daily tests. With facilities at breaking point, it was impossible to turn round results in time, so the players were told they would instead have to submit to a quicker test, involving a probe up the nostril and down the throat. Those who did it said it was hugely uncomfortable, and there was a revolt when they were told their wives and children would have to endure the same procedure. This was while England were facing defeat at the MCG, where they surrendered the Ashes after three Tests. Any focus on the cricket had vanished. The fact that England drew in Sydney without Silverwood – and even then only just, thanks to rain – did not help his chances of avoiding the sack.

Australia, meanwhile, played only nine Tests in the Covid period, all at home, shut away and isolated from the rest of the world. No wonder they were fresher than England. Before the return leg in 2023, Broad irritated Australians with a revisionist take on the 2021–22 series in his *Mail on Sunday* column: 'In my mind, I don't class that as a real Ashes. The definition of Ashes cricket is elite sport with lots of passion and players at the top of their game. Nothing about that series was high-level performance because of the Covid restrictions. The training facilities, the travel, not being able to socialise. I've written it off as a void series.'

This was Broad *in excelsis*, getting under his opponents' skin while maintaining the straightest of faces. But the virus could be blamed only so far. England made errors in selection, and repeatedly buckled under pressure. In April 2021, Giles had sacked Ed Smith as national selector, leaving Silverwood in overall charge of selection, while coaching both the white- and red-ball teams. It was all too much, and the gamble would eventually cost Giles his job. Smith had some success as selector and was bold in picking young players such as Sam Curran and Pope, but he rubbed too many up the wrong way, particularly senior players, including Broad, who felt he interfered beyond his remit.

Giles described selection panels as outdated and harking back to the amateur era. He may have been right, but his relationship with Smith had grown strained. After aligning himself so closely with Silverwood, Giles had to go once the head coach was so badly exposed. He had wanted to promote an Englishman after the tenure of Australian Trevor Bayliss, and there was plenty of encouragement to do so from the ECB as they looked to justify the millions spent on their coaching programmes. Silverwood was steeped in the county game, and in the Yorkshire traditions of getting your head down, making big scores and ploughing a furrow outside off stump.

Insiders say he was always striving for approval from his players, perhaps desperate to convince himself that he was good enough to coach an England team in transition. He always put his players' welfare first, and was well liked, both inside and outside the squad. But, too often, hard work and commitment trumped imaginative leadership. 'I'm the head coach of England but I'm also an England fan,' he said as pressure mounted in Australia. 'I'm passionate about England

and love the fact I can get involved and help. I want to continue doing this job, I think I can do this job. I'd like to see changes that would help us do the job better.' His go-to cliché – 'know what I mean?' – added to the sense that he was constantly seeking validation.

In truth, he had lost the players before the Ashes were surrendered in Melbourne. Rory Burns had been incensed before the match when he learned of his dropping by reading the English papers. Silverwood launched a mole hunt, perhaps forgetting he had himself let the news slip to the media during a chat by the MCG nets. Even Woakes, the nice guy of the touring party, struggled to defend the coach. Asked if Silverwood retained the faith of the players, he was non-committal: 'Who am I to talk about people's futures other than my own, to be brutally honest?' But Woakes happily sprang to Root's defence. 'Joe is a great cricketer. He's got a great cricket brain. His record as England captain is pretty good. It definitely feels like Joe will continue.'

The MCG nets are outside the main arena, so fans can watch the players train. It is a very public space, with cameras and media watching closely through the wire netting. And it was here that Ant Botha, the South African-born former Derbyshire and Warwickshire all-rounder who had been drafted in to throw left-handed and replicate Mitchell Starc's angle of delivery, put England's struggling openers, Burns and Haseeb Hameed, through a different kind of drill. It involved them batting on one leg, in a bid to improve their balance, though two legs had so far served neither particularly well: Burns had averaged 12 at Brisbane and Adelaide, Hameed 14. Botha's advice was well-meaning, but it smacked of desperation, with England looking for quirky answers to familiar problems. And it provoked yet more mockery, which was the last thing they needed.

Silverwood had promised his team would arrive in Australia 'fitter, faster, leaner, more ready than ever before'. To achieve this, he and the management had bought into a rest and rotation policy, long before the first Ashes Test. It had all started so positively, with a comfortable 2–0 win in Sri Lanka, where Root scored 228 and 186. Full of positive energy, England flew to India for a four-match series. Root had endured a tough 2020 with the bat, his first calendar year without a hundred, but he primed himself for the biggest 12 months of his life by going back to the drawing board, spending long hours on his technique at Headingley. He was fitter, and his footwork against spin was more decisive: he got forward or back with greater purpose, and had complete control of the sweep, both conventional and reverse.

In his 100th Test, at Chennai, he scored a superb 218 as England started the series in spectacular fashion, with Anderson bowling a magical over of reverse swing to spark a thousand Twitter memes and undermine India's resistance. But they had prepared a flat pitch, with little turn – and now they learned. The pitches became sandtraps, the ball turning square. In the next three Tests, spinners Ravichandran Ashwin and Akshar Patel struck 50 times at an average of under 11, as England were bowled out four times for 135 or fewer, wickets falling as quickly as players came and went from the squad. They used 17 across the four games as part of their rotation policy; inevitably, some were thrown in undercooked. Only Root averaged above 27.

Jonny Bairstow had played well in Sri Lanka, then went home for a break; by the time he returned, he had mislaid his form, and made three ducks in four innings, casting doubt over his career. Jos Buttler played the first Test but was sent home to keep him fresh for the one-day series. Moeen was picked for the second Test, where he took eight wickets and smashed 43 in 18 balls, but then went home for a pre-planned break, before returning for the one-dayers. Root clumsily said he had 'chosen to go home', having not said anything similar about others leaving the tour. Root apologised to Moeen, but by now everyone was rattled.

England were their own worst enemies in Ahmedabad, where the ball swung in the nets as they prepared for a day/ night Test. Kidded by the conditions in practice, and wedded to a plan cooked up before they arrived, they picked four seamers. They were barely used. India's spinners took 19 wickets as the ball ragged from the first over and, despite Root picking up a remarkable five for 8 with his part-time off-breaks, England lost in two days.

Their dogmatic approach would be repeated in Adelaide later in the year, when England stuck to a pre-planned attack for another floodlit Test – with a similar outcome. This was their problem in 2021: the sweet moments, such as Chennai, quickly turned sour. It continued at Lord's at the start of the summer against New Zealand, when debutant Ollie Robinson lined up with team-mates in front of the pavilion in a black T-shirt bearing an anti-discrimination message. It was a gesture of support in the Black Lives Matter era, and all the players bought into it. The previous summer against West Indies, England had taken the knee. That was too much for some, so the T-shirts were the compromise.

Robinson started with four wickets, outperforming everyone on what should have been a proud day for him and his family. But while he was bowling at the Pavilion End, word spread in the media centre about unpleasant tweets in which he had used racist and sexist language. They were nearly a decade old and had been written when he was a teenage cricketer who struggled with authority and was sacked for unprofessionalism by Yorkshire. Robinson was pitched headlong into the culture war, held up as a totem by those disgusted that remarks from the past could be used as a stick with which to beat him in the present. The ECB – already facing a brewing racism row at Yorkshire – were compelled to take action. Robinson had spent a career in the backwaters of county cricket. Suddenly he was a national story, featuring on the night-time news bulletins and the front pages of the papers. Mentally shot, he was not considered for the next Test at Edgbaston. Eventually he was banned for eight matches, five suspended.

A Test match that had started so well ended with Root being booed on the final day, when he decided against chasing a target of 273. Instead, his eye was on the future: rather than win the game and entertain the first post-Covid crowd at a Test in England for nearly two years, his team ground their way to 170 for three from 70 overs. Dom Sibley batted for 207 balls and more than five hours, hitting only three fours in an unbeaten 60. It was a passage of play that would never leave Root. A year later, freed of the captaincy, he masterminded a thrilling run-chase at the same ground against the same opponents to kickstart the Stokes era. Here, though, he hesitated, and a full house at Lord's let him know what they thought. Root wanted a blocker like Sibley to build confidence and stay at the crease. Under Stokes, Sibley was banished to county cricket.

Meanwhile, the ECB launched a Twitter trawl, going through old messages posted by the players in a bid to prevent any shock revelations before Edgbaston. The players were on edge, worrying what they might have said in the early days of social media. The ECB revealed they were investigating 'a number of historical social media posts by other individuals' in the England set-up; the Wisden website dug up an offensive tweet by one player when he was 16 but chose not to name him.

Root's team were distracted from the cricket, and up against a strong New Zealand side preparing for the World Test Championship final against India, which they would go on to win. England's defeat at Edgbaston felt inevitable: as they lost on day four, another series slipped away. James Bracey, handed a Test cap at Lord's to keep in place of the injured Ben Foakes (Buttler was at the IPL), summed up the decline. He started with two ducks and was close to tears in front of his team-mates. He was not picked again.

The high point of the 2021 summer was the Test series against Virat Kohli's India, whose strong seam attack – Jasprit Bumrah, Mohammed Shami, Ishant Sharma and Mohammed Siraj – would provide England with a strong indication of where they were ahead of the winter in Australia. Despite the defeat by New Zealand, they were upbeat. Root was working well with Silverwood, who felt up to the challenge of his workload and even booked a family holiday in July, hoping to miss a one-day series against Pakistan. That plan was scuppered by the Covid outbreak, which meant Stokes stepped in for Eoin Morgan as captain, leading England to victory. But, for Root, came another blow, when Stokes announced on 30 July that he was taking a break from the game: England would face India without him. 'I just want my friend to be OK,' said Root, as he prepared for the first Test at Trent Bridge, but the news added to the feeling that everything was stacking up against him. He made a second-innings hundred in Nottingham but needed bad weather to save England from defeat.

They were tense going into the Lord's Test. They had not won all summer, and Stokes's absence had ruined the balance of the side, leaving Root unwilling to pick Jack Leach, who did not play a home Test in 2021. Rumblings about the winter and Covid restrictions in Australia were starting to emerge: while trying to concentrate on beating India, an exhausted Root was leading negotiations with Cricket Australia on behalf of his players.

India, by contrast, were unified under Kohli. At Lord's, a partisan last-day crowd – they were not cheering for the home side – provided further evidence of cricket's changing power base, and fired up the players as India won a bad-tempered Test. Root and Kohli had exchanged angry words in the Long Room at the end of the third day, after a bouncer barrage from Bumrah to Anderson. Then, in the team huddle before England's second innings, Kohli told his players in Hindi that 'for 60 overs they should feel hell out there'. England were bowled out for 120. They levelled the series on a greentop at Headingley, where Robinson and Anderson were supported by Craig Overton, and Root scored a wonderful hundred on his home ground. It was England's finest performance of the summer, even if it was achieved in helpful conditions. India had exploited home advantage earlier in the year, but England were striving to improve on flat pitches, and this win did little to suggest they were the better team. On a less helpful surface at The Oval, they picked Overton, despite the conditions nullifying him, rather than the promising – and quicker – Saqib Mahmood. They were defeated again, with Bumrah's pace exposing England's batsmen, and leaving India on the verge of a historic series win. Covid provided its final twist at Old Trafford, where India pulled out hours before the Test was due to start following an outbreak in the squad.

Their decision left thousands of fans disappointed, and the ECB worried about a £40 million black hole in their finances. It would be a year before the series would finish.

All the while, England were racked with uncertainty over the Ashes. Harrison revealed the players had 'demanded assurances' from Cricket Australia that their families would be granted visas – not a foregone conclusion, since the country was still closed to foreigners. Buttler was the most vocal, effectively saying he would not go to Australia without his family. Bubble-weary players were concerned about quarantine conditions in Australia, as well as the travel restrictions once they arrived. Scott Morrison, the Australian prime minister, said there would be 'no special deals' for the England families, seemingly throwing the tour in doubt, though the message was aimed at his home audience.

Behind the scenes, frantic negotiations were going on between government officials and the ECB. Eventually the players settled on a spell of quarantine at a golf resort in Queensland for themselves, and a hotel in the Yarra Valley in Victoria for their families, who would emerge from isolation for Christmas in Melbourne. Most probably wished they had pulled out by the time the tour limped to its sorry end in Hobart. 'Honestly, everyone has got a story about how shambolic it has been,' said one player.

Preparation had indeed been a shambles, and not of England's making. The squad was split between those who had played at the Twenty20 World Cup in the UAE in the autumn of 2021, and the Test specialists. Because the T20 players arrived later, their two-week quarantine period delayed the squad's unification. The bubbles made it harder for players to train, and logistics were complicated by Covid rules on social distancing from people outside the touring party.

When England finally played their warm-up match at the Ian Healy Oval in Brisbane, the scoreboard failed, the analyst was unable to film the action because of Wi-Fi issues, and rain cut short the game, turning it into middle practice. More rain forced the bowlers to attune to conditions in the indoor nets: with no form to go on, selection for the first Test was a gamble. Pope was picked at No 6 ahead of Bairstow, and England had to rely on the physio and medical staff to decide on the fitness of Anderson, who had pulled out of the 2019 home series after only four overs. There was no appetite for a repeat.

On a green Gabba pitch, England left out Anderson and Broad, and selected an attack that had never played together: Wood, Woakes, Robinson and Leach. Root won the toss and, in perfect bowling conditions, opted to bat. He was wary of the criticism levelled at Nasser Hussain for bowling first at Brisbane in 2002–03, and had himself poked fun at Hussain in the past. But this was a bowling day – and England were throwing in their underprepared batsmen on a lively surface against the best pace attack in the world.

In advance, Burns had been asked by the media if he had thought about the prospect of facing the first ball of the Ashes. 'Nah, not really,' he replied. And the first ball did not go well, as Starc bowled him round his legs. England were skittled for 147. Then David Warner, relieved not to be facing Broad, who had dismissed him seven times during the 2019 series when he often went round the wicket, helped himself to a morale-boosting 94; only Wood, briefly, replicated Broad's angle of attack. The cameras picked up Anderson and Broad bowling in the nets next to the Gabba. The series had barely begun, and England were already a laughing stock.

Selection problems did not end there. During the first Test, the England Lions were playing Australia A in Brisbane, which offered players not in the XI for the first Test — such as Bairstow — a chance for time in the middle. Instead Mo Bobat, the performance director in charge of the Lions, picked the team 48 hours earlier, before the Test side had been finalised. England realised their error only on day one at the Gabba, where Bairstow, Dan Lawrence and other squad reserves were running the drinks in their hi-viz bibs. By contrast, Australia's second-choice cricketers — the likes of Usman Khawaja, Scott Boland and Michael Neser — managed valuable match time for the A team. Khawaja and Boland would go on to play important roles in the Ashes.

England had agreed before the series that, when Leach came on, they would set defensive fields, knowing Australia would attack him. Back in the team because the return of Stokes had created room, he was chosen at Brisbane, one of the hardest venues in world cricket for a finger-spinner. But when Leach came on, Root caused stunned looks among the senior players by bringing up the field and attacking, despite having so few first-innings runs on the board. Leach was hammered: he conceded 102 runs in 13 overs, affecting plans for the next Test. Not that the selection process was any less fraught, with senior players frustrated that James Taylor — the former Nottinghamshire and England batsman who had recently made the transition from selector to head scout — had so much influence while sitting at home, thousands of miles away.

Even so, England were still confident. They had targeted the Adelaide Test, because it would be played with a pink ball under lights — helpful, in theory, for Anderson and Broad. The question was what to do with Leach. His confidence had been shattered, and England were intent on picking their seamers. Wood was rested, despite being the sharpest bowler in Brisbane. Robinson was retained, and Broad and Anderson recalled, with Woakes playing ahead of Wood. England had picked an attack full of right-arm fast-medium bowlers. Two days before the game, groundsman Damian Hough was asked about the surface. 'History says that the pitch will spin,' he said, but England laughed it off as mind games, thinking Australia would love nothing more than to face Leach again.

England justified leaving out Wood because they wanted to hold him back for the third Test in Melbourne. He was their most dangerous bowler – and perhaps their only player to enhance his reputation all tour – and yet he bowled more overs when the series was dead (75.4 at Sydney and Hobart) than alive (45.3 at Brisbane and Melbourne). 'Selection is a marathon, not a sprint,' said Silverwood, but in Australia touring teams have to get ahead first, then race for the line. Instead, the hosts were out of sight before the first bend. England were predictably poor in Adelaide. Broad and Anderson bowled too short with the new ball as their conservatism took hold, and – in Leach's absence, with the pitch confirming Hough's hunch – Robinson was reduced to bowling off-spin. Buttler, Root's rock behind the scenes, looked frazzled. England took just two wickets on day one of the Test, and Buttler twice dropped Marnus Labuschagne on his way to a hundred. His tour never recovered, though he tried to save England in the fourth innings. They lost by 275 runs.

Back in 2017–18, when England picked Woakes, Anderson and Broad at Adelaide, they managed 13 wickets for 335 – though only four for 230 in the first innings, when Australia took control. This time, they had collective figures of six for 315. Root blamed them for getting their lengths wrong. 'We needed to bowl fuller,' he said. 'As soon as we did in the second innings, we created chances. That's frustrating. We did it four years ago and didn't learn from it. We have to be better.'

Anderson, writing in the *Daily Telegraph* a few days later, did not take the criticism kindly: 'We can't just go after the game "we should have bowled fuller". If we are bowling too short, at lunch we need information back saying we need to push our lengths up.' The criticism was aimed at Root, Silverwood and the bowling coach, Jon Lewis. Anderson had little time for their management styles.

Silverwood reacted to the Adelaide fiasco by making the batsmen sit through footage of their dismissals, putting 14 of the 20 wickets on the big screen, as an angry, open-ended discussion took place in the dressing-room. Stokes and Buttler, in particular, spoke out, but England were emphasising their failings, dwelling on the negative – an approach Stokes would never countenance when he took over. Silverwood was facing questions about his future and did little in the post-match press conference to instil confidence, refusing to admit any mistakes. 'There is always going to be divided opinion,' he said. 'I was happy with the skillset we had in the pink-ball Test, so I would pick the same team again.'

When the tour reached its festive leg, in Melbourne and Sydney, nobody was in the mood to celebrate. Because of the spread of the virus, the players were banned from having haircuts outside the team hotel and confined to bubbles with their families. A sombre Christmas Day meal was arranged at St Kilda, but England would soon have plenty of time on their hands, losing in Melbourne inside three days after they were bowled out for 68 in their second innings by Scott Boland, who took an extraordinary six for 7.

Silverwood insisted he was the man to carry on, then caught the virus himself, which left Thorpe in control for

Sydney. It emerged Strauss had been put in charge of the end-of-tour review by Harrison, who was in Australia to see the disintegration at first hand. Giles arrived in the country and held a tense pre-match press conference at the SCG. He was upset that Strauss, his predecessor, had been put in charge of reviewing his performance, and sensed the writing was on the wall. He blamed the system. 'You can change me, change the head coach, change the captain,' he said. 'But we're only setting up future leaders for failure. That's all we're doing. We're only pushing it down the road.'

England rallied slightly during the fourth Test, avoiding a potential whitewash thanks to a belligerent century from Bairstow, and rain, which shaved seven overs off the final day; it ended with Broad – who had taken a five-wicket haul – and Anderson blocking for a draw. Whatever fight England summoned, however, vanished at Hobart, as Tasmania hosted its first Ashes Test (Western Australia, with the strictest Covid rules in the country, had been closed to visitors). Hobart was another day/nighter, which left plenty of time in the mornings for players and coaches to wander the cafés and quayside close to the team hotel. In a compact city centre, they were often seen huddled together over breakfast. Despite that, England were now at the stage where it was every man for himself. Anderson feared he would be blamed, Broad too. Silverwood was gloomy, and Giles spent hours walking the coastal path brooding over his end-of-tour report, which he hoped would save his job.

It is not unusual on tough Ashes tours for solace to be sought at the bottom of a glass, and this trip was no different. Some sought it more regularly than others, and by and large the team restricted themselves to days off. Some of the senior players were surprised by the amount of drinking by the coaching staff, though while the cricket was on no serious incidents came to light.

The fifth Test was a doom-laden affair from start to finish. England recalled Burns, and Robinson passed himself fit, despite a back injury that had dogged him all tour as it became clear his fitness and conditioning were not good enough for international competition. He started well, removing David Warner and Steve Smith for ducks, but went off after lunch. When he returned, his pace had dipped to 70mph. Lewis, who knew him from his time at Sussex, expressed the management's frustration: 'If he's going to perform consistently over a long period of time at this level, he will need to be a fitter bowler, 100 per cent. We've had those conversations, we've been pretty frank with him. And now it's up to him to go and do the work.'

Robinson was not alone. England were not fit enough in general, and the management had been weak with some players. One had started the tour by refusing to take the mandatory skin-fold test. When they insisted, he told them he was being 'fat-shamed'. The test never took place.

England surrendered limply in Hobart, sliding from 68 without loss in their second innings to 124 all out. The series ended appropriately, with Robinson backing away as he was bowled by Cummins, the ninth wicket to fall in a session. Root trooped across the Bellerive Oval to speak to the travelling media, and blamed county cricket's shortcomings. It was clear the management felt constitutional change was necessary in English cricket, but they knew they could influence proceedings only so much. There was truth to what Root was saying, but it overlooked the mistakes made on tour.

Asked what needed to change in county cricket, he replied: 'How long have you got?' He added: 'What incentives in county cricket right now are there to open the batting? What incentives are there to be a spinner? And what incentives are there to bowl fast? There don't seem to be many, the way it's set up, with first-innings average scores of 250. I'm not going to make excuses for a performance like this, because it was not good enough for Test cricket. But what I will say is, anyone that's coming into this Test team at the minute is doing it *in spite* of county cricket, not because of county cricket.'

That night, players from both teams drank beyond dawn, with police intervening at 6 a.m. after they were called by hotel staff when Thorpe lit a cigar indoors, breaking anti-smoking laws. It was something of nothing, but it emerged shortly after newspaper headlines in the UK about England's drinking culture. Hours before the team were due to go home, it was the final humiliation.

It was a miserable end to a miserable 12 months, in which only Root averaged above 31. Apart from him, only Burns and Bairstow scored hundreds. In 2021 alone, England made a record-equalling 54 ducks, and were bowled out for under 200 on 13 occasions. Zak Crawley had scored 267 against Pakistan in 2020 but averaged below 11 in 2021. Extras were the team's third-highest scorer.

England had agreed to a 'Project Ashes' podcast with the BBC, which outlined the detailed planning that had gone into the trip, but that was all thrown into chaos as soon as they arrived in Australia. This all had to have consequences. On 3 February, Giles was sacked. 'Off the back of a disappointing men's Ashes this winter, we must ensure we put in place the conditions across our game to enable our Test team to succeed,' said Harrison. Just 24 hours later, Silverwood was gone too, quickly followed by Thorpe. Strauss was put in temporary charge, and would hire Giles's replacement, leading the 'red-ball reset' that would continue in the West Indies, with Root clinging on.

There is a scene in *Ben Stokes: Phoenix from the Ashes* – the 2022 film directed by Chris Grubb and Luke Mellows – in which Stokes is lying on his hotel bed. The room is silent, apart from the hum of the ceiling fan. The clip was designed to show how lonely touring can be, how much time a player has to think about life and cricket, especially when results are going badly. It was filmed in Stokes's room at the Radisson in Grenada. Just a few doors down, Root was going through his own turmoil. The reset had not worked. India, New Zealand, Australia and now West Indies had broken the England team, and the spirit of its captain. Even if it didn't feel that way at the time, West Indies did England a favour by winning that third Test so comprehensively. It precipitated change that would echo beyond English cricket and offer glimpses of a new future for the Test game.

The 2023 Ashes

First Test, Edgbaston

As if to confuse the Australians, the Bazball Ashes were officially opened by one of the most un-Bazball players in England's history. In 2010–11, at the peak of his relentless accumulation, Alastair Cook had faced a total of 1,438 balls at Brisbane, Adelaide, Perth, Melbourne and Sydney, scoring 766 runs at an average of 127 and a strike-rate of 53. He was so good at this kind of thing that he had since become Sir Alastair. As he walked out between two rows of flame-throwers on the Edgbaston outfield and placed a replica urn on a plinth, he was still England's leading Test run-scorer. Ben Stokes, though, had already suggested he wouldn't have made his team; later, up in the media centre where he now worked, Cook was not alone in quietly wondering about the wisdom of Stokes's first-evening declaration. The two England greats shared a mutual respect, if not a cricketing philosophy. But, for the moment, honoured and incongruous, Cook was declaring the 2023 Ashes open for business.

It's safe to say Zak Crawley sees the game differently. And when he hammered Pat Cummins's loosener through the covers, he kickstarted a series in which he would score more quickly than anyone and confirm his status as Bazball's favourite project. It was the beginning of a memorable day, on which both sides marked out their territory. For the next six and a bit weeks, England would not quite be the irresistible object, and Australia far from the immovable force, but the clash of styles was always engrossing.

The Australians had begun in un-Australian fashion, with a deep point for the first ball. When Crawley clipped the first delivery of the next over, from Josh Hazlewood, to the square-leg fence, Cummins redeployed third slip at cover. By the fifth over, there were three on the fence – not yet half an hour into a five-match series. Ben Duckett had gone for 12, fiddling Hazlewood to Alex Carey, but there were open spaces to exploit for Crawley and Ollie Pope. Before the recent World Test Championship final against India at The Oval, Cummins had suggested his 'field placings might have to change a little bit' for the Ashes. But going on the defensive almost before a ball had been bowled? English observers detected a blow to Aussie machismo.

For the rest of a bright and breezy Friday, the pendulum twitched repeatedly, as it would throughout the series. Their boundary options limited, England stole 54 singles before lunch – the average for the first session of a Test was said to be 18 – and Australian commentators queried their side's tactics. Ricky Ponting was restless; Mark Taylor felt it was 'almost like a one-day game'. Pope reached 31, but was leg-before to a straight one from Nathan Lyon, before Crawley nibbled at Scott Boland and was caught behind for 61 in the morning's last over. Of the 26.4 bowled by Australia, not one was a maiden. For those charged with scoring each session as a boxing judge scores each round, a total of 124 for three was problematic: England had lost at least one more wicket than they would have liked after winning the toss, but had scored perhaps 40 more than par. Not for the first time, their approach would render traditional judgements almost meaningless.

At 175 for three, they were on top, even if Hazlewood had just completed the day's first maiden, at 2.25 p.m. But two wickets fell for one run. Harry Brook, after reaching an assured 32 on Ashes debut, was somehow bowled by Lyon, the ball looping skywards off his pad after a defensive leave, over his head and back down on to the stumps. Stokes quickly edged a big drive off Hazlewood. At 176 for five, the Bazball obituarists were flexing their fingers.

Two Yorkshiremen saved them the bother, Joe Root and Jonny Bairstow adding 121 in just 23 overs before Bairstow was stumped for a run-a-ball 78. Moeen Ali followed suit for 18 – two players stumped on the opening day of a Test in England hadn't happened since 1950. It was a Bazball stat, if ever there was one. Even so, Root completed his first Ashes century for eight years, and England were closing in on 400 – reviving memories of their 407 here on the first day of the 2005 Ashes – when Stokes pulled the plug. He wanted Stuart Broad to reopen the wounds he had inflicted on David Warner four years earlier, when he had removed him seven times at a personal cost of 35 runs. But four overs from Broad and Ollie Robinson went unrewarded, handing extra ammunition to critics of the declaration. Their bullets would be fired for the rest of the series.

Opinion was divided between those who felt Stokes was right to seize small windows of opportunity against the world champions, and those who felt the decision showy and unnecessary. Hadn't he declared eight down in England's first innings two Tests earlier at Wellington, with Root deep into a century, and lost? Surely, they argued, England would have been better off chiselling out more runs, rather than make them in the second innings.

Defenders of the declaration felt it was worth trying to unsettle Australia's openers – Warner in particular – on the series' first evening. They later argued that, because of time lost to rain, the Test might otherwise have been drawn. But that was with hindsight. Perhaps there was a stronger case: without Bazball, England wouldn't even have been in a position to declare, and if you were happy to accept the pick-me-up of five runs an over, you had to accept the occasional side-effect. Stokes knew Bazball might fail if he watered it down. And so, daringly, he declared, leaving Lyon – who had been serenaded by the Hollies Stand with chants of 'You're just a shit Moeen Ali' – with the busy figures of four for 149 from 29 overs. He would later say he had seen no evidence of Bazball.

Stokes's decision, though, did give England two cracks with the new ball – one that evening, the other next morning. And if the first didn't work, the second gave them control of the Test. Broad quickly removed Warner for the 15th time, bowled via a horrible drag-on, then had Marnus Labuschagne caught behind first ball, pushing at one he should have left. Batting experts noted Labuschagne's off-stump guard, and sensed a hangover from his stint at Glamorgan, with county cricket's slow, low pitches obliging him to take lbw out of the equation. The dismissal also meant first blood to Broad, who had spoken in advance of a new away-swinger to target Labuschagne and Smith – part compliment, part con trick. To add to the chaos, Stokes brought on Brook to bowl to Smith, who blocked him with the care and attention of a man who knew dismissal would mean a lifetime of Twitter memes.

Instead, it was Stokes who removed Smith – at the site of his twin centuries four years earlier – for 16. Umpire Erasmus gave him leg-before, and Smith reviewed, in vain. Australia lunched at 78 for three, 46 adrift of where England had been the day before, from 4.2 more overs. Australia had managed 13 singles in the session; England had bowled seven maidens.

After the break, Usman Khawaja and Travis Head, Australia's lone Bazballer, counter-attacked in a stand of 81 – only for Head, on 50, to pull Moeen to Crawley at midwicket. It was Moeen's first Test wicket since removing India's Rishabh Pant in September 2021, and his first to benefit from Stokes's insistence on an inner ring of catchers. Previous captains might have pushed Crawley back to deep midwicket, and Head would have trotted a single.

Two balls later, Cameron Green advanced naively at an off-break, partially unsighting Bairstow as the ball spun back through the batsman's defences. The missed stumping was the start of another subplot: was Bairstow, not long back from a career-threatening leg injury, a better bet to keep wicket ahead of Ben Foakes in England's most important series of the new era? After tea, he would drop Carey on 26 off Root; next morning, he would drop him on 52 off Jimmy Anderson. And on the fourth evening, in the first over of Australia's chase, Bairstow wouldn't so much as flinch when Khawaja edged Anderson low to his left, bisecting him and Root at first slip.

Before all that, Khawaja brought up a classy first hundred in England, cathartically throwing his bat in the air by way of celebration. England's afternoon got scrappier when Broad bowled him on 112 in the first over with the second new ball, moments before replays showed he had overstepped. Australia closed on 311 for five.

Anderson bowled Carey for 66 next morning with a nip-backer from round the wicket, ending a sixth-wicket stand of 118. But Khawaja was still there, prompting

Robinson and Stokes to reprise a tactic they had used in Pakistan: an umbrella field, with three men on each side of the wicket, waiting for the drive. Sensing a chance to score square, Khawaja advanced at Robinson, but lost his off stump. A masterful innings of 141, made from 321 balls in just under eight hours, was finally over; for England, only Root had lasted longer than two.

Khawaja deserved better than to hear Robinson turn the air blue, triggering another theme that lingered. Robinson already had a point to prove to many Australians after struggling with his fitness during the 2021–22 Ashes. Now, he was swearing at – or at least near – Australia's hardest-working batsman and, it was pointed out, their only Muslim. Since he had earned a suspension two years earlier when old racist, sexist and Islamophobic tweets resurfaced during his Test debut, his behaviour invited speculation, though the likelier explanation was that he had sworn out of frustration at Khawaja's resilience. That evening, Robinson further enraged his Australian critics by suggesting England had spent years soaking up abuse in the Ashes, so what was the odd expletive in return? Searching for a name by way of evidence, he chose Ponting, who was not amused.

A few hours earlier, Robinson and Broad earned England a seven-run lead by taking Australia's last four for 14. The closeness of the two first innings offered a snap judgement on the workings of Bazball: England had scored 393 for eight in 78 overs at a rate of 5.03, having played out two maidens; Australia replied with 386 in 116.1 at 3.32, having played out 22. And yet here they were at lunch on the third day, level pegging. Rain limited the afternoon to 10.3 overs, but not before Australia knocked over Duckett and Crawley under the darkest skies of the series, a wicket threatening to fall almost every ball. As the Ashes progressed, some argued Australia repeatedly suffered the worst of the conditions, but Birmingham's bleakness had given them a way into the game.

The fourth morning began outrageously. At last, Cummins had attacked in the field, so Root – still on nought – tried to reverse-ramp his first delivery over a packed cordon. He missed, and the ball passed harmlessly through to Carey, but not before Jonathan Agnew and Phil Tufnell had a near-coronary up in the *Test Match Special* box. In the next over, from Boland, Root whipped a boundary through midwicket, then pulled out two more reverse-ramps in succession, this time collecting six and four. Immediately, Cummins moved second slip to a very fine fly slip – for Root, the desired outcome.

But Australia's attack was too good simply to be manipulated at will, and the day turned into a string of missed English opportunities. Root was stumped, for the first time in his first-class career, off Lyon for 46; Brook fell to the same bowler for the same score, pulling a ball to midwicket that wasn't there for the stroke. Bairstow failed to connect with a reverse-sweep, and Stokes was out-manoeuvred by Cummins. Robinson made handy runs, but when Australia's chase began shortly before 4.45 p.m., they needed 281 – tough, but gettable. Previously a metronome, Boland finished with match figures of two for 147 off 26 overs, and played only one more Test. His six for 7 on debut against England at Melbourne in 2021–22 felt like another world.

This game, and possibly the series, might have turned out differently had Bairstow lunged for the edge offered by Khawaja off Anderson. Instead, an opening stand of 61 was riches for Australia. But ascendancy remained a fleeting concept. Robinson removed Warner for 36, and Broad had both Labuschagne and Smith caught behind, for 13 and 6, to make it 89 for three.

Birmingham awoke to rain on the final morning, another element in the drama. When play started at 2.15 p.m., Australia needed 174 more with seven wickets in hand. The first of the series' four tight finishes was about to unfold. Boland, the nightwatchman – no nighthawk frivolity for the Australians – made a useful 20, before Head fell to Moeen again, edging an off-break to slip for 16. Green provided useful company for Khawaja, who had now batted on each day of the Test. At 192 for five in the final session, Australia looked the likelier winners. But Green chopped on trying to dab Robinson to third man, and Stokes conjured up a 72mph leg-cutter to remove a disconsolate Khawaja for 65, made at slower than a run an over. Had Australia lost, his steadiness might have invited scrutiny, though that would have been unjust: without his diligence across both innings, England would have won easily.

And they became favourites once more when Root held a return catch to see off Carey: 227 for eight, with 54 still to get. Perhaps 19 times out of 20, such a scenario would have led to victory for the bowling team. But England weren't peppering the lower order with bouncers, as they had done in the first innings, and Stokes delayed taking the second new ball: Anderson was off-key, the pitch had offered nothing all game, and the old ball was harder to hit. Moeen's spinning finger had been incapacitated by a blister, so Root stayed on, and Cummins pumped him for two straight sixes in an over. With 37 needed, Stokes's logic almost paid off: Lyon flapped at a short one from Broad, and the ball looped high into the leg side. Crawley ventured in off the fence, but Stokes was already haring back from square leg. He leapt with an outstretched right hand, momentarily caught the ball, then allowed it to slip from his grasp as he returned to earth. After Australia retained the Ashes at Old Trafford, Stokes would describe the drop as his only regret of the series.

He finally took the new ball with 27 required, preferring Broad and Robinson – England's two best bowlers throughout the Test – to Anderson. But Cummins and Lyon had their eye in, and got more value for their strokes now that the old ball had gone. At 7.20 p.m., Cummins chopped Robinson towards third man, where Brook was unable to prevent the boundary. Australia had won by two wickets, leaving Stokes to reflect on cricket's karmic wheel. Four years earlier, Lyon had fluffed the run-out of Jack Leach that would have earned Australia a one-run win at Headingley; next ball, he was deprived of an lbw verdict against Stokes by umpire Joel Wilson. Moments later, Stokes pummelled Cummins for the winning four. Now, Cummins and Lyon were on the right side of a thriller. One game in, and the 2023 Ashes were already living up to their billing.

ENGLAND v AUSTRALIA (1st Test)

At Edgbaston, Birmingham, on 16, 17, 18, 19, 20 June 2023.
Toss: England. Result: **AUSTRALIA** won by two wickets.
Debuts: None.

ENGLAND

Z.Crawley	c Carey b Boland	61		c Carey b Boland	7
B.M.Duckett	c Carey b Hazlewood	12		c Green b Cummins	19
O.J.D.Pope	lbw b Lyon	31		b Cummins	14
J.E.Root	not out	118		st Carey b Lyon	46
H.C.Brook	b Lyon	32		c Labuschagne b Lyon	46
* B.A.Stokes	c Carey b Hazlewood	1		lbw b Cummins	43
† J.M.Bairstow	st Carey b Lyon	78		lbw b Lyon	20
M.M.Ali	st Carey b Lyon	18		c Carey b Hazlewood	19
S.C.J.Broad	b Green	16	(10)	not out	10
O.E.Robinson	not out	17	(9)	c Green b Lyon	27
J.M.Anderson				c Carey b Cummins	12
Extras	(LB 6, NB 3)	9		(LB 9, NB 1)	10
Total	**(8 wkts dec; 78 overs)**	**393**		**(66.2 overs)**	**273**

AUSTRALIA

D.A.Warner	b Broad	9	(2)	c Bairstow b Robinson	36
U.T.Khawaja	b Robinson	141	(1)	b Stokes	65
M.Labuschagne	c Bairstow b Broad	0		c Bairstow b Broad	13
S.P.D.Smith	lbw b Stokes	16		c Bairstow b Broad	6
T.M.Head	c Crawley b Ali	50	(6)	c Root b Ali	16
C.D.Green	b Ali	38	(7)	b Robinson	28
† A.T.Carey	b Anderson	66	(8)	c and b Root	20
* P.J.Cummins	c Stokes b Robinson	38	(9)	not out	44
N.M.Lyon	c Duckett b Robinson	1	(10)	not out	16
S.M.Boland	c Pope b Broad	0	(5)	c Bairstow b Broad	20
J.R.Hazlewood	not out	1			
Extras	(B 4, LB 6, NB 15, W 1)	26		(LB 10, NB 8)	18
Total	**(116.1 overs)**	**386**		**(8 wkts; 92.3 overs)**	**282**

AUSTRALIA	O	M	R	W		O	M	R	W
Cummins	14	0	59	0		18.2	1	63	4
Hazlewood	15	1	61	2		10	1	48	1
Boland	14	0	86	1	(4)	12	2	61	1
Lyon	29	1	149	4	(3)	24	2	80	4
Green	6	0	32	1		2	0	12	0

ENGLAND	O	M	R	W		O	M	R	W
Broad	23	4	68	3	(2)	21	3	64	3
Robinson	22.1	5	55	3	(3)	18.3	7	43	2
Anderson	21	5	53	1	(1)	17	1	56	0
Brook	3	1	5	0					
Ali	33	4	147	2	(4)	14	2	57	1
Stokes	7	0	33	1		7	2	9	1
Root	7	3	15	0	(5)	15	2	43	1

FALL OF WICKETS

	E	A	E	A
Wkt	1st	1st	2nd	2nd
1st	22	29	27	61
2nd	92	29	27	78
3rd	124	67	77	89
4th	175	148	129	121
5th	176	220	150	143
6th	297	338	196	192
7th	323	372	210	209
8th	350	377	229	227
9th	-	378	256	-
10th	-	386	273	-

Umpires: Ahsan Raza (*Pakistan*) and M.Erasmus (*South Africa*).
Referee: A.J.Pycroft (*Zimbabwe*).　　　　Player of the Match: U.T.Khawaja.
Close of Play – Day 1: A(1) 14-0; Day 2: A(1) 311-5; Day 3: E(2) 28-2; Day 4: A(2) 107-3.

4

'Do you have the nerve to do this?'

The greatest revolution in England's Test history began with an abusive text message, then a hopeful phone call. Both were speculative – and both intrigued the recipient. The text was from Andrew Strauss to Rob Key, not long after England had returned, bedraggled, from Australia in early 2022. The call, a few weeks later, was from Key – by now the ECB's managing director of men's cricket – to Brendon McCullum, who was at the IPL coaching Kolkata Knight Riders, and was chatting about the problems faced by English cricket at the precise moment Key phoned with the offer of a chance to solve them. England had recently ground to a halt. Somehow, they had to set the wheels in motion once more.

Strauss and Key had needed little introduction, having teamed up for the last seven of Key's 15 Test caps, first in 2004 – the summer of Strauss's England debut – then in South Africa that winter. In their first match together, against West Indies at Lord's, they had put on 291 for the second wicket, with Key going on to a double-century, the only three-figure score of his England career. Had he played under Stokes and McCullum, it's hard to imagine he would have been dropped for good only two Tests after making 83 against a strong South African attack in Johannesburg. Instead, it was Strauss who became the more decorated, leading his country in 50 Tests, and winning the Ashes both home and away, as only Len Hutton and Mike Brearley had previously done as England captains. Key, meanwhile, continued to play for Kent until 2015, before forging a career as an engaged and engaging pundit for Sky. His on-air sparring with Mike Atherton and Nasser Hussain – not all of it tongue in cheek – became part of his broadcasting persona. But jocularity could not disguise a sharp cricket brain. He was about to put it to the test.

'Strauss texted me and said: "Would you be interested in a real job rather than talking shit for a living?" I said: "I could be interested, mate." And that was it.' Strauss phoned him to find out more, before a Zoom chat also involving Jim Chaplin, a headhunter from London-based consultancy firm SRI, who had worked with the ECB in the past. Key was relaxed, allowing his natural sunniness to shine. 'I said to Jim that I had a great job: I loved working for Sky. I was not bothered if I didn't get it. I said: "If you think you might go for somebody else, just drop me out. I'm fine. I have a better life than going in the lions' den with you lot."'

Other interviews followed with high-ranking board officials: ECB chief executive Tom Harrison, almost the only member of England's hierarchy still standing after the Ashes; Clare Connor, the former England captain who was now managing director of women's cricket; and Martin Darlow, a non-executive director on the board who would soon take over as interim chair. They were all struck by how uncorporate Key was. In one interview, he was asked to outline his management style. He said he didn't have a clue, then talked freely about how he worked. Connor said: 'That sounds like a highly collaborative process, Rob.' Key said: 'OK then – that's my style.' There were no airs or graces, no jargon, no KPIs or spreadsheets. And Key felt his broadcasting career had served him well: 'Sitting around with Nass and Ath, and having to argue with two ex-England captains, was much harder than this – in their eyes, they're always right. I was relatively prepared. It was a great way to do an interview – basically, I don't care if you take me or not. I was not going to just tell them what they wanted to hear. If I do it, this is how I will do it.'

The message he conveyed was exactly what the board needed to hear after a winter of failure on the field, and bloodletting off it. 'I said I wanted to take pressure off people. I want them to see the opportunity and think positively, because – in my simple scientific terms – your brain works faster that way. If the ball is coming out at 90mph, you need your brain to work quicker. When you think properly, your defence is better. If you are thinking positively, you trust your game, and your brain will make decisions quicker.'

For Strauss, Key was the stand-out candidate. 'We'd known a lot about Rob through the work he'd done with Sky and as captain of Kent, so it wasn't a case of needing loads of references,' he says. 'The more we saw of him during his broadcasting career, the more we could see the depth of his thinking and understanding. He's a guy who comes across as very unflustered, quite light-hearted. But there's a lot of thinking that goes on underneath. The other thing Rob had shown throughout his career was an ability to deal with detractors and criticism, a clear-headedness and a sharp cricket brain. All of that came together to make him the obvious candidate.

'We were looking for a new direction for English cricket. The Ashes had been such a timid affair. It wasn't just the losing:

it was the way we lost. Keysy articulated very strongly what a significant impact the England team, their method and style, could have on cricket played throughout the country. He was talking in the interview process about the approach of the Australian team in the 1990s and the 2000s – why it had been so successful for them, and why he felt English cricket could adopt it.

'He felt that was the obvious next stage for our game, and that was exactly my view. It had worked so well for us in white-ball cricket, so it was just a case of embedding that in Test cricket, though obviously that was easier said than done. You need complete alignment between director of cricket, captain and coach, and that was Rob's challenge – to find a coach and a captain who were willing to play that way.'

Strauss had been one of Key's predecessors, taking over as MD from Paul Downton after England's disastrous performance at the 2015 World Cup in Australia and New Zealand. One of his first acts had been to back the white-ball captaincy of Eoin Morgan, who had taken over from Alastair Cook so soon before the start of the competition he had no time to implement the aggressive strategy that would lead to World Cup success four years later. Strauss had not forgotten the lesson.

'What we learned from the Eoin Morgan situation was that, whatever you're trying to do, you can't half-do it,' he says. 'We were trying to do something with our white-ball thinking, and we needed a captain who could embody it. It was clear Rob had that vision too. You've got to be relatively open-minded during that interview process and listen to people's thoughts and philosophies. But I was looking for something that was clearly articulated, and that prospective candidate believed in strongly. Of course, there are always going to be detractors and negativity, and you can get knocked off course easily. So to see it through, you've got to believe it deeply, and that's what I felt with Rob.'

Key's openness paid off. 'He's very easy to underestimate from an intellectual perspective,' says Chaplin. 'But he spends time thinking things through. England were at a pretty low ebb when he was appointed, and he brought that optimism, a can-do attitude. He said not *everything* is wrong with English cricket: it just needs a mindset shift. It was a bit like when Strauss replaced Downton. Strauss brought something different: gravitas, and an ability to communicate with a broad church of people, including coaches, media, board directors. Rob is the same, and he's so likeable. He has time for everyone. That bit of the job is quite important.'

One England player who knew Key well was his former Kent team-mate Sam Billings, who despaired at some of the sniping that followed Key's appointment: 'The amount of people who said it was jobs for the boys. Loads of people wrote it. I thought, *you guys have no clue: you haven't had time to go and talk with Rob Key.* Anyone who had a pair of ears and listened to the Sky stuff – he spoke the most sense out of all of them. If you put Keysy's opinions on Ricky Ponting's face, the credibility would be huge.' Billings intended that as a compliment.

Key was unveiled on 17 April, three weeks after England's defeat in Grenada, and two days after the resignation of Joe Root. The chronology was important, because it meant Key had nothing to do with Root's decision. His slate was clean, which also mattered to Stokes, a lieutenant so ferociously loyal he was almost a Praetorian Guard. Now, appointed by an MD who had played no part in Root's departure, Stokes could proceed with a clear conscience – and Root's backing.

Not that Root ever thought it was an issue. 'It did not even need to be discussed,' he says. 'He will always have my back, and I will always have his. It was never going to be awkward or difficult.'

Even so, Key respected Stokes's principles: 'Ben had decided he was only going to go for captain once Joe had decided he didn't want to do it. He didn't want the job if he was taking it off his mate, which I thought was such a great trait.' Despite some concern – not shared by Key – that the captaincy would be a burden too many, there was an inevitability about Stokes's appointment, confirmed on 28 April. 'I always wanted him to do it,' says Key, 'and he wanted to do it too.'

That was the easy part. Now he just needed to find a coach with a similarly aggressive outlook, a natural capacity for thinking positively against the 90mph ball. Ever since Strauss had first been in touch, Key had been contemplating how he might transform England's fortunes. Having been signed up to commentate on Australia's three-Test series in March 2022 in Pakistan, where the evenings were long and the nights out few, he had time for reflection.

'My view had always been that English cricket had a negative way of thinking,' he says. 'When I was a young player, we always thought: "Glenn McGrath's a good bowler – we'd better watch out for him, and not do anything stupid." But then the Australians came into the county game – Steve Waugh, Shane Warne, people like that. They were the opposite. Their view was that the harder things are, the more aggressive you become. As a player, I couldn't necessarily do that all the time myself, but it was in my philosophy too.

'Then I thought, well, who else would do that? Brendon was the one. To me, it was so obvious. He'd done this with New Zealand. He'd got a side punching above their weight by the way he led, and that was what it was about. It wasn't about how do we win the Ashes? It was about how do we change a mindset and a mentality? Mentality is the most important thing in sport. I felt every other potential coach would be just another version of a similar thing. Whereas I felt that Brendon – and it was a hunch because I didn't know him that well – would be on that sort of wavelength.

'The Test team needed someone with huge credibility. They didn't need someone who was going to come in and say: "Right lads, what do you think?" They needed someone with gravitas, who would also be given time. With the likes of McCullum, you start off with respect, and it's yours to lose, as opposed to someone without the name who has to earn everyone's respect.'

Among the brains Key picked was Billings, who had made his Test debut at Hobart in the dying days of the Chris Silverwood era and had got to know McCullum in the Kolkata Knight Riders dressing-room. Billings was in a Covid bubble in India when the call came through. 'What's Baz like as a coach?' asked Key. Billings replied with what he calls a 'pretty resounding character reference'.

Having seen McCullum up close, he was unequivocal. 'He's an incredible human being,' says Billings. 'He was, in his own way, a great of the sport and achieved everything he wanted, but he understands how difficult the game is, its complexity, and the battle and the inner turmoil people go through. His appreciation of that element was so different. I mean, he's just so un-ECB, after a set-up which was *so* ECB. That's the best way I can put it.'

The captain, of course, needed to be on side, but when Key ran McCullum's name past him, Stokes was 'all over Brendon'. This was more a relief than a surprise. 'I had the hunch it would work with Brendon, but I didn't know exactly how aligned they would be,' says Key. 'Tactics and philosophy are one thing, but actually how they manage people is very similar. They are great players who understand people's failings, which a lot of great players don't. When I used to play with a great player, they would ask: "Why can't you do this?" Because I'm not as good as you, mate!'

In fact, Stokes had approved of McCullum long before they joined forces. In his 2016 mini-autobiography, *Firestarter*, he writes: 'You can tell you are up against a Brendon McCullum team by looking around the field. You won't see conventional and defensive field settings. There will be three slips, two gullies and no mid-on, and that might be the case in one-day cricket, as he showed in the 2015 World Cup, as well as Test matches. Some captains place their hands over their faces when things don't go well for them. Not Brendon. There's no biting of nails, cursing or grunting, just a smile and a positive attitude. One of his signatures is to chase the ball as hard as possible until the second it hits the boundary. He's totally carefree and it's a great way to be.'

Speaking a year into the new regime, Key could fully appreciate the skills McCullum and Stokes had brought to the table. 'They have such a good radar for when someone is struggling, and that is when they are on them. Most coaches and leaders are all over you when you are flying. But they don't do anything for the bloke in the corner who thinks the world is coming to an end, who is struggling like mad. Then when they find form they're all over them again, and you just think: *what a dick*. But these guys are the opposite. They're always there for them.'

Back in the spring of 2022, freshly appointed as MD, Key rang McCullum. The call interrupted a chat McCullum was having with Wayne Bentley, a genial South African who has worked as England tour manager and had experienced at first hand the Ashes meltdown under Silverwood. Perhaps Key's ears had been burning: the topic of conversation was English cricket.

'Wayne started laughing because he knew why I'd called. I asked Baz: "Are you interested in one of the England jobs?" I think I'd thrown him a bit because it wasn't even on his radar. I said we needed someone to change the mentality: I think you're the right person, I think it would be fun. This was the start of me convincing him that I was all in too. It's all well and good saying "I want someone to change the mentality", but you've got to have people who are brave enough to do that, because it can fall flat on its face.'

McCullum listened and reflected. He spoke to his wife – Ellissa, an Australian – who was keener about the idea than he expected. A couple of days later, McCullum called back to find out more. 'We were very aligned about how we think,' says Key. 'He asked me whether I had the nerve to do this: how risk-averse are you? I said I'm fine, I'm not going to do it any other way. If this is the way you want to do it, I'll back you.'

McCullum made it clear he wasn't interested in the white-ball job, because he loved Test cricket and wanted to get his teeth into a bold project. England's white-ball side had already undergone their revolution, making the transition from dead weights to world champions after Morgan had taken note of the change his close friend McCullum had brought about with New Zealand. For McCullum, the potential upside of England's one-day and T20 teams was not as exciting. Besides, for all his white-ball pyrotechnics, he had a deep affinity with Test cricket, never forgetting how the whole of New Zealand had ground to a halt one Tuesday morning in February 2014, when he resumed a match-saving innings against India at Wellington on 281. Twenty-three years after Martin Crowe had fallen for 299 against Sri Lanka at the same ground, McCullum soon brought up his country's first Test triple-century. White-ball cricket could set the pulse racing, but it was Test matches that brought people together. Armed with an open mind, McCullum also knew how important it was for the global game that England's Test side remained strong. What Key said struck a chord: 'I convinced him that I was prepared to stick with this and be brave. That was the start of it all, of him thinking this was a realistic option.'

During their playing days, Key had come up against McCullum only a few times, but listened closely whenever he spoke in the media, and was impressed by his essential belief that cricket was less about technique than it was about understanding people. One instance stood out, after McCullum's New Zealand had humiliated England during a World Cup group game at Wellington in 2015. First Tim Southee took seven for 33 as England were skittled for 123. Then McCullum thrashed 77 off 25 balls. New Zealand won in 12.2 overs. *Wisden* reckoned Morgan's team 'resembled the last stragglers of Stalingrad', which was putting it kindly.

Key, like Stokes, noted the fields McCullum had set. Full of slips, it was not what anyone expected in a one-day international. 'He'd worked out that England were under so much pressure that he went to a Test field – and he attacked the life out of them. Then he came out and smashed it. I remember thinking, *that's someone who's smart.* The person in the street could analyse a player's technique and say: "He's falling over and getting lbw." But Brendon could work out where someone was mentally, just by their body language.

That's what coaching is. It's saying the right thing at the right time. If you could understand where a person's mindset is, then you might be able to help them improve that mindset.'

Despite beginning his own career in 1998, at a time when conservatism still ruled English cricket, Key was heavily influenced by the group of players who went on to win the Ashes for the first time in a generation. Many of the heroes of 2005 – the year Key was dropped from the Test team – shared a faith in the power of positivity, without which an all-time-great Australian side would never have been beaten. Key believes Strauss, the only player in that summer's series to score two hundreds, has been 'as bold a decision-maker as England's ever had'. He adds: 'He doesn't get anywhere near enough credit for what has happened, and there's almost this thing of "Straussy's left [the ECB] now, and that's a good thing". Actually, that's not a good thing. Straussy, since 2015, has been a catalyst. I wouldn't be here without him. You talk about courage: Strauss has had lots of courage in all his decision-making. He's never been afraid.

'There's a whole mob of us, and I think it's from 2005. Whether it's Freddie [Flintoff], Michael Vaughan or Kevin Pietersen – your brain works better when you think more positively, more aggressively. Brendon's the same. He was out in Australia when he was young – his wife was from Sydney – and he spent a lot of time with the Waugh twins at New South Wales. We'd all had this upbringing that was very different to what county cricket was back then. Yes, they were bloody good players, but there was an alignment.'

Sensing he and McCullum shared an outlook, Key sat down to interview him formally on Zoom. Chaplin, Strauss and Mo Bobat were also on the call. McCullum wore a T-shirt and baseball cap; he was softly spoken but clear. Key felt it was like doing a podcast, not an interview for England head coach. He asked McCullum to explain how he thought Test cricket should be played. His answer came in three parts: batting, bowling and fielding.

Key takes up the story. 'He said: "Batters have got to have the ability to put bowlers under pressure, and the courage and fortitude to soak it up when needed." I thought, *yep, that makes absolute sense.* In English cricket, we'd often had the courage and fortitude to soak it up, but we'd not put opponents under pressure.

'Then he said bowlers should look to take wickets, which was always Warney's thing: you can have every man on the boundary, but you should still have one slip and try to nick 'em off. It sounds so simple, but it encompasses everything, whereas I felt England had been a bit like, "we're going to stop them scoring". But actually, the question of how you're going to get them out, and take wickets, is the same thing. It just gives you more options, and you always want more options in sport. If, when you're batting, you look to survive, you either survive or you get out: two options. If you look to score, you either score, survive or get out. That's one more option, and I'll take that.'

Then came fielding, and here Key needed more persuading. 'The one I didn't get straight away was "chase every ball hard to the boundary". I was a bit like: *whatever, I never did that.* But then I started watching. It's such a simple instruction, and you find out whether someone cares or not. If you want to find out how committed someone is, watch how they chase the ball to the boundary.' England had a chuckle about this when, in the sixth over of the new era, against New Zealand at Lord's, Jack Leach hared after a thick edge from Devon Conway, and hurled himself at the ball just before it touched the boundary foam at third man. He saved one run, but landed awkwardly and was ruled out of the Test with concussion. Not that McCullum was going to let one mishap derail an entire philosophy.

Leach's misadventure was still weeks away. Back in the interview, Key was enjoying the simplicity of McCullum's vision. 'It was three rules. It wasn't a 15-minute lecture on Test cricket. It was three very simple views on batting, bowling and fielding, and it made complete sense to me. On TV, you're told to talk in soundbites, and he had that: it meant he could communicate. Cricketers don't want some long-winded plan. They just want bang, bang, bang. I thought, *that's exactly what I want too.*'

There were broader perspectives as well – not least the need for English cricket to change its mentality, which McCullum had been discussing with Bentley when Key called him in India. Now he expanded on it. Chaplin says: 'He said, "you English are always looking at the negatives. You've actually got some bloody good players. You have the raw materials and the resources. What's holding you back is the negativity and the English way of looking at the downside." Rob was a very good interviewer – his media training helped – and he probed him hard. But Brendon was very persuasive and eloquent about how he'd changed the mentality in New Zealand. It was a remarkable interview, and he had this extraordinary charisma and likeability, but also this clarity.'

For Root, the appointment of McCullum felt like the ideal way to draw a line under the old era – a generous view, given his involvement with what had gone before. 'The beauty of it was that we were in a perfect situation,' he says. 'We were just out of Covid, we'd had a rough time on the field as well, and everyone was ready for a fresh start, to buy into something new. It was the perfect time for a new captain and coach to take things in a completely different direction. Keysy was very brave and smart in his appointment of Brendon. He could have easily gone with an established name in Test cricket. I imagine it's a very appealing job for a lot of coaches out there. To go for an unknown entity in Brendon might be seen as a bit of a risk. But it was a perfect fit, really.'

Later, Key decided to simplify England's selection process, after the messy ending to Ed Smith's tenure as national selector in April 2021. James Taylor was moved on as head scout in June 2022, shortly after McCullum's arrival, and Luke Wright – the former Sussex and England white-ball all-rounder – named as a new 'England Men's selector' in November. He became part of a panel that, as well as the coach and captain, included Key, Bobat and David Court, the ECB's 'player ID lead'. If Smith had been too independent for the liking of some, the new arrangement kept things tighter. 'The role of selector changed in my mind,' says Key. 'I wanted a selector, but not one to lead the process and be the head selector – someone to give us a steer on the county game, and input into it, rather than run it. It made sense for the captain, coach and myself to lead it, with all the scouts and national selector.'

McCullum, meanwhile, set his sights on changing Test cricket as a whole. Chaplin again: 'He said, "I love Test cricket, and Test cricket needs England to be good. At the moment, they're not very good." He said it was a massive opportunity to transform Test cricket. I thought: *wow!* It was bold and engaging.'

Key was equally impressed. 'Brendon is a very open book. He had a great line about having a bigger purpose than winning. He said: "Test cricket needs England more than anyone else, and if we get this right it will keep Test cricket on the map." It was so much more powerful than "let's win the Ashes". That resonated with me, and when he said that I was thinking, *shit, it's not that we're so pretentious we think we can save Test cricket, but it will help take pressure off, and will help people follow you more.*

'There was no intensity to him. I didn't want someone who was going to be intense. Everyone is under so much pressure with England. There's never a time when someone's not trying hard; you're generally trying *too* hard. You don't play for England and toss it off. You might think: *this is too hard for me.* But you don't play for England and think: *I need someone to put me under more pressure*, because there is no more pressure you feel than playing for England in a Test match, and that's more than for a T20 or a 50-over game. But Brendon makes it all sound so simple.'

Key had long wanted to split the head coach's job: red-ball Test cricket on the one hand, white-ball ODI and T20 cricket on the other. Both tasks had become untenable for Silverwood, with different squads sometimes playing simultaneously on different continents. For a while, the speculation was that Gary Kirsten, the dogged former South African opener who had coached both his own country and India, was in line for the Test job, leaving McCullum as favourite for the limited-overs role. Kirsten had missed out to Silverwood three years earlier following the departure of Trevor Bayliss – in part because Ashley Giles wanted an English coach. Now, Kirsten's apparent status as favourite suited Key, since it allowed McCullum to go under the radar.

'I had another really good candidate,' says Key, alluding to Kirsten. 'People stopped guessing who it was going to be, because they all thought it was going to be him. He was a bit more of a reserve candidate, so I had the one I was really going for, and someone who would be bloody good and interviewed really well, but would be slightly safer. He would have been a more than capable option if Brendon didn't want to do it.'

As for the argument that McCullum lacked experience – he had never coached a red-ball team – Key was having none of it. 'I always had the view that experience is the most overplayed thing,' he says. 'I find it so frustrating when people tell you they've got to have experience. It's the same with players: if they're good enough, it doesn't matter. Experience can be negative as well as positive. If you chase experience, you end up on this coaching treadmill, where you never give anyone new a chance because they don't have experience. So how are you going to get experience?'

Not that the recruitment process wasn't thorough. Key texted Ricky Ponting, ex-captain of one of the great Australian sides, but heard nothing back. (Ponting later said he had turned down the job.) Stephen Fleming, the former New Zealand captain, was approached, but he was happy at Chennai Super Kings in the IPL. Justin Langer was a free agent again after coaching Australia to their Ashes victory, but Key had heard he wasn't interested. In any case, the suspicion that Langer was too intense had been reinforced by his starring role in the Amazon Prime docuseries *The Test*, which charted his time in charge of the Australians. There were whispers about Ottis Gibson, who had previously been England's bowling coach, and had since taken charge of his native West Indies, and South Africa. But all roads led back to McCullum – with his love of Test cricket, his clarity of thought, his ability to inspire.

'There were some good candidates,' says Chaplin. 'Rob would have been very comfortable appointing Kirsten: he had a good track record with India and South Africa, and he spoke well. But Brendon brought this sparkle and excitement. The attitude was that it would be a high-risk, high-reward appointment, which aligned nicely with Rob.'

During the recruitment process, Strauss – with one of the winter's Test series in mind – asked each candidate the same question: 'How are you going to win in Pakistan?' Key can't recall McCullum's exact reply but, after England won the first Test at Rawalpindi in early December in spectacular fashion, Chaplin texted him. 'If Baz had answered Straussy's question by saying we score at five an over, then declare to leave a 50-50 game, would we have given him the job?' Key's response? 'Probably not.' Some scenarios, it seems, are too outlandish – even for Brendon McCullum.

5

A man in full

It seems strange to imagine, but not everyone was convinced Ben Stokes was the man to replace Joe Root. The doubts had nothing to do with how he might fare as a leader: even while Root was in charge, Stokes was the dressing-room's life force. He had charisma, authority and a grasp of people. He also had an acute cricket brain, though quite how acute would not become apparent until he embarked on the job. Equally, there was no question he would say no to the captaincy: he was not one to duck a challenge, as the England management had recently seen for themselves.

In July 2021, a Covid outbreak had forced the selectors to name a new squad almost overnight for a one-day series against Pakistan. Stokes, who had just sat out some white-ball matches against Sri Lanka – when the virus spread through the England camp – was the obvious candidate among the unquarantined to take over from Eoin Morgan. 'My job needed me to do something, so I had to stand up and do it,' he said with characteristic matter-of-factness. Stokes has always been ambitious, but a sense of duty runs even deeper, as it had when he stepped in to lead the Test side against West

Indies at Southampton in 2020 while Root was on paternity leave. England lost that game, though the selection of both Jofra Archer and Mark Wood provided an early hint about his preference for all-out pace. It remains the only Test England's two fastest bowlers of the modern era have played together. Now, a year later, Stokes's impact was instant. 'When he captained in that Pakistan series,' says Rob Key, 'word was coming out of the dressing-room about how positive they were being.'

No, what concerned some outsiders was that he already had too much on his plate – so much, in fact, that Sam Billings, who had only just won his first Test cap, was touted in some quarters as Root's successor. 'It was quite laughable, wasn't it?' says Billings. 'People were sending me stuff about it. Stokesy was always odds-on favourite, but I was second-favourite with the bookies. Laughable, really. It was always going to be the right decision to go with Stokesy.' Stuart Broad was mentioned, too, though mainly in passing.

But the concerned outsiders had a point. Within three weeks of leading England's reserves to a 3–0 win over a full-strength Pakistan, Stokes had announced he was taking an indefinite break, to look after his mental health. There was also the matter of his left index finger, which had failed to heal properly after he broke it playing for Rajasthan Royals at the IPL. And by the time he replaced Root in April 2022, it had been only a few months since his return to international cricket. The concerns were perfectly reasonable.

It wasn't as if Stokes's comeback had galvanised England, either. In Australia and the West Indies, he averaged 26 with the bat and 43 with the ball. This was Stokes-lite, not the colossus who had bestrode the summer of 2019. And yes – those concerns. He was already the most talked-about cricketer in the country, as well as his team's leading all-rounder and beating heart. And because he was guaranteed a small fortune each year at the IPL, that meant little time off between international assignments – part of the reason he temporarily quit the ODI format in 2022. If he had been willing to bowl 15-over spells for Root, as he did against Australia at Headingley in 2019 before his heroics with the bat, who was going to tell him to take it easy when he was captain?

Key was relaxed. 'I just felt that if he did struggle, he would stop doing the job,' he says. 'I was thinking: *if he does it for the summer and doesn't enjoy it, we will give it to someone else.* I had no real expectation. My job was to take things off him, but not big decisions: people like Ben want to be involved in things that matter. The things you take off them are more irrelevant, like functions or bits of speaking. But at times I get more input from Ben than I do from anyone else, and that is great. He is speaking to players all the time: that is what he loves. You don't take that off him.'

For some on the outside, precedent played a part in the nervousness. This was not the first time England had handed the captaincy to their alpha male, and their track record was underwhelming. Ian Botham had lasted barely a year, stepping down after he made a pair in the second Ashes Test at Lord's in 1981 and walked off to a contemptuous silence from MCC members. Freed of the yoke of leadership, and urged on by his successor, the captain-cum-psychoanalyst Mike Brearley, Botham spent the rest of the summer making history, which seemed to confirm he should never have got the job in the first place. Then there was Andrew Flintoff, whose 11-game reign ended in a 5–0 defeat in Australia in 2006–07 – only the second such whitewash in Ashes history – and a breakdown in relations with his coach, Duncan Fletcher.

In both cases, there was mitigation. Nine of Botham's 12 games in charge had been against the unstoppable West Indians, the other three against Australia. (Brearley avoided West Indies altogether during his 31 Tests in charge, a reminder that luck has always been integral to leadership. He once advised Botham to try captaining England against someone else.) Flintoff, meanwhile, was unfortunate to come up against an Australian side still foaming at the mouth after losing the Ashes in 2005. Key was adamant the past was a different country: 'We have to judge Ben Stokes by Ben Stokes's standards, and not by previous all-rounders who have captained the England cricket team.' But English cricket has rarely taken risks. Even as it celebrated his rise, it crossed its fingers.

Stokes was also emerging from a period of his life which might have persuaded others to quit the game altogether, and led to his decision to take a break. In *Phoenix from the Ashes*, Clare Stokes reflects on a decade of married life: 'We've never had a year without something exciting or dramatic happening.' For most couples, this might mean moving house, the birth of a child, perhaps a pay rise. But the Stokeses were not most couples.

Most dramatic of all had been a six-day trial for affray at Bristol Crown Court in August 2018, the result of a drunken late-night punch-up the previous September which had left one man with a fractured eye socket and another with a concussion. Both men – members of the public – also stood charge for affray, and both – like Stokes – were acquitted. Had he been found guilty, he would have faced a three-year prison sentence and the end of his career. And though he emerged from court with his liberty, the experience left him drained, disheartened, suspicious. During a meeting at a motorway service station near Harrogate with Clare and Neil Fairbrother, the former England and Lancashire batsman who was now his agent, Stokes said he never wanted to play for his country again. As he put it in the film: 'I was thinking I was playing for the wrong people. I was like, I'm not walking out on to the field and putting in my energies and efforts for these guys.'

Fairbrother talked him round: 'He lost the desire, and it just wasn't Ben. So we talked about who you play for and why you play. I had to get over to him that he was playing cricket for himself, his family, his team-mates. That was what he played for. That was why he was so good, and that's what we had to get back to.' The idea of a trusted cohort of insiders would be central to Stokes's captaincy; outsiders with a half-baked, ill-informed opinion were less welcome.

English cricket remains grateful Fairbrother talked him off the ledge: in 2019, Stokes enjoyed the summer of his life. It began on an impossibly dramatic day against New Zealand at Lord's, when he helped England win the 50-over World Cup for the first time. Stokes recalls being asked for a selfie by a senior ECB official he felt had let him down at the time of his trial: 'I told him to fuck off. If this person didn't know how I felt towards them then, they did know the night of the World Cup final.' His suspicion of the men in suits never quite left him: when he was asked in 2023 not to wear England's new bucket hat at pre-match press conferences, he rejected the suggestion.

A couple of hours after England had won the 2019 World Cup, a tired but jubilant Fairbrother admitted his relief in a nearby pub: had England lost, Stokes really might have quit. It was an allusion to the painful near-miss that had haunted him for nearly three years – the four sixes he conceded to West Indies' Carlos Brathwaite in the last over of the T20 World Cup final at Kolkata's Eden Gardens. The experience was made worse by the gloating of his nemesis, and player of the match, Marlon Samuels. In a remarkable press conference, Samuels – still wearing his pads – placed both feet on the table bearing journalists' recording devices, and taunted Stokes: 'He never learns.' Luckily for England, he did.

Victory over New Zealand helped dilute that memory and paved the way for Stokes's second miracle of 2019: six weeks later, against Australia at Headingley, he completed with the bat what he had started with his marathon bowling stint, hitting 135 not out and taking England to a series-squaring win. Jack Leach's share of a last-wicket stand of 76 was 1 not out – a scampered single to level the scores. As the crowd went berserk, Stokes's awestruck team-mates greeted him in the middle as if paying homage to a higher force. The sight of Archer clinging to him from behind, resting his head on Stokes's shoulder, was as touching as it was revealing: Stokes had become the team's spiritual leader, if not yet their captain. In the press conference soon after, Root struggled to put his gratitude into words. The Ashes were alive, and Stokes's stock could not have been higher.

But there was a problem. His experience in Bristol – first on the streets outside Mbargo nightclub, then inside the courtroom – had taken his fame to another level, the sort which makes the front page as well as back. English cricket had been here before. In the 1980s, Botham's off-field appetites had persuaded the tabloids to send news reporters on England tours to accompany the cricket correspondents, in case a bed was broken with Miss Barbados, or the wrong kind of roll-up smoked. This development spelled the beginning of the end for regular fraternising between the players and the press, with consequences that still linger. Flintoff, too, had made the transition to the news pages, having been spotted by a member of the public taking a pedalo out to sea during the 2007 World Cup in the West Indies; when the *News of the World* was tipped off, all hell broke loose. The 'Fredalo' episode became emblematic of Flintoff's messy finale. Stokes's challenge, post-Bristol, was to remain on terra firma.

Two days after England squared the Ashes series for a second time, with a 135-run win in the fifth and final Test at The Oval, the *Sun* ran a shocking front-page story headlined 'Hero Ben's brother and sister were shot dead'. It recounted the murder in New Zealand – three years before Stokes was born – of two of his half-siblings by the first husband of his mum, Deborah. (The husband shot himself.) The story had long been a matter of public record but had vanished from sight, having first been published in New Zealand in the pre-internet era. For the Stokes family, its regurgitation more than three decades on was profoundly painful. Stokes called the decision to publish it 'despicable' and couldn't finish reading his mum's victim-impact statement; two years later, the *Sun* paid the Stokeses substantial damages. It was limited consolation.

Early 2020 brought further turmoil, when Stokes's dad, Ged, was diagnosed with terminal brain cancer. He was 64. To make matters more poignant, Ged and Deborah lived nearly 12,000 miles away in Christchurch. Ged's career as a rugby league coach had taken his family from New Zealand to Cumbria when Ben was 12; nine years later, his parents returned home, and stayed put.

The distance was a wrench, but it had not weakened the bond. Whenever Stokes scores a century, he celebrates by bending the middle knuckle of his middle finger: Ged had the joint cut off his left hand after breaking it during a game of rugby. The alternative – undergo an operation, and miss the rest of the season, including match fees – was no alternative at all. (For years, he told Ben and his older brother, James, that he had lost the finger to a crocodile, which the boys happily believed.) And when Stokes helped deny the country of his birth in the World Cup final, Ged joked that he was 'probably the most hated father in New Zealand'. Aware that time was running out, Stokes flew back to be with his family after the first Test against Pakistan in the Covid summer of 2020. Once the trip to New Zealand was over, he knew he would not see his dad again. Ged died in December.

Stokes was rested from the two-Test tour of Sri Lanka at the start of 2021, but the modern schedule is unrelenting, and on 5 February he was out in the middle once more, scoring 82 to help set up England's shock win in the first Test against India at Chennai. After that series, which England ended up losing 3–1, it was off to the IPL. By the time he stepped in for the one-day internationals against Pakistan, he was running on fumes. Not only was his finger a concern, but he had yet to process the death of his dad, to say nothing of the *Sun* story or his trial in Bristol. Any one of these experiences would have been hard to deal with. To endure all three in quick succession pushed him to breaking point.

As the film's executive producer Sam Mendes puts it during an interview in *Phoenix from the Ashes* when Stokes was in the depths of unhappiness: 'Your dad's died, your mum's been through an incredibly stressful period, Bristol, global pandemic – *anyone* is going to think it's an incredibly stressful period. It's very clear in a way all the things that have gone into it.' Stokes was unaccustomed to discussing his inner life, but quietly agreed. Slowly, he began to heal.

It was cold and grey in Chester-le-Street on the day he was unveiled as England's 81st Test captain, but Stokes spoke with a clarity and a warmth that had been missing from the thousand-yard stare seen by Mendes. When Stokes watched that interview back a few months later, he had all but forgotten its contents – as if a disconnect had emerged with his depressed self. He had cut himself off from others, too, throwing himself into video games and failing to return calls from even his closest team-mates, including Root.

Yet the experience had not been in vain. He was older now, perhaps a little sadder, certainly wiser. 'There's always a negative feeling around mental health,' he said in Chester-le-Street. 'But I see it as a positive. Having gone through what I went through last summer, and even before that, I've got a huge amount of experience in what the game and life can throw at you.'

Those close to him noticed the change. 'It certainly made him much more professional when he came back to cricket,' said Broad, who spent time with Stokes during his break from the game. 'It made him grow up really quickly in a very brutal way.' In the film, Fairbrother echoed him: 'Ben is a different person to who he was pre-Bristol, without a doubt.'

Jimmy Anderson has been a first-hand witness of Stokes's entire Test career, starting with the Ashes at the end of 2013 – a year in which he had already been sent home from Australia by Andy Flower after too many late nights out on an England Lions trip. Flower's words in the disciplinary meeting struck a nerve: 'You don't want to play for England. You just want to piss it up the wall with your mates and have a good time.' Stokes angrily disagreed and vowed to prove Flower wrong – just as Flower hoped he would.

'I feel like he is who he is now because of what he has been through,' says Anderson. 'It has helped him become the person he is. He wants to make sure everyone is looked after, so he gets rid of any outside noise. There was a prime minister's event in Pakistan we were all meant to go to after a day in the field.

He said: "The bowlers are not going. They are staying at the hotel and recovering. A few others and the coaches can go." He's very strong with that, which is great for the players. He has a great manner about him in the dressing-room. He puts his arm around lads and picks us up if we need a lift. He is really relaxed, but I don't think the lads knew how sensitive he could be.'

Wood goes even further back, to his and Stokes's early days in Durham age-group cricket, and has seen him develop from a 'loose cannon of a captain' to what Wood calls – a pinch of salt may be necessary here – a 'mature adult'. Wood goes on: 'He's a guy who's been through the highest highs and the lowest lows. Maybe one or two players in the dressing-room will undergo *one* of the things that has happened to him during the course of their careers. He's had four or five major things happen while he's been playing cricket: World Cup finals, trouble in Bristol, his dad, his mam. So much has happened. So when he talks, you believe him, because he's been through it all.'

At the heart of Stokes's change were new levels of empathy, apparently at odds with the machismo of international sport. He had made mistakes and emerged on the other side. He had experienced off-field trouble of a different magnitude and learned that cricket wasn't everything. Most of all, he had grasped a truth: the *realisation* that cricket wasn't everything could help your cricket. Athletes often talk about the importance of perspective. Having gone through hell, Stokes had taken this a step further, turning theory into practice: play as if there is nothing to fear – the holy grail in any sport. Many had espoused it, but few had successfully implemented it. Fun was supposed to be anathema to the seriousness of professional sport. But, if it replaced fear, perhaps it could unlock some vital force. Deep down, he had always known this. One of his many tattoos reads: 'Being the best that you can be is only possible if you desire to be a champion and your fear of failure is non-existent.' Inked on his left biceps was the essence of Bazball.

During an interview for the *Daily Mail* with Nasser Hussain, Stokes expanded on the extent to which his experiences had shaped him. 'I think the things I've been through make me more relatable to people, not just from a cricket perspective but a day-to-day perspective,' he said. 'I feel I have an understanding of quite a lot of things that can happen to people. If anything, it's all made me more open and honest with myself, which allows me to be more open and honest with individuals. I still struggle with certain things – I find speaking to an individual harder than speaking to a group, because I worry I might say something wrong to an individual. But being relatable does make captaincy a bit easier, I guess.'

Even before he took over, Stokes had been honing his people skills. As Archer prepared to defend 16 in the super over at the 2019 World Cup final against Jimmy Neesham and Martin Guptill, Stokes drew on his memory of Eden Gardens. Rather than advise Archer to avoid full tosses or long hops, he told him: 'Whatever happens will not define you as a cricketer.' Archer started with a wide and was then launched into the Tavern Stand by Neesham. But thanks to the last-ball run-out of Guptill, he kept New Zealand to 15. He later said it was the best advice he could have received, briefly removing him from the pressure of the moment.

In the lockdown summer of 2020, England divided much of their time between the on-site Hilton hotels at Southampton's Ageas Bowl and Manchester's Old Trafford. It eased playing arrangements, but presented challenges to those who weren't used to spending so much time cooped up in their rooms.

When Stokes noticed one member of the backroom staff struggling with the claustrophobia, he generously gave him his room, the spacious captain's suite. The old Stokes, too, might not have donated his match fees on the Test tour of Pakistan – nearly £50,000 – to the country's flood-relief appeal. A few months earlier, when he and his team-mates attended the London premiere of *Phoenix from the Ashes*, Stokes walked on stage and addressed the room engagingly. His turmoil was about to appear, very publicly, on a big screen, but he might as well have been watching a different man.

Again and again during the first year of his reign, he combined a motivational bon mot with an awareness of the bigger picture. Shortly after his appointment, he hit 34 off an over during a championship match for Durham against Worcestershire at New Road – five sixes plus a one-bounce four. The bowler was Josh Baker, an 18-year-old left-arm spinner in his ninth first-class match. That evening, as Baker broke down at home with his parents following some heartless comments on social media, a WhatsApp message arrived from an unknown number: 'Hey Josh, Ben Stokes here. Hope you don't mind me sending you a message pal. Please don't let today define the rest of your season. These days social media is relentless and a vile place for keyboard warriors and people who are jealous of us that we are professional cricketers and they didn't make it. You've got serious potential and [I] think you'll go a long way… Most important opinion is from the lads in your changing-room and they will always have your back. This coming from someone who got meeeeeeeelted in a T20 World Cup final.'

Baker was blown away. 'He's a world-class cricketer and it's his job to score runs, so it was a big shock to get it – and really nice,' he says. 'It felt like it came from him, as well – it wasn't like a generic, robotic message. I messaged him back, and we had a bit of a chat next day about what I could have done different, which was really nice. I asked him when did he want to hit me for six sixes, and he said: "From ball one. Even if it was Nathan Lyon, I'm still going to try to take him on." I was in the wrong place at the wrong time, but I took massive confidence from it as well. It shows his character. He's a fierce competitor on the pitch, but off it he's a really good bloke. You've seen that from his documentary as well. He just seems so down to earth – not big-time. He's got the time of day for a teenage cricketer.'

Whatever qualities Stokes might have lacked when he became captain, empathy was not among them. Key knew this: 'He'd had his own issues, but England needed him not for the player he was, but the way he was as a person.' As Anderson pointed out, and the message to Baker confirmed, Stokes had also stopped caring what others thought, beyond his closest circle. The idea of unhelpful 'outside noise' became a team tenet, with the point often made to reporters responsible for much of it. And when Stokes was interviewed before the toss on the first morning of the first Test against New Zealand at Lord's, he made it explicitly: 'This isn't the media's team. This isn't the *Daily Mail*'s or the *Telegraph*'s team. This team needs a bit of Brendon McCullum really making everyone feel massive. He's very, very good at doing that.'

Stokes's view was that everyone had an opinion, and most opinions were irrelevant. He later told Hussain: 'Pundits and commentators have a job to do and that's fine, but it's not what we need to worry about. The players have the backing of me, Brendon and the dressing-room, and that's what matters. Not the opinion of those writing articles or commentating on you while it happens. Understanding we are in the entertainment business has really freed everyone up.'

And if McCullum quietly paid attention to what was in the media, grasping their use as a means of connecting with the public, Stokes's attitude towards the press might best be characterised as amused – possibly bemused – tolerance. If he decided a press-conference question wasn't quite as exalted as Frost meets Nixon, he would happily respond with a one-word answer, and a polite but unambiguous smile.

Stokes had been an England cricketer for over a decade when he got the job, giving him time to observe how other leaders behaved. He believed, for instance, that Peter Moores – who had two stints as England coach – was too analytical. He also felt Silverwood sometimes spoke for the sake of it. Stokes thought cricket at the highest level could be simplified.

He had learned, too, to appreciate the importance of backing players in public, drawing strength from the assessment of Trevor Bayliss after the 2016 World T20 final that Stokes was the 'heart and soul of the team'. When England's bowling coach Jon Lewis publicly criticised the fitness of Ollie Robinson at Hobart, Stokes disapproved, even if Lewis's words had the desired effect. Stokes, though, had always rated Robinson – even while other team-mates felt he needed to work harder – and believed these matters were better handled in-house.

When he and McCullum first addressed the team, in the Lord's dressing-room ahead of the New Zealand game, neither spoke for long. And what little Stokes did say was not proscriptive. 'Under my captaincy,' he told his players, 'I want you to feel like you are not gripping the bat too tight, and your hands are loose.' The advice fell somewhere between literal and metaphorical, between technical wisdom and the description of a vibe. 'Good vibes' would, for some, become a stick with which to beat Bazball, since it suggested style over substance, the prioritisation of a mood at the expense of runs and wickets. But Stokes knew how much pressure the players already felt. His job was to ease it.

McCullum's team talk was just as brief. Broad recalls: 'There was no presentation. Five minutes before training, Baz said: "Look guys, my philosophy is no dickheads, don't end up on the front page of the papers, and I really want to entertain people. Test cricket is on the edge, and we need people to have fun. England is crucial to Test cricket in the world: entertain the people who watch us. If we have a goal of entertaining, the results will look after themselves. You also buy yourself a bit of clout if you give it a go."'

That last point was important. McCullum knew his task would be eased if England could take the public and the press with them – especially in a country whose first cricketing instincts were usually conservative. However much Stokes wanted his side to exist in a vacuum, McCullum kept an eye on the outside. Validation mattered.

So did simplicity. The resources available to English cricket had always meant plenty of hands on deck, often to the mirth of less wealthy opponents. Were England a bit cosseted? Certainly, McCullum's New Zealand background had been more modest. He and Stokes decided to clear out clutter. Long team meetings disappeared. The backroom staff was trimmed, and those not considered central to on-field performance kept at arm's length. An exception was made for David Saker, the sociable Australian who had worked so well with England's fast bowlers during the Flower era, and was respected by Anderson and Broad; he also likes a beer, which in McCullum's mind did not count against him.

The practice of inviting county coaches to take part in training sessions was ended, to avoid too much advice from too many sources. Except for cap presentations, huddles on the outfield were abandoned: McCullum regarded them as a waste of time, wallpaper to display to the outside world. Everything that needed to be said could be said in the dressing-room. Golf became almost as big a part of pre-match preparation as cricket, with McCullum's handicap falling dramatically during his first year in charge. (He was, though, still a few shots behind both Zak Crawley, a member of the prestigious Sunningdale course whose handicap at one stage was 1.2, and Anderson, who played off two.) McCullum wanted to create memories – the wisdom of the Instagram generation transplanted into the furnace of international sport.

Players could turn up on the morning of a Test whenever they liked, within reason. Under Silverwood, they had arrived two hours in advance. Now, it might be 30 minutes. When Robinson got stuck in traffic one morning in Manchester, missing a planned interview with Sky, it was more like 20; no one batted an eyelid. Net sessions could be as long or as short as the players chose, since they were trusted to know what worked best for them. Naughty-boy nets were made to look like the gimmick they always were. And Stokes removed the curfew that had obliged players to return to the team hotel by midnight on the eve of a game. Adults were treated like… adults. Not until England went 2–0 down in the Ashes was their new relaxed attitude called into question, with former fast bowler Steve Harmison among those who wondered whether the dropped catches and no-balls that had marred the performances at Edgbaston and Lord's stemmed from their laissez-faire approach.

The players denied this, though there was no doubt England's discipline improved as the Ashes progressed: after 41 no-balls in the first two Tests, they bowled just ten in the last three. 'Practice is still taken seriously,' says Chris Woakes, a Bazball latecomer. 'The guys are just given more of a free role in terms of what they feel they need to do to perform. There is still some guidance from the coaching staff, but there's more onus on the player to figure it out for himself. I've been around the game for quite a while now, but in terms of preparation, the most important thing – and some people will disagree with this – is the six inches between your ears. You have to be clear and refreshed and ready for the hard yards of Test cricket. If you end up prepping for weeks on end, by the time you get to the game you're frazzled.'

For some in the dressing-room, the new mood was especially important. Jack Leach had not enjoyed the last year or so of Root's reign. He had not been picked at all during the home summer of 2021, but was still thrust into the first Ashes Test on a greentop at Brisbane, where he was mauled by David Warner and Travis Head. In the Caribbean, he sent down over after over to the obdurate West Indies opener Kraigg Brathwaite, giving away little but rarely threatening to bowl England to victory. In the first innings at Bridgetown, his analysis of 69.5-27-118-3 recalled the accusation once levelled by Shane Warne at Monty Panesar, another England left-arm spinner: he hadn't played 30 Tests, he had played the same Test 30 times. Perhaps more than anyone in the team, Leach needed to be freed up, to be told he was the man, to be made to feel integral to England's chances. Stokes grasped the importance of all of this and set about making Leach feel 'ten-feet tall', as per McCullum's wisdom.

The process took place off the field as well as on it, with Leach asked to make the final observation at the (now brief) team meetings. Sometimes, he would offer a deadpan 'No, nothing', which would raise a laugh. On other occasions, he would come up with something more serious. That would get a laugh too. Leach loved it: 'It's perfect. That's what they're big on: not taking things too seriously. Playing for England *is* important, but I really feel like I'm playing with my mates.' One Leachism did stand the test of time, when he observed: 'We may not be the best, but we'll be the bravest.' Stokes approvingly quoted that more than once.

On the morning of the delayed third Test against South Africa at The Oval in September 2022, Leach had another thought. The first day had been washed out, and the second cancelled because of the death of the Queen. 'I said to Baz as I was warming up that I had something. I decided to make a speech about the Queen and her life. I'd been listening to people talk about her on TV, and how it was extremely positive. The country wasn't always in a great place, but what they loved about her was the way she went about things. I said we were trying to change our way too, and not be worried about the result: people were enjoying the way we were doing it. We should keep that in mind for the game.'

By lunch, England had six South African wickets in the bag, and were already on their way to winning the series. There were no prizes for guessing who was taking the credit. 'I said to Baz: "We should do that more often – that was genius, wasn't it?"' says Leach. 'He was loving it.'

The players also grew to appreciate Stokes's on-field acumen. 'The way he captained in Pakistan won us that series,' says Ben Duckett. 'I knew he was going to be a good leader, but I didn't realise how good. It was like he was always one step ahead. That comes with backing the bowlers, and the bowlers have to take a lot of credit too. It takes a lot to attack how he did – every day, all day long. Other teams might start attacking, then think: *This isn't working, we'll go defensive now.* He continued to try to take wickets throughout, and it had a massive impact on the Pakistani players. Baz sets the foundation and says how he wants to play his cricket, and Stokesy goes even more over the top.'

His declaration at tea on the fourth day at Rawalpindi may yet go down as the high point. England had scored at a rate of knots all game – at 6.50 runs an over in the first innings, and 7.36 in the second, the highest in their history for an innings of longer than five overs. Stokes knew that England's aggression was the only way to overcome the flatness of the pitch and give his team enough time to dismiss Pakistan twice. He also knew he had to set a target that would encourage them to chase the runs. And so he left them 343 in four sessions. His predecessors would not even have been in the position to declare, since their teams scored much more slowly. But, had they faced the same scenario, they would almost certainly have batted on, leaving Pakistan with no option but to play for a draw. On a surface as lifeless as Rawalpindi, they would doubtless have achieved it, too.

'I didn't think you could get a result on a wicket like that,' says Leach, who on the fifth evening, with only minutes to spare before the sun set, removed Naseem Shah to secure one of the greatest wins in England's history. 'It shows the value of how quickly we batted in the first innings. We created so much time to take 20 wickets.'

Roaring Test-match finishes can sometimes make up for four-and-a-half days of cat and mouse. England's win in the dark at Karachi under Nasser Hussain 22 years earlier was a case in point. Pakistan made 405 in 139.4 overs, and England replied with 388 in 179.1. Then, on a fast-forward final day, Pakistan were bowled out for 158, before England chased down 176 in 41.3. But Stokes's strategy meant Rawalpindi was absorbing from the start, when Crawley took 14 off the first over, to the finish, with nine men around the bat. And they were setting their sights outrageously high. During a chat before play on the second day, when England resumed on 506 for four, McCullum had an equation in mind: add another 300 in 30 overs, then stick Pakistan in. That morning, Stokes belted the second ball back over Naseem's head for six, before falling in the same over. Harry Brook hit another six in the next over, before Liam Livingstone hit his seventh ball as a Test cricketer for six more. England eventually settled for 657.

Not all his gambles paid off. At Wellington, he boldly called a halt to England's first innings at 435 for eight, with Root unbeaten on 153, to allow his bowlers seven overs before lunch. When New Zealand replied with 209, Stokes sent them in again. Had England batted instead, with a lead of 226, they would probably have won, and almost certainly not have lost. But his commitment to moving the game forward took priority: New Zealand dug in to make 483, setting England 258. Stokes's team lost by one run. It felt apt, somehow, that the occasional chaos of Bazball should include on its CV only the fourth instance of a team losing a Test after enforcing the follow-on.

Then, in the first Ashes Test at Edgbaston, Stokes did it again, declaring on the first evening at 393 for eight, with Root on 118, cut off in his prime once more. Again, England lost. Again, Stokes had no regrets. He was all in: any backward step, in his view, would weaken England's potency. It took a strong mind – stubborn, some argued – to ignore the brickbats on the outside.

But Stokes was there for the tough times. After one long day out in the middle in Pakistan, he turned the hardship into a positive, telling his players: 'I looked round the field today and I could honestly say I trusted every single person on the pitch. I knew you'd put everything into it, and that's a really empowering feeling for me.'

His ability to take them along for the ride, clutching them close in a manner that felt warm not suffocating, had been on show the previous summer after Jonny Bairstow's power hitting on the last afternoon against New Zealand at Trent Bridge – the day England first spoke about 'running towards the danger'. At tea, with England 139 for four as they chased 299, Stokes had told his team: 'We're either winning this game or losing it.' Later, he began to inflate their tyres: 'With this group of players, the sky's the limit. We can probably go further than that.' He also paid them the indirect compliment of placing the win above his two 2019 tours de force. It was a cute piece of psychology, an emphasis of the collective. The 'vibe' had been 'awesome', the 'enjoyment of every minute incredible'.

After England completed a 3–0 win at Headingley, Stokes used his press conference to speak to the nation's first-class cricketers. 'These last three games should have sent the message to people who aspire to play Test cricket for England over the next two or three years at least,' he said. 'It's about the way you're going to play – not your stats. It's not just about us at the moment: it's about the future as well. And what I think we've done over the last three weeks is make people enjoy watching Test cricket again. If we were on the wrong side of these results, I would have walked off a very happy captain with the way everybody's applied themselves. I'd like to think that people watching know what they have to do to try and bang the door down and get in this team.' England's captain had sounded the Bazball klaxon. When Australia visited a year later, touring journalists would ask their English counterparts to sound the klaxon in the press box whenever they suspected Stokes's team were about to move through the gears.

McCullum was blown away by what he had seen in his first few weeks. 'I'm aggressive, but I think he [Stokes] might have me covered,' he said. 'He came in last night and we'd been set 296 with 40 overs left, and he was like: "We'll just knock them off tonight – extra half hour as well, it's only seven an over!"'

Despite his occasionally outrageous calculations, Stokes encouraged his players to pay less attention to the score, as if it were a distraction. This applied especially when England were in the field and trying to focus on taking wickets rather than fret about giving away runs. As Leach puts it: 'We're not looking to control the scoreboard.' There were even moments when Stokes's fascination with the process seemed to override everything else. After England knocked off 378 to beat India at Edgbaston, he said: 'There was a bit of me that wanted India to get to 450 to see what we would do.' He *did* care about winning. But the perception that he might care less than other captains was unsettling for opponents.

Early in the tenure, Stokes was criticised for selling himself short as a batsman, scoring at quicker than a run a ball against New Zealand at both Trent Bridge and Headingley. In the first of those games, he had fallen for 46 off 33 deliveries, miscuing a huge slog-sweep off Michael Bracewell as England replied to New Zealand's 553. Later, he rationalised his approach: 'Another half-hour or hour of me playing in the way that I did would have turned the game upside down, I guess.' He also knew that the best way to spread the Bazball gospel was to practise what he preached. If that meant sacrificing his own stats, so be it.

But he also knew he owed it to his team to score meaningful runs. Perhaps only Root has a better defensive technique, and few eyebrows were raised when Stokes walked out at No 3 for England's final innings in the Ashes because of an injury to Moeen Ali. Back in 2022, against India and South Africa, Stokes calmed down, and scored consistently at a rate between 63 and 71 per 100 balls. In fact, he only once went quicker than a run a ball after that New Zealand series, thrashing 41 off 18 on the first evening at Rawalpindi, where he had walked out to bat at 462 for four. Otherwise, he struck a balance between aggression and caution, between derring-do and derring-don't.

For a while, the runs didn't flow: 30s and 40s, yes, but nothing more. During the Wellington game, where Stokes made 27 and 33, Root provided some context. 'His own performances will come,' he said. 'You know he's that kind of big-game player. There will be a situation where we'll be up against it, and he'll deliver. Ultimately, it's more important the contribution he's making as leader, because he's getting the best out of ten other players. That in itself is massive for this team.' Sure enough, a few months later, Stokes played two of the Ashes' most memorable innings: 155 at Lord's, which was unable to prevent defeat, and 80 at Headingley, which set up victory. In those, he hit 14 sixes, but defended doggedly too – hybrid batting of the highest quality, and the captain's own take on Bazball.

In 18 Tests since taking over, Stokes scored 1,056 runs at an average of 39, and at a rate of just under 70 per 100 balls. Despite hitting 34 sixes, more than any of his team-mates (Brook was next with 23), he had one of the lowest strike-rates in the side; among batsmen, all-rounders and wicketkeepers, only Moeen, Billings, Alex Lees and Ben Foakes scored more slowly. But it was still an uptick on Stokes's pre-Bazball numbers: an average just shy of 36, and a strike-rate of 57. He had both improved his own game, and set his team an example, going over the top at first, then showing his players how the method might be finessed. It was leadership in the truest sense.

Another factor emerged, slowly but painfully. The chronic tendonitis in his left knee was beginning to play up on a more regular basis. In Pakistan, he had bowled 20 overs in the second innings at Rawalpindi because the ball was reversing – a skill at which he is adept. But at Multan and Karachi, he did not send down a single over. In two Tests in New Zealand, he bowled only nine. He didn't bowl at all against Ireland, and against Australia managed 14 at Edgbaston and 15 at Lord's, where a 12-over spell of bouncers in the second innings seemed to finish him off. For the rest of the Ashes, he was a batsman only, prompting questions about how he would best manage the problem in the long gap before England's next Test assignment, in India in late January 2024. Just over a fortnight after the Ashes came an answer of sorts, when his one-day retirement was ended by his inclusion in England's squad for the World Cup in India in October and November.

But his inability to bowl put another slant on his evolution with the bat. Was Stokes, who turned 32 in June, preparing for life as a specialist? He clearly had the game for it, but any such development would also leave England struggling for balance – and they have often fared best when they have six bowlers to choose from, Stokes included. Intriguingly, he was spotted before and during the Oval Test bowling off-breaks in the nets, under the tutelage of spin-bowling coach Jeetan Patel. Was he seriously thinking about adding off-spin to the many strings on his bow? The idea seemed far-fetched. But then so did Bazball.

The 2023 Ashes

Second Test, Lord's

Jonny Bairstow is reluctant to talk about the S-word. It is nearly a month since he was stumped during the second Test at Lord's – a moment of sharp practice or clever thinking, depending on where you sit in a debate in which everyone has had their say. The Lord's Test brought out the best and the worst of Bazball. It also brought out the worst in others: many who were there on the final day later reflected on their behaviour with regret.

Chatting after a net session at The Oval, Bairstow has had time to consider the incident that changed the mood of the Ashes. He has spoken only once since Lord's, during a spiky press conference after his unbeaten 99 at Old Trafford in which he defiantly replied 'no comment' to questions about the stumping. Even now, in the presence of a single Dictaphone, his instinct is to pull down the shutters.

'Jonny, we would not be doing our jobs if we didn't ask you this. Lord's – how do you look back on it now?' There is no need to mention the stumping: he knows what we mean.

'I don't want to give any comment on it. Not until way down the line.'

'Can you give us anything?'

'No, no. It was just one of those things.'

'Do you wish you'd stayed in your crease?'

'I'm not answering it... I was so close to saying something there. No, no, no.'

'Go on. Can you give us one line?'

'No comment. It is what it is.'

Then he begins to talk. 'It wouldn't come into my mind, you know, because you're stood in your crease. If you're starting in your crease, then it wouldn't even enter my mind to do that. If you're batting out of your crease...'

He is referring to Marnus Labuschagne. As the row raged, Australians pointed out online that Bairstow had previously thrown at the stumps when Labuschagne was batting. But, for Bairstow, that was different, because Labuschagne had taken guard outside his crease. Bairstow was *in* his crease when he ignored a bouncer from Cameron Green, looked up and cursorily marked his guard. He hadn't yet left it when Alex Carey underarmed the ball towards the stumps. By the time the ball hit them, Bairstow was walking towards Ben Stokes for some routine mid-over conversation.

'They're two different things,' he says, warming to his subject. 'If you're starting out of your crease, you're trying to gain an advantage. If you start in your crease, and not trying to take a run, and you finish in your crease... That's the bit – if you try to gain an advantage, then it's fair game. But if you're starting in your crease, you've ducked, tap, tap, scratched. I've even dragged my bat, looked up, and then gone.'

England claimed they would have withdrawn the appeal, with Stokes saying: 'Would I want to win a game in that manner? The answer is no.' It is not the done thing in English cricket to game the laws in that way, which is why there is such an aversion to run-outs at the non-striker's end – 'Mankads', before the word became taboo, though many Australians dislike that dismissal too. But did Bairstow unwittingly become a pawn in a culture war? Is the stumping not the kind of thing that happens in Australian grade or club cricket all the time?

'Does it?' he says. 'First time I've heard that. I've never seen it happen from someone starting in their crease. I don't think you want that filtering down into kids' cricket. Look at the Mankads and everything like that. You want young kids to be out there batting and having fun, not thinking about whether the fielders might do this or that. It might tarnish people's enjoyment of the game that we're trying to get kids into. You want to be out there batting and bowling, rather than thinking about the 11 different ways you can get someone out.'

Was he surprised by the Australians' lack of contrition? Certainly, Bairstow had been furious behind the scenes, telling his opponents what he thought of them in the players' shared dining area, where the incident was replayed on the TV screen in the middle of the room. Bairstow shouted across to Alex Carey and Pat Cummins, asking them how they would feel in his position. He also picked out David Warner, his former IPL opening partner at Sunrisers Hyderabad, and Steve Smith, and wondered why they wouldn't look at him. Eventually his frustration boiled over. He slammed down his cutlery and stormed out, muttering expletives.

'There's nothing I can do about it,' he says. 'The decision was that I was out, and I moved on. I've not brought it up since. I've kept quiet. It's on them. If that's how they want to go about it and win a cricket game or what have you, then so be it. Ben's said what he said, and he's right. There have been other bits. There's conjecture around everything. Fingers underneath the ball when the ball's still touching the ground. Celebrating when the ball has touched the ground. Marnus celebrated at Edgbaston at short leg. Then the one that Rooty fell to at Lord's, when [Smith] said his fingers were underneath the ball. However, they were splayed widely. But that was given out, that's fine – it's part and parcel of the game and the decisions the umpires give.'

With a Test still to go, and grievances still fresh, Bairstow is getting things off his chest. Back at Lord's on that final day, phonecam footage and scenes filmed by Sky Sports revealed anger in the Long Room and the pavilion. The MCC chief executive, Guy Lavender, gave the members a ticking-off over lunch, and launched an investigation into allegations the Australian players were abused on the stairwell leading to their dressing-room. Usman Khawaja and Warner were drawn into unprecedented finger-jabbing rows with members who usually offer nothing more boisterous than polite applause.

It was one of those rare moments when a cricket controversy mushrooms into a piece of social commentary. This was not a football crowd losing its mind at an off-side decision: it was MCC members, the so-called ruling class, in theory immune to such partisanship. In the *Guardian*, Emma John – a member herself – compared their behaviour to Oxford University's boozy Bullingdon Club. In *The Times*, Gideon Haigh wrote of 'puce-faced MCC snobs. Lord's is a place of privilege, in almost every respect, and one of those privileges is that members can stand in the Long Room within touching distance of the players as they walk through and on to the field.'

The Australian team released a statement saying their players had been 'verbally abused, with some being physically contacted, as they made their way to lunch through the members' area'. An investigation was launched. Three members were suspended, and a whistle-blowing hotline was opened. That it all happened in the week an independent report into racism, sexism and classism in English cricket was released, with MCC attracting heavy criticism, added to the urgency of the club's response. When a spoof tweet invented the names of the suspended trio – Bartholomew Frinton-Smythe, Humphrey Wingbert-Porter and Quinten Breckenridge – it said plenty that many believed it.

By the laws of the game, Bairstow was out. But, for many English observers, this went beyond a line call. At the heart of their objection was what they regarded as Carey's sneakiness, evoking the old phrase 'it's just not cricket', used about an immoral or dishonest act. The raging by MCC members, and shouts of abuse at Australia's players, ensured the story would lead the evening news bulletins and next morning's front pages.

The Spirit of Cricket is a vague set of principles that can be read in many ways and disregarded or applied to suit a team's perspective. An initiative led by Ted Dexter and Colin Cowdrey, former England captains and MCC grandees, it was introduced as a preamble to the laws of the game in 2000, when the code was redrafted. It was designed to remind players that cricket is to be played with sportsmanship and fairness in mind. It also reminds them to respect the umpires' decision.

As the incident unfolded, Zak Crawley was picked out by the Sky cameras watching replays of it on his iPad. He looked as bemused as Bairstow. 'It was bewilderment at first,' he says of the mood in England's dressing-room. 'We were all asking each other what we thought. Nobody knew what to think. But quickly it turned into the fact that we were not happy with it. We were discussing whether we would have done it as a team. We all knew it was out: there was no debate on that. It is just the spirit of the game, and we felt we would not have done it.

Each to their own. They chose to do that under pressure and that is the way it went. I actually got out like that myself when I was 15 in club cricket, and I thought it was weird then, let alone at Lord's in the Ashes. There were some emotions in the dressing-room for the next couple of hours.'

Moeen Ali, sitting out the game, was watching on television at home. His thoughts echo those of most of his teammates: Australia missed a chance to prove they had changed since the ball-tampering scandal at Cape Town more than five years earlier. 'I thought, *oh my God, this is going to kick off now – Bluey [Bairstow] is fuming here,*' says Moeen. 'My view was it was out, obviously. I just thought it was a great opportunity for Pat Cummins to put to bed a lot of the things that have happened previously. Not just put to bed, but take away that label they have had for a while with Sandpapergate. Firstly, if I was captain, I would hate to win a game like that. And secondly, a great opportunity missed for Australia.'

The Australians ended up winning by 43 runs, but with their character under question, as a cry of 'Same old Aussies, always cheating' echoed round Lord's. Carey, an unassuming character far removed from the Rod Marsh–Ian Healy image of Aussie keepers, was unsettled; it seemed no coincidence that his series fell away. The likeable Cummins – a new-age captain of Australia, and a climate-change campaigner who has modelled hoodies made from seaweed and been derided as 'woke' – was clearly unnerved. For once, it was England who had the alpha-male captain. Now, Cummins was projected as a hypocrite because he had said Australia had changed since Sandpapergate. Presented with his first moral dilemma, he seemed more like an old-school Aussie captain. That, at least, was the excuse many in the crowd needed to boo, though they needed little encouragement.

It all overshadowed Australia's best performance of the series, in which they out-thought England for the only time. The margin of victory looked closer than it was, because Stokes channelled his rage to score a breathtaking 155 from 214 balls with nine sixes – breaking the Ashes record he had set at Headingley in 2019. With England six down and still 178 short, Bairstow had been replaced in the middle by Stuart Broad, forming with his captain a challenging combination for the Australians: Stokes, looking to take his anger out on the bowlers, and Broad, the arch Aussie baiter who had never been forgiven for refusing to walk at Trent Bridge in 2013. Now, he had a free hand to wind them up, and the support of nearly 30,000 spectators. He told Carey: 'That's all you're ever going to be remembered for, that.' He repeated the taunt. Carey replied: 'Yeah.' Broad then turned to Cummins: 'Literally, that's the worst thing I've ever seen in cricket, and those boos are for you.' And he tapped his bat inside the crease at the end of each over, shouting 'in', as if fooling around on the beach.

Three weeks later, Broad leans back in his chair in the Old Trafford media centre and spills out the story as if giving evidence in the witness box, forensically going through every moment. It does not require a Perry Mason cross-examination to elicit the details: unlike Bairstow, he needs little prodding.

'You could tell there was a bit of anger brewing, even a minute after the decision, which maybe connected with my red mist when I got out there,' he says. 'When I saw it on the screen in our dressing-room, I stood up and thought: *what's happened there?* I thought, *they're going to revoke that, surely* – it was just a given. There's no way they'll keep that. And when they did, the crowd booed.

'For me, I wasn't really that angry about it. I've seen loads of things on the cricket field. But it was a good way of getting involved, creating a bit of chaos and putting doubt in their mind. Because ultimately they'd won the game at that point. So it was to try to take them away from what they were doing, and cause carnage. That was our only way of getting a win – we needed nearly 200. And it worked. It affected them, and they bowled differently. They were very stand-offish. You could almost see the cogs turning, and they were like: *could we have done something differently here?* I was saying: "I've never heard Lord's like this – these are cricket fans, listen to what they think of your decision."'

'I pointed at Pat quite a lot. I was shouting at him: "You hear all these boos – they're for you. Your one decision, they're for you." Again, I didn't really believe it – it was just a way of me changing the game up and seeing what would happen. At lunch, Stokesy had got his hundred – there was a massive cheer when we walked in the Long Room first. Then we turned our corner. I've been booed by 50,000 people at the Gabba, and I reckon the Long Room was louder. It was unbelievable. I was like, wow! Then we saw Sky's most-watched Twitter clip ever: the members having a go at the Aussies. I couldn't hear what they were saying – the boos drowned it out. But I'd never heard boos like that.'

Was there tension in the players' dining-room? 'I wasn't there, because I was batting, but I've heard about it. The awkward thing about lunch is you've got a table where England sit, then a little gap, then a table where the Aussies sit. In the middle, there's a TV on the wall. They were obviously showing it on Sky. All the players were watching it, including Jonny. He hadn't been up for lunch all week – he always has it in his spot in the dressing-room. But he went up that day to see what was going on.

'I think Zak was... not winding Jonny up, but going: "I can't believe they've done that. They can't be happy with that." I

think he said: "You should ask them if they're happy with that."
Within point five of a second, Jonny says: "You happy with that,
lads?" They were like: "Yeah, pretty happy." But the members
were lined up all the way from their changing-room to the lunch
room as well. They must have thought: *have we got this one
slightly wrong, maybe?* The Australians later said it was Warner
who replied to Bairstow's question, prompting teammates –
their backs to the England table – to dissolve into a fit of giggles.
It might just as easily have been the primary-school canteen.

Before lunch, Stokes moved to his hundred with three
successive pulls for six off Green. After it, he hit the second ball,
from Hazlewood, for six more, this time down the ground.
Smith dropped him in the same over at deep backward square
on 114, but he kept hitting out, even with nine on the fence.
And while Broad was busy annoying the Australians, Stokes
preferred a menacing silence.

'He didn't say a word,' says Broad. 'He was revving me
up. I was saying: "Do you think I've got to calm down here,
Stokesy?" He said: "No, keep going. I think they're properly
rattled." The Aussies weren't talking to each other. They were
just turning round and bowling. I was just being that facetious
prat that I turn into on the odd occasion.

'Hazlewood was bowling into the wind with the short
boundary, so I said to him: "It's nice the captain bowling you
at this end, isn't it? Bet he'll drop you next week. He'll bowl
that end, and you'll get dropped. I promise you. You watch."
Starc told me to eff off at one stage. It was me in red-mist,
competitive mode. I hate batting – I can't bat. But I thought
if I get into some sort of battle… Like when I blocked 50 balls
off Jimmy [Anderson] at Trent Bridge in a county match a
few weeks earlier. Something in my brain was saying: "I am
not going to get out."'

Broad wore the bouncers, which were many, and says they have 'only just healed'. He reckons he picked up eight bruises, and points to his right arm, where he was cut by the ball's seam. 'Very bravely, I had one in the middle of my back as well, which Rooty loves.'

As sporting theatre, it was riveting, England's indignation the support act to Stokes's star turn. Until then, he had struggled for rhythm with the bat, and when Bairstow was dismissed he had 62 from 126 balls. With Broad at No 8 – England were fielding an all-seam attack for the only time in the Bazball era – they had a longer tail than usual. You can hardly blame Australia for their ruthlessness. They knew Bairstow and Stokes were capable of obliterating the target and, with Headingley 2019 in mind, were taking nothing for granted. They also knew Stokes would have to take risks once Broad arrived. And, against the short ball, they suspected Broad would not last long. These were reasonable assumptions. Now, they just had to do something about them.

Instead, Stokes went on the rampage, pummelling eight sixes in ten overs, all towards the short leg-side boundary by the Tavern and Mound Stands. Lord's can be quiet. Now it was febrile – the hum replaced by a roar. Stokes barely celebrated his century: he was in the zone, and business needed to be concluded. Everyone knew defeat for Australia would be worse than Headingley four years earlier.

Cummins brought together his senior players at the end of the 66th over. It proved a profitable chat, and they proceeded to bowl wider of off stump, making it harder for Stokes to cart them over leg. After smashing 85 from 60 balls, he slowed down, his next eight coming from 28. At a drinks break, he spoke to Broad: he felt he needed to go for it. With 70 needed, Stokes tried to heave Hazlewood towards the longer boundary, and was left hunched over his bat as Carey held the skyer. A raucous stand of 108 in 20 overs, of which Broad's share was 11, had come to an end.

England still had three wickets, but Ollie Robinson and Broad fell in successive overs. Josh Tongue and Jimmy Anderson cobbled together 25 for the last wicket, giving Australia one last, brief worry. 'We got close,' says Tongue, who was finally bowled by Starc trying to make room. Soon, the Australians were out on the field at a deserted Lord's, playing with their children – a touching contrast to the rancour.

'The drinks break came at a bad time for us,' says Broad. 'I regret now… perhaps at one stage, with everyone on the boundary, we should just have taken singles. If we go at four an over for an hour here, they might have to change tack. Stokesy's a freak, but it was hard to keep doing sixes. When he's in that mode, he doesn't call. He just says: "Watch what I do." But it was amazing as a sports fan for me to be out there and watch him in that mode. It was really cool – one of my best mates in the ultimate zone, and not being fazed by what I was doing or the Aussies were doing, but just being clear in his own plan.'

The stumping debate dominated the post-match wash-up. 'I can't imagine we'll be having a beer anytime soon, if that's what you're asking,' said Brendon McCullum. This from a man who had grown up at Albion Cricket Club in South Dunedin, where a beer with opponents is part of an unwritten code. There is no greater insult.

Cummins was unrepentant. 'I thought it was totally fair play. That's how the rule is. Some people might disagree. That's how I saw it.' Stokes said 'yeah' when asked if he would have withdrawn the appeal. 'When is it justified that the umpires have called over?' he asked. 'Is the on-field umpires making movement… is that signifying over? I'm not sure. Jonny was in his crease, then out of his crease. I am not disputing the fact it is out. If the shoe was on the other foot, I would have put more pressure on the umpires and asked whether they had called over, and had a deep think about the whole spirit of the game, and would I want to do something like that? For Australia it was the match-winning moment. Would I want to win a game in that manner? The answer for me is no.'

McCullum was soon denounced as a hypocrite, as the whataboutery began in earnest. He had, for instance, once run out Sri Lanka's Muttiah Muralitharan during a Test match after Murali left the crease to celebrate a century by Kumar Sangakkara while the ball was still live. In 2016, he apologised while delivering MCC's Spirit of Cricket lecture at Lord's. But he had had years to think about his decision – Cummins had a couple of minutes, in the heat of an Ashes battle. Australians sensed McCullum was being holier-than-thou.

Even politicians became involved. 'The prime minister agrees with Ben Stokes,' said a spokesman for Rishi Sunak. 'He said he simply wouldn't want to win a game in the manner Australia did.' This prompted a response from Anthony Albanese, his Australian counterpart. 'When I was learning to play cricket, as every Australian does at primary school, the nuns at St Joseph's Camperdown knew: put your bat behind the crease. Stay in your crease. It's not hard.' He also tweeted: 'Same old Aussies, always winning.' Two weeks later, at a NATO summit, Albanese presented Sunak with a photograph of the stumping. 'I'm sorry I didn't bring my sandpaper with me,' deadpanned Sunak.

Does the stumping have anything to do with Bazball? Arguably, it strikes at the heart of how McCullum and Stokes want to play. They believe – even if it sounds pompous – that they want to win in the 'right way'. They see themselves as role models. One day, they will be tested by a Spirit of

Cricket incident. After the Lord's hoo-ha, their response will be watched closely. The Australians were a bit crafty, that's all. England may easily be hypocrites in the future.

What about the rest of the Lord's Test? It started with Bairstow lifting up a Just Stop Oil protester after three ran on the pitch in the second over. Picking him up as if tucking a bat under his arm, he carried him over the rope and – to cheers from the crowd – dumped him on the sidelines. A colleague managed to deposit orange powder on the square, though it was easily hoovered up. Nothing, not even the prospect of climate Armageddon, was going to stop the Ashes.

By then, England had won the toss in good bowling conditions, having stuck by Anderson after his difficult first Test, but they put down both openers in the first hour, and a dark mood descended. Again, Australia were slow, making 39 off the first 16 overs, but batting was not easy. Tongue, playing because Moeen's spinning finger had not recovered after Edgbaston, struck first, bowling the becalmed Khawaja in the last over before lunch, then Warner soon after, for 66 – his highest score of the series. Robinson removed Labuschagne for 47, but it was a stand of 118 between Travis Head and Steve Smith that made this Australia's day. Head took on a bouncer barrage and won, making 77 off 73, though when he and Green fell in the same over to Joe Root, England were clinging on.

Smith, 85 overnight, moved to his eighth Test century in England – behind only Donald Bradman's 11 among visiting batsmen – and Australia made 416, their largest total of the summer. Tongue took three for 98, but Anderson and Broad managed only two for 152, while Anderson later dropped two catches – including, crucially, Khawaja, only 19 runs into his second-innings 77. Once more, England were paying for their laxity.

They did, though, set about their reply with gusto, as Crawley and Ben Duckett put on 91 inside 18 overs, before Crawley was stumped for 48 off Nathan Lyon, the first bowler to play 100 consecutive Tests. It left Lyon only four short of 500 Test wickets, but proved his last of the series. Duckett played superbly at times, scratchily at others, but a slow pitch suited his dabs, and he made swift progress on the ground where he had hit 182 against Ireland a few weeks earlier.

Australia were getting desperate as he and Ollie Pope worked them around, so Cummins changed tack. Recognising the two-paced nature of the pitch, the quick bowlers went short, suspecting England would take on the challenge. It led to a passage of play that lost England the Test, but cost Australia dear, too. When Duckett swatted another bumper from Green towards the Grand Stand, Lyon ran in for the catch, but pulled up in agony, having ripped his calf. Distraught, he was helped round the boundary by medical staff, straight into an ambulance. The immediate comparisons were with Glenn McGrath, who had twisted his ankle treading on a stray ball on the morning of the Edgbaston Test in 2005. But while McGrath played two more games in that series, Lyon's summer was over – bar a brief reappearance with the bat in Australia's second innings.

Moments later, England reached 188 for one. Against an attack lacking its champion off-spinner, control of the game beckoned if they could see off the bouncers. But the Bazballers lost their heads. Pope failed to read the situation, tried to hook Green and was caught on the boundary. He had an excuse of sorts: he had dislocated his shoulder fielding (an injury that would end his series) and could not quite get under the shot, toe-ending it to Smith. In which case, though, why play it? Duckett fell for 98, playing his fourth uncontrolled hook in a row just as the engraver was poised over the honours board. Then Root was bounced out for 10, having been caught off a Green no-ball on 1. England had lost three inside eight overs.

At the end of play, Duckett took part in an excruciating interview with the BBC cricket correspondent, Jonathan Agnew, who wondered whether England should have batted with more nous. 'What about the general mood in the dressing-room, that three frontline batsmen get out in that fashion with such a clear [bouncer] plan, and with the spinner off the field injured?' he asked. 'I'm not sure how to answer that,' said Duckett. 'I'm surprised about the question. We've played positive cricket for the past 12 months and we're certainly not going to change.'

It was the wrong tone. Humility can help, especially at 1–0 down, and even more so with 2–0 on the horizon. And England did learn from it, whether they cared to admit it or not. McCullum watched everything unfold from the players' balcony, but did not flinch. 'He was happy,' says Tongue. 'That is what Baz is so good at. He backs everyone 100 per cent, whatever your gameplan is.'

Despite the outcry about England's batting, they got to stumps on 278 for four, with Stokes calmly ignoring the short stuff to reach 17 off 57 balls. They were still in the game. But Starc removed him with the second delivery of the third day, before Brook became the latest to fall to the short ball, slapping Starc to cover for 50 – an egregious shot after the events of the previous afternoon. England were soon all out for 325, and chasing the game.

Armed with a lead of 91, Australia had latitude, and Khawaja survived the drop by Anderson, at midwicket off Tongue, to build on their advantage. England hit back with their own prolonged spell of bouncers, including 12 overs in a row from a half-hobbling Stokes – his final bowl of the series. Robinson got stuck in, and Broad chipped away, before Lyon dragged himself out to bat on one leg, and helped Starc put on 15 for the last wicket – a courageous act which provoked winces and grimaces on the Australian balcony. The contrast with England's approach at Edgbaston was telling: where Stokes declared early to have two new-ball sessions, Australia chose to squeeze out every run, whatever the cost to Lyon's fitness. He even pulled Broad for four. It had been brutal, draining cricket. After England's first-innings collapse, seamers on both sides had banged it in continuously. The ball struck body, glove or helmet 52 times, as 32 per cent of deliveries were pitched short, the highest since ball-tracking data began in 2006.

England's chase began disastrously. Starc reduced them to 13 for two with the wickets of Crawley, feathering down the leg side, and Pope, thrillingly yorked. And when Cummins worked over Root, then bowled Brook with a beauty, it was 45 for four. As stumps beckoned, Australia thought they had Duckett for 50 after Starc caught him at fine leg, but rubbed the ball along the ground as he slid on his knees. The third umpire, Marais Erasmus, ruled that he did not have control over his body before the catch was complete, sparking anger among the Australians. They later accepted Erasmus's ruling, but through gritted teeth, and not before Starc had berated Duckett, who next day went on to make 83.

Did Australian resentment at Erasmus's interpretation spill over into the stumping of Bairstow? It is hard to say. But with Duckett's reprieve following the bouncer warfare, it was perhaps unsurprising that Australia should refuse to budge over Bairstow. And so Lord's turned into a Roman amphitheatre, baying for blood on an unforgettable final day.

ENGLAND v AUSTRALIA (2nd Test)

At Lord's, London, on 28, 29, 30 June, 1, 2 July 2023.
Toss: England. Result: **AUSTRALIA** won by 43 runs.
Debuts: None.

AUSTRALIA

D.A.Warner	b Tongue	66	(2)	lbw b Tongue	25
U.T.Khawaja	b Tongue	17	(1)	c sub (M.J.Potts) b Broad	77
M.Labuschagne	c Bairstow b Robinson	47		c Brook b Anderson	30
S.P.D.Smith	c Duckett b Tongue	110		c Crawley b Tongue	34
T.M.Head	st Bairstow b Root	77		c Root b Broad	7
C.D.Green	c Anderson b Root	0		c Duckett b Robinson	18
† A.T.Carey	lbw b Broad	22		c Root b Robinson	21
M.A.Starc	c Bairstow b Anderson	6		not out	15
* P.J.Cummins	not out	22		c Duckett b Broad	11
N.M.Lyon	c Tongue b Robinson	7	(11)	c Stokes b Broad	4
J.R.Hazlewood	c Root b Robinson	4	(10)	c Root b Stokes	1
Extras	(B 12, LB 14, NB 12)	38		(B 14, LB 9, NB 6, W 7)	36
Total	**(100.4 overs)**	**416**		**(101.5 overs)**	**279**

ENGLAND

Z.Crawley	st Carey b Lyon	48	c Carey b Starc	3
B.M.Duckett	c Warner b Hazlewood	98	c Carey b Hazlewood	83
O.J.D.Pope	c Smith b Green	42	b Starc	3
J.E.Root	c Smith b Starc	10	c Warner b Cummins	18
H.C.Brook	c Cummins b Starc	50	b Cummins	4
* B.A.Stokes	c Green b Starc	17	c Carey b Hazlewood	155
† J.M.Bairstow	c Cummins b Hazlewood	16	st Carey b Green	10
S.C.J.Broad	lbw b Head	12	c Green b Hazlewood	11
O.E.Robinson	c Carey b Head	9	c Smith b Cummins	1
J.C.Tongue	c sub (M.T.Renshaw) b Cummins	1	b Starc	19
J.M.Anderson	not out	0	not out	3
Extras	(B 9, LB 4, NB 7, W 2)	22	(LB 3, NB 4, W 10)	17
Total	**(76.2 overs)**	**325**	**(81.3 overs)**	**327**

ENGLAND	O	M	R	W		O	M	R	W
Anderson	20	5	53	1		19	4	64	1
Broad	23	4	99	1		24.5	8	65	4
Robinson	24.4	3	100	3	(4)	26	11	48	2
Tongue	22	3	98	3	(3)	20	4	53	2
Stokes	3	1	21	0		12	1	26	1
Root	8	1	19	2					

AUSTRALIA	O	M	R	W		O	M	R	W
Starc	17	0	88	3		21.3	2	79	3
Cummins	16.2	2	46	1		25	2	69	3
Hazlewood	13	1	71	2		18	0	80	3
Lyon	13	1	35	1					
Green	9	0	54	1		13	3	73	1
Head	7	1	17	2	(4)	4	0	23	0
Smith	1	0	1	0					

FALL OF WICKETS

Wkt	A 1st	E 1st	A 2nd	E 2nd
1st	73	91	63	9
2nd	96	188	123	13
3rd	198	208	187	41
4th	316	222	190	45
5th	316	279	197	177
6th	351	293	239	193
7th	358	311	242	301
8th	393	324	261	302
9th	408	325	264	302
10th	416	325	279	327

Umpires: Ahsan Raza (*Pakistan*) and C.B.Gaffaney (*New Zealand*).
Referee: A.J.Pycroft (*Zimbabwe*).   Player of the Match: S.P.D.Smith.
Close of Play – Day 1: A(1) 339-5; Day 2: E(1) 278-4; Day 3: A(2) 130-2; Day 4: E(2) 114-4.

6

On the couch with Bazball

In the book-lined basement study of his North London home, Mike Brearley is trying to make sense of it all. The insights shared here are usually for the benefit of the patients who visit him for psychoanalysis. But Brearley, possibly the best reader of people ever to be a Test captain, is fascinated by what Ben Stokes has been up to. On the surface, the two could scarcely be more different. Brearley is the scholar from Cambridge who used to write Shakespearean sonnets on his wrist before taking the field for Middlesex. Stokes is the lad from Cumbria who left school at 16 with a GCSE in Physical Education and has rap lyrics tattooed on his arms.

And yet both have an interest in the inner life, using it to forge their identities as captain. Brearley won 18 Tests out of 31 between 1977 and 1981, and lost only four. At the time of our conversation, Stokes has won ten out of 12. Both believe a captain must understand his players, and Brearley – who decodes hidden urges and unknown motivations for a living – gently ponders the origins of Stokes's style of leadership.

'I had this idea that maybe it was to do with being depressed,' he says. 'McCullum said the same – he'd been depressed, he'd lost his drive for top-class cricket. In Stokes's case, I think with his father's death and with his illness and the court case and probably other things, he'd become depressed. Well, he said he had: Mendes's film showed that. I wondered if it was a sort of new lease of life, which has a very slightly manic quality to it. I'm not saying he's bi-polar or manic, but I'm saying there's a trace of it. It's slightly gung-ho. You wouldn't want a surgeon to be gung-ho, but the important point is it's only a game – and it's one game at a time.'

Brearley is theorising, but he may be on to something. On the third evening of the third Test against Pakistan at Karachi, England had been set 167 to win, and given a good start – 87 in 11.3 overs – by Ben Duckett and Zak Crawley. Rehan Ahmed walked out as England's first official 'nighthawk', the nickname given by McCullum to Stuart Broad – who missed the trip to take paternity leave – in a bid to encourage him to be a different sort of nightwatchman. In the dressing-room, Stokes had put on his pads. Mark Wood asked him what he was doing. Stokes replied: 'I'm going to try to win the game.' Wood looked baffled: 'Stokesy, there's two days left!' Stokes said: 'We can win it tonight.'

Wood remembers: 'I was a bit shocked. Do I say to him "let's not give them a chance", only for him to tell me to eff off and say: "This is not what this team is about"? I was reluctant to say anything, which is not like me. I usually say what I'm thinking, but this time I raised my eyebrows, and said: "All right." That was the first time I realised this was proper different.'

When Ahmed fell for an eight-ball 10, and with the light fading, Stokes marched out, and spoke briefly to Duckett: 'He said the way me and Zak had batted, he was so giddy,' says Duckett. 'He thought he could hit six sixes and win the game that night.' At one point, Stokes tried to launch Pakistan's left-arm spinner Nauman Ali in the direction of the Arabian Sea, only to lose control of his bat, which described a parabola towards square leg. So, yes: 'manic' feels about right.

In the main, Brearley speaks admiringly of what Stokes has done, though he thinks he is wrong to discount draws, and says cricket should still find room for caution, citing Alastair Cook and Geoff Boycott, who between them scored over 20,000 Test runs without too many risks. Is it right to suggest Stokes discounts draws? Not entirely: he just doesn't want his team to play for them, because he fears it will breed caution. Instead, he wants his players constantly thinking about how they might win. But his threshold remains unclear. When he was asked before the second Test at Multan whether, with 20 needed off the last over and England nine wickets down, he would encourage Jimmy Anderson to go for the runs, he didn't hesitate: 'Yes.' Five reverse-sweeps for four? 'Yes.' Trying to work out when, if ever, he might shut up shop became a parlour game, and it was never resolved – mainly because the scenario never arose. Not until the Old Trafford Test against Australia, the 17th of his tenure, did England draw, and that was only because rain ruined the last two days.

Brearley's point about Cook was a different matter. In a pre-Ashes interview, Nasser Hussain – another England captain from the old school – asked Stokes whether the likes of Cook, Mike Atherton and Jonathan Trott would have found a place in his team. Stokes said he respected the way they had played, but added: 'In this day and age, while I'm captain and Baz is coach, that is not something we're looking for.' It was why Duckett eventually replaced Alex Lees. Back in November, before England headed off on tour, a piece by Cook for the *Sunday Times* was headlined: 'Will Stokes stick to all-out attack? I'd advise against it in Pakistan, where patience is key.' The piece did the rounds on the England team WhatsApp group. Their run-rate in Pakistan was 5.50 – a record for a Test series of more than one game.

Back chez Brearley, and the 2023 Ashes have not yet begun. When they do get underway, it's easy to imagine him questioning the wisdom of Stokes's first-evening declaration at Edgbaston, or England's headstrong hooking at Lord's. Brearley was revolutionary in his time, but even he feels faintly uneasy about Stokes's shredding of the rule book.

It is not immediately obvious whether he is simply applying the wisdom of another era, or has got to the heart of Bazball, a philosophy whose greatest strength may also be its biggest weakness. Freedom, yes – but what about responsibility? In his latest book, *Turning Over the Pebbles*, Brearley recounts the First World War experiences of Wilfred Bion, a giant of psychoanalysis. After Bion – whose wartime CV included Ypres and Passchendaele – was awarded the Distinguished Service Order for courage under fire, he remarked: 'I thought I might with equal relevance have been recommended for a court-martial. It all depended on the direction which one took when one ran away.' Was England's decision to tackle the Australian bouncers at Lord's the Bazball version of Bion's conundrum? Would it have been more courageous to duck under the short ball for half an hour?

As Brearley alludes to, McCullum's attitude was also shaped by adversity, and his own disillusionment with cricket. When he took over the New Zealand captaincy, he could do nothing about the fact that the country's cricketers were always in the shadow of the All Blacks. But he was determined to change the perception of his team as overpaid prima donnas lacking in national pride.

If that felt like a local issue, the death the following year of Australian batsman Phillip Hughes, who burst a vertebral artery after being hit by a bouncer in a Sheffield Shield game in Sydney, caused McCullum and his New Zealanders to reassess their approach at a deeper level. News of Hughes's death reached their dressing-room before the start of the second day of the third Test against Pakistan in Sharjah in November 2014. Play was abandoned, allowing McCullum and his team time to reflect on a tragedy that touched the entire cricket community. In an interview with his former national coach Mike Hesson, McCullum said Hughes's death 'changed everything'.

He went on: 'It was such a difficult thing to know how to navigate the team through, because nobody had been through it before. The time we spent together in that initial 24 hours, when the game was delayed a day, and the closeness of the group and relationships that started to knit together, was something that stuck with us for a long time. The result became irrelevant and it was about playing for your mates and not worrying about competition.'

When the Test resumed on the third day, New Zealand took Pakistan's last seven first-innings wickets for 66, but as a mark of respect refused to celebrate each breakthrough. They then set about one of the most remarkable batting performances in their history. At stumps that evening, they had reached 249 for one from 45 overs, with McCullum unbeaten on 153. Next day, they added another 388. McCullum eventually fell for 202 from 188 balls, and Kane Williamson for 192 off 244. By the time they were dismissed for 690 on the final morning – made at a rate of 4.81 an over – they had hit 22 sixes, beating the old Test record, held by Australia, by five. McCullum alone hit 11, as he did in New Zealand's next game, against Sri Lanka in Christchurch – by far the most six-heavy two-innings burst in Test history. (Next is Stokes, with 14 against Australia at Lord's and Headingley in 2023.) Meanwhile, Pakistan had been dismissed for 259, to lose by an innings and 80.

As McCullum told Hesson: 'The fact we went on to hit 22 sixes and beat Pakistan, who had just hammered Australia in the same conditions – and did it in that style of cricket, it opened our eyes to the fact that we could take away the fear of failure and play as a unit. It was a terrible time, and you feel sorry for those more heavily involved in it, but it defined us as a team.'

Between the start of the Sharjah game and the end of his Test career 16 months later, McCullum scored 1,002 runs at an average of 50 and a strike-rate of 100 (until then, his strike-rate had been 60). And he made New Zealand, traditionally a team of grafters, one of the most watchable sides in the world. Their visit to Lord's in May 2015, two months after McCullum had taken them to the World Cup final in Melbourne, was a classic – even if he fell first ball in New Zealand's second innings, his stumps rearranged by Stokes. And he signed off from Tests with 145 off 79 against Australia at Christchurch in February 2016, including that world-record 54-ball hundred.

Just as New Zealand's thrashing of England at the 2015 World Cup had inspired Eoin Morgan to tear up England's white-ball strategy and start all over again, so the seeds of Stokes's Test revolution could be found in what the New Zealanders had learned about removing the fear of failure.

Stokes told Hussain that the moment McCullum's name came up as a possibility for the Test job, 'it was a case of putting everyone else out of my mind. I knew he would be absolutely perfect for where I wanted to take the team, having played against him over the years and knowing what he was about. I'm not saying it wouldn't have worked with another coach, because you never know. But in terms of coming in and having an impact straight away, it was definitely a lot easier having Brendon.'

Shortly before the start of the home Test series against New Zealand in 2022, Rob Key was in a meeting to discuss Andrew Strauss's wide-ranging but controversial high-performance review of the English game. Also there was Dave Brailsford, who had revolutionised the fortunes of British cycling and presided over six wins in seven years at the Tour de France with his stable of Team Sky riders, Bradley Wiggins, Chris Froome and Geraint Thomas. Brailsford stood up and drew a graph, with 'winning' along the x-axis, and 'likeability, respect and brand' along the y-axis.

According to Key, Brailsford said: 'If you are winning but nobody likes or respects you, it ends in disaster. At Team Sky we were all about winning, but people think you are doping or whatever, and you think: *Why are we bothering with this?* It was the same with the Australians and Sandpapergate: they beat everyone, but it ended badly and the world comes for you. But if you lose, and people think you are weak and cowards, then nobody likes you: you get hammered. That is a nightmare. If you lose with courage, and have style and the right attitude, people will go with you.'

Pointing to the top right-hand corner of the graph – where winning meets popularity – Brailsford continued: 'This is what they call Top Right Racing. Winning with style, respect, brand of entertainment. That is the dream. That is what you have to get to.'

Key took it all in. 'I remember thinking: *that is exactly it.* I realised Brailsford had just articulated better than me what I think. Then throughout that year, his graph played out. Against New Zealand at Trent Bridge, when England needed 160 in the last session, Baz was like: "We are going for this regardless." If we had lost that game being brave, then Brailsford's graph would have worked anyway. With a sell-out crowd, the last thing you could have done is block out for a draw. That would have been such a let-down, and sport is so much more important. They ended up winning and getting Top Right Racing.

'I have shown this to McCullum, but not to Stokes. Everything he talks about – entertaining and being rock stars – is on him. He just does it. But I believe that graph plays out every time. If you focus on those things like entertaining and style, the result is an outcome "focused on the process", to sound like a management dick. Steve Waugh says focus on the process, and that is what they do naturally – not because I told them about this bloody graph, but because they are authentic. All of us listen to people who are authentic.'

Later, McCullum himself remembered the importance of that teatime chat in Nottingham. 'From the start to that point, we had been talking about this, and that moment lent it to how serious are you about this?' he told the ECB website. 'Are you going to shit the bed and go back to normal or are you true to your word? The skipper walked in and said: "Baz, now is the time to nail the message." I was the mouthpiece at the time able to reinforce that. What followed from there nobody could have scripted. Ridiculous. Anyone who watched the game at Trent Bridge or around the world, they walked away entertained.

'All I want to do is make sure we never take it for granted. The opportunity passes us by so fast that there has to be a period where you are able to stop and smell the roses. The boys take the piss out of me because I say "be where your feet are". That is the message I have got for the group. It is really humbling. The history of English cricket, the talent we have got and the opportunity to bring relevance back to Test cricket, is the greatest opportunity.'

One of the reasons McCullum was more drawn to the Test than the one-day job was because he felt he was better at turning a struggling team into a good team, rather than a good team into a great team. He was, by his own admission, not a technical coach, but a student of people. Back on the day he was unveiled at Lord's, looking relaxed in dark jeans and white trainers, he outlined his basic position with a candour that might not have been possible from an English coach reared on respect for institutions and orthodoxy.

'My first job is to try to strip away some of the stuff that doesn't really matter but can affect you as a person, and to keep things as relaxed as possible,' he said. 'If we can do that, talent can come to the fore. Everyone's got a fear of failure to a degree, but it's probably just a little more English than others. That's one of the beauties of it, because that's where a lot of my skills are, taking a lot of those pressures off people. It's not going to be easy, I understand that, and there'll be some guys who get there quicker than others. But when you do get to that state where you're playing the game for the game's sake, because you enjoy it and you're invested in it, you immerse yourself in that moment and it's a great game to play. It's not a great game when you're worried about all the other stuff which goes on.'

In a WhatsApp message to England's backroom staff headed 'My philosophy', he pointed out that his style was 'pretty relaxed', which it turned out would often feel like an understatement. He wanted to 'get the best out of everyone', to 'have some fun on the road'. He said he valued 'relationships, hard work, loyalty and ambition', adding: 'I am an optimist and believe in doing things that make you happy.' He outlined his pet hates, among them 'job justifying, long meetings, bullshit and doing things for the sake of it. Realism is a nice balancer but pessimism I'm not into.' Then he got to the heart of the matter: 'It's meant to be the time of your life at top-level sport, and if we're putting into the team, have a smile on our face and we can handle pressure, then we will create the environment needed.' He ended by encouraging those who needed anything to 'flick me a message', and signed off as 'Baz'.

The players gained an instant insight into McCullum's style. On the first playing day of his reign, at Lord's, England had responded to New Zealand's 132 all out by slipping from 59 without loss to 116 for seven at stumps. Was the new era, in fact, the same as the old, just dressed up more snazzily and embellished with buzzwords? In the dressing-room, there was apprehension among the players about how their new coach would react. But McCullum was upbeat: 'What a day, boys! You should all be proud of yourselves. Tomorrow's another day, and we'll go better.' From a different coach, the message might have sounded disingenuous, even desperate. But McCullum, the players felt, was being genuine. The contrast with Adelaide six months earlier, where Chris Silverwood had made his batsmen rewatch their dismissals, was lost on no one.

McCullum was also following through on his pledge to back the players if things went awry. It tallied with his insistence that he wanted to speak to the media only after England lost: he would be the bulwark between the players and the press when times were hard, but shove them front and centre after victory. As he told one insider: 'You'll need me when the shit hits the fan, and when that happens I'll be backing the boys.'

England did indeed 'go better' at Lord's, and McCullum reiterated his approach at the hotel bar that night. 'It's like golden eggs,' he said. 'They're really precious and valuable. I don't want to waste the golden eggs by speaking too often.' Partly, he was being modest – as he would be again on the outfield at Karachi a few months later, when he insisted after England's 3–0 whitewash that 'I don't do much, really'.

If he wasn't doing much, he had a funny way of showing it. Repeatedly in the months that followed, the players would talk about England's new 'environment', as if McCullum was planting ideas, sowing seeds, tending the green shoots of recovery. The metaphor isn't far-fetched: he really was encouraging them to reconnect with their roots, to relocate the little boy who had once fallen in love with cricket. Authenticity wasn't a slogan nicked from a management dossier: it was central to McCullum's attempts to free up the talent he believed lay close to the surface in the English game. This was troubling for some, who detected a whiff of new-age nonsense, perhaps even the workings of a cult, as if any successful sporting team didn't have a strong leader with a clear set of values. But – and this was what mattered – the players loved it.

Does he offer much by way of technical assistance? 'Not a great deal,' says Duckett. 'I certainly don't think he'll be shouting "Shot, Ducky" from the back of the net when I play a block or a leave. But every time I pull someone over midwicket for six, or switch-hit the spinner over extra cover, he seems quite vocal. So I know what drives him, and I know what he enjoys watching.'

If sceptics detected a slight hint of evangelism about Bazball, they were not necessarily alone. Wood had missed the 2022 summer through injury, but joined the squad for the last game of the season – the Oval Test against South Africa. 'I'd been watching on the telly and people were saying this is the best thing ever, and I was thinking, *how can it be that different?* They're just bigging it up something rotten here. It will be good, but it cannot be what they're saying. They're overegging it, and it's starting to get on me tits. Oh, what a gig, what a gig!

'And then I got into the group, and I couldn't believe how different it was. It was so trusting and relaxed. Stokesy and Baz were very clear. I was smiling. When I went home, I thought I cannot believe what that was like. I cannot believe we're a professional team. We *were* professional, but it was different to how we had done it before. It was hard to describe. You will think I'm making it sound unprofessional, but it wasn't. It was just like it didn't matter – whatever the result. Ah well, we'll hit a few fours, hit a few sixes, always try to take wickets, positive option. It's easy to say them things, but the way Baz delivers it, he makes it feels like it's reality.'

A few weeks earlier, after England had completed their whitewash of New Zealand, McCullum had explained how pushing the boundaries was integral to the new approach. Asked whether England could ever take things 'too far', he replied: 'I hope we take it too far, because then we'll know exactly where that line is. Until you do that, you're not really sure. We've seen it with the England white-ball stuff. There have been times where they've probably pushed too hard, and then they know. I think it'll be the same with us, and we've got to keep exploring what that line is.'

Observers trying to distil the spirit of Bazball settled on the nighthawk, which had quickly entered cricket's lexicon.

Broad begins by pointing out that the nickname was 'not my choice'. But he could understand what McCullum was doing.

'We were at Trent Bridge,' says Broad. 'Rooty and Popey were batting really nicely. I got myself a coffee and a chocolate digestive, because I knew where they were at my home ground. I went upstairs to watch the cricket quietly, and Baz came walking in and said: "Broady, get your pads on." I was like: "What?" He said: "The guys are batting beautifully, but look around the ground, everyone is just a bit quiet. It is a bit sedate, they need a boost. Get your pads on, try and hit the first ball for four, get the crowd roaring. If you get out, you get out." I said: "You want me to pad up ahead of Ben Stokes and Jonny Bairstow?" This was at three in the afternoon. Reluctantly, to start with, I went along with it. I had my pads on all the way to the second new ball.'

'Nighthawk', though, was yet to be used. Broad again: 'We played India at Edgbaston, there were ten overs left in the day, and the light was going. Baz came into the physio room and told me to get my pads on. The theory was to attack when your opponent is sleeping: they will think you're a nightwatchman and will set attacking fields. Go and whack 30, and it will knock 30 off our chase. I said: "So it is not nightwatchman?" And he said: "No, you need a different name." I said: "What attacks its prey at night?" He said: "A hawk." That is how it came about. Every time I have walked into the changing-room since, he says "morning, hawk" or "afternoon, hawk".'

Even the nighthawk needed to lay down a few conditions. 'One of my rules as the hawk is I'm not going to go out there and get caught at deep square leg, then Stokesy comes in and nicks one,' he says. 'Then I will look like a prat. So if I get out, Leachy has to come in and shut the day down. He calls

143

himself the owl because he is more watchful. It is a bit of a piss-take. It is like a club team.'

After Ahmed graduated to the role in Karachi, McCullum texted Broad: 'Confirming the nighthawk is back for the New Zealand tour. See you soon, boss. It will be one of the great tours.' Broad replied with a message for Ahmed: 'Looking forward to it. Congrats on a great series. Please pass on to nighthawk junior that although the ultimate goal of the nighthawk is to hit a six first ball, the fullest use of feet and slap back past the bowler is the next best thing. The strike-rate keeps our breed in the positive and we made our intentions clear.'

Broad finally got a chance to spread his wings on the second night of the floodlit first Test against New Zealand at Mount Maunganui. Crawley had just fallen for 28 in England's second innings, and there were a couple of overs to go before stumps. Their lead was 87. Out walked Broad, who charged Scott Kuggeleijn's first ball and took a blow to the ribs. Next ball, he top-edged a heave, then watched in disbelief as Kuggeleijn and wicketkeeper Tom Blundell left a simple chance to each other. The ball plopped to earth, and Broad trotted a single. In the next over, he crashed Southee over cover. He fell next morning for 7, but his job was done.

'The idea is to cause complete chaos, which I did a little bit then,' he says with a glint in his eye. 'It buys into the light-hearted nature of the changing-room and takes the pressure off thinking it is really serious the whole time. Obviously, we do take our performances seriously, but Baz wants you to wake up every morning feeling like you are 12, when you used to open the curtains before a game on a Saturday morning and – yes! – it's sunny. I have had that feeling for a year. For a couple of years prior, I didn't.'

Broad's admission underlines one of McCullum's most vital achievements: he reinvigorated the senior players, not all of whom had been uplifting presences during the 2021–22 Ashes tour. As Sam Billings puts it: 'Broady wouldn't be bowling bouncers and not moaning about it a year ago, would he? That's the perfect analogy, seeing the change in behaviour in someone like that.'

Even Anderson, into his third decade as a Test cricketer, was enjoying the sense of a spring clean. 'It did feel like a fresh start, because both positions had changed, and Keysy had come in as well,' he says. 'It felt nice to have a line drawn under the previous few years, when the results were pretty poor, and start again.' The sense of renewal allowed him to deal with the disappointment of England's one-run defeat at Wellington, where he walked out to join Jack Leach with seven needed for victory. Leach swiped a single off Neil Wagner, which gave Anderson an idea. 'I'd never thought this in my life before, but I was thinking: *I can win this with one shot, and how good would that be?* I ran down to Wagner, but ended up turning my wrists on it, so it went down.' Even so, Anderson had connected well enough to collect four, leaving England two short of victory and one short of the tie that would have guaranteed a series win.

'Leachy faced the next over and I thought: *surely he will get a nick for four. Just get some bat on it!* Once you had faced a bit of it, we were confident. Then you get in two minds as you get closer. Do I slog it or do I try and play properly? I ended up playing properly and getting out.'

Anderson was caught behind down the leg side as he tried to glance Wagner for the winning runs, but it was the ball before his demise – very short and very wide outside his leg stump – that exercised him. Umpire Rod Tucker remained unmoved, as did his square-leg colleague, Chris Gaffaney. 'It definitely sailed over my head and I was looking at the umpire waiting for the arms to go out but nothing happened,' says Anderson. 'I asked if I could review it. They said no. It was frustrating but because of this environment...'

He pauses to remember the Headingley Test of 2014, when he fell in the final over against Sri Lanka, having fended off 54 deliveries. 'I was devastated getting out off the penultimate ball in that game. This time I was pissed off, but as we walked off the field I saw Stokesy smiling. We had been involved in such a great game, and all the fans left happy.'

What did he say to Tucker? 'I can't remember exactly. I feel like I said: "Thanks, mate. I wouldn't watch that back again." The umpires left with their tail between their legs. I've never seen umpires leave the ground so quickly, even before the trophy presentation. They scuttled out.'

Joe Root, too, quickly relished the fresh approach. 'Having a different outlook on the game has been the most beneficial thing from my experience with Brendon,' he says. 'I just like the way he talks about it. Instead of worrying too technically about things, where your hands are, where your feet are – the majority of the time there's one thing that doesn't feel great – it's about how are you going to solve the problem? You can be technically perfect, and still get a good ball. Watching how he operates with both the younger players and the senior players, and still manages to get the same level of commitment and excitement out of both groups, is really impressive.'

Root also enjoyed the fact that the coach and captain decided he would bat at No 4, come what may. He had never shaken off the question of whether he should go in a place higher, especially during the days of Trevor Bayliss, who felt the best player belonged at No 3. But Stokes and McCullum ended the debate. When Ollie Pope dislocated his shoulder during the second Ashes Test at Lord's, England tried three others at first drop – Harry Brook, Moeen Ali and Stokes himself – but not Root.

As England approached the 2023 Ashes, the players spoke more freely in the press about their hopes and dreams, and their intentions for the Australians. This was a subversion of the usual dynamic, in which Glenn McGrath would roll out his 5–0 prediction or Shane Warne would come up with a new name for the one that didn't turn, instantly causing panic in English ranks. And since McCullum's only rules of media engagement were to avoid the front page (for the wrong reasons, presumably), and since England were now winning more often than not, the players felt emboldened to have their say.

Broad's claim that he had been working on an outswinger to combat Steve Smith and Marnus Labuschagne summed up the new chutzpah. 'Maybe I just had the confidence to say something when I haven't in the past,' he says. 'My record against Smith and Marnus was average. I had to bowl a lot of balls at them to get a wicket, so I needed something to create a little bit of difference. I knew Marnus would read it.'

At Edgbaston, Labuschagne edged his first ball, from Broad, into the gloves of Bairstow – instant gratification and vindication, it seemed, for the new plan. Then he had him caught behind again in the second innings, for 13. Come the second Test at Lord's, it was on everyone's minds. 'We were waiting for him to change gloves,' says Broad, 'and Marnus said: "I've been practising for that outswinger. I'm ready for it." It was like, oh cool, have you? I said something like: "Well, you only saw one of them at Edgbaston." Just typical pathetic chat. But he was obviously aware of it.

'Rob Key has played a big role in that. At Sydney in the previous Ashes, I made a facetious comment about how it doesn't matter what bowlers you play if you only score 200. I said we have got to stop being obsessed with the Ashes. We have to enjoy the present, instead of always looking at four years' time. Gilo [Ashley Giles] was not happy, Spoons [Silverwood] was not happy and I got a bit of "you should not have said that, it was out of line". So I was a bit repressed. Whereas Keysy has such a relaxed nature. He could just call you up and make you feel at ease. Although he is your boss, he is a good people person. He will text you if you have a good or bad day, whereas no other director of cricket has done that. You feel like you're his player rather than his employee.'

Broad's new delivery wasn't England's only attempt to unsettle Smith, whom he dismissed for 6 in Australia's second innings at Edgbaston. In the first, Stokes had implemented a strategy cooked up with Brook during England's pre-Ashes golfing jaunt to Scotland. In New Zealand, Brook – who bowls wobbly 68mph mediums, almost off the wrong foot – had collected a distinguished first Test scalp when Kane Williamson feathered one down the leg side to Ben Foakes to end an innings of 132. Stokes decided Brook should be used against Smith.

'The plan was to get him out of his bubble,' says Brook. 'It put him off slightly having a frog in a blender run down at him and chuck a ball. Stokesy said to me when we'd had a few drinks a few weeks before: "Brooky, you are going to bowl at Smith as soon as he comes in." Bear in mind this is when we were drunk in Scotland. Baz was there and he said: "Yep, you're coming on to bowl." I thought they were taking the mick. But then I come on to bowl to him in my first Ashes Test. It was quite funny. There were no nerves because I knew it was coming.' Amid widespread hilarity, Smith suspiciously defended his first five deliveries, before tucking a single off the last. Brook later bowled a couple of tidy overs before the second new ball to Usman Khawaja and Alex Carey, and finished with figures of 3-1-5-0. He bowled only three more overs all series.

Perhaps we're back to Brearley, and an observation in *The Art of Captaincy*: 'I still squirm to think of opportunities missed, of hunches *not* acted on.' After concocting his Brook plan in Scotland, Stokes might not have forgiven himself had he failed to try it out. And if Smith survived easily enough, Stokes had correctly calculated that he was unlikely to risk a big shot, with all the embarrassment a dismissal would entail. Later in his book, published in 1985 but still pertinent today, Brearley writes: 'I am convinced that cricket... must avoid too much solemnity or pedantry. Captains have a responsibility to keep the game fun, however serious.'

Nearly four decades on, he smiles as he considers the success Stokes's England have enjoyed. 'I'm astonished it could happen so dramatically and so quickly,' he says. 'I'm full of admiration for him. If everyone were to try the same as him, the same proportion of teams would win and the same proportion would lose. He's a shrewd judge, on the whole. To see the transformation is fantastic.'

7

'What about that percentage, mate?'

The crack of bat on ball might have been a cannon going off. The noise of the Edgbaston crowd roared along Harborne Road, possibly stopping shoppers in their tracks at the Bullring Centre. Zak Crawley, left foot plonked down the pitch, bat arcing through the off side, had just belted a Pat Cummins half-volley through the covers. It was not just any ball, either, but the first of the 2023 Ashes series. The last time an England opener had faced the first ball against Australia, Rory Burns had his stumps detonated by Mitchell Starc at Brisbane. A lot had changed in English cricket between 8 December 2021 and 16 June 2023. Given the field Crawley faced, with a man at deep point, it seemed a lot had changed in Australian cricket too.

'There is the first question answered,' said Ricky Ponting on Sky Sports. 'Will they continue on playing that way? What a start to an Ashes series!' The cameras panned to the England dressing-room. Ben Stokes, his bucket hat and ginger beard making him look like a bass player in a 1990s indie band, was wide-eyed and open-mouthed. 'Even looked like the captain was surprised,' said Ponting.

Normally, supporters take a while to make their way to their seats at the start of a Test, and there were roadworks both in Birmingham city centre and close to Edgbaston. Not this time. Because of England's stirring cricket over the previous 12 months, everyone knew the first ball could be a moment in time. The queues at the bars were short. It seemed every seat was taken.

But if Stokes looked surprised, Crawley – who, unlike Burns at the Gabba, had already played the shot a million times in his mind – was not. 'I always watched the first ball of the Ashes growing up, whether in Australia or in England,' he says. 'I saw the Harmison wide [in 2006–07], I was there in Brisbane when Burnsy got out. I thought there was a good chance I could be facing the first ball, and it was in the back of my mind that I could have a good moment if it was in the right area. I was looking to be positive, and I managed to hit it well. But I didn't hear the crowd. Everyone spoke about it afterwards, but I was in the bubble. It was weird I didn't hear anything. I was in a daze.'

Under almost every other regime, and by his own admission, Crawley would not have been standing at the crease that day. He would have been sent back to county cricket to learn the basics of red-ball batting and building an innings. His form had been patchy; no other player in the team divided opinion quite like he did. But he justified his place against Australia, whose fast bowlers suited his batting, scoring 480 runs – more than any of his teammates – at an average of 53 and a strike-rate of nearly 89, giving England starts in seven innings out of nine, and lifting his career average by three to 31. He was now transferring more weight on to the front foot, and leaving more judiciously.

It changed perceptions and silenced those who saw him as the privileged public schoolboy, the jazz hat from Kent, who owed his place in the team to the fact his father is a golf buddy of some big names in English cricket – including Rob Key. Crawley can be a flashy player, and the numbers do not obviously back up the faith shown in him by McCullum and Stokes. While he plays for England, say his critics, many are grafting hard in the county game, churning out the runs. But they are not snazzy enough for the Bazballers.

To others, he is a special talent, a purveyor of outrageous shots who pours the rocket fuel in the Bazball engine, and has been part of England's three-fastest century opening stands to prove it. His 86-ball century in Rawalpindi was the quickest by an England opener, and helped the team break a 112-year record for the most runs on the first day of a Test. Don't forget, either, that England made those runs – 506 for four – from just 75 overs. The old record – 494 for six by Australia against South Africa at Sydney in 1910–11 – had come from 99. In other words, England had scored at 1.76 runs an over more quickly than the previous best. This was a paradigm shift.

Speak to those close to Crawley, and they describe a popular figure who plays selfless, aggressive cricket against the new ball to set the team on their way. Inevitably, it is a method which risks sacrificing a good average, but McCullum and other members of England's coaching staff have stressed that Crawley is not in the team for his consistency – an argument that has raised eyebrows.

His father, Terry, is a multi-millionaire, having once earned £100 a week as a carpet fitter in Bermondsey, before earning his fortune on the 1990s London futures market. Because of his money-making knack, he was known in the City as 'Terry the Till', one year reputedly picking up £23 million. The tabloids wrote up his story as 'Rugs to Riches'. It all helped put his son through Tonbridge School, alma mater of the Cowdreys, but Zak has also been taught to make his own way. 'They're not pushy parents,' says Key. Being a decent teammate certainly helps when the runs dry up and earns a bit more patience from the selectors. But Crawley himself acknowledges he has been lucky: 'I have feared for my place a few times. They obviously see something in me they like.'

He is not alone. Among England's top three, Crawley, Alex Lees – the first player dropped by the new regime – Ben Duckett and Ollie Pope have all been shaped in different ways by the new management. Moeen Ali ended up at No 3 for the second half of the Ashes, but only because England needed to get inventive after Pope dislocated his shoulder. In total, seven players have batted at No 3 in the Bazball era, including two nightwatchmen and two injury replacements: Harry Brook at Headingley, then Stokes at The Oval. But while the personnel may have changed, the approach did not.

Sent out to set the tone, the trio of top-three regulars had to be made to feel secure. They were being asked to attack the new ball, which brings risk, and so requires a certain selflessness. Four years earlier, ahead of the previous home Ashes, England had taken a punt on Jason Roy: with few other viable candidates in county cricket to open the batting, coach Trevor Bayliss hoped Roy could translate his white-ball brilliance into the Test arena. He made 72 off 78 balls on debut against Ireland, but didn't pass 31 in eight innings against Australia, before he was dropped for the final Test. In private, Bayliss believed England had bottled the decision. Certainly, McCullum might have given Roy a longer rope.

And, as the 2023 Ashes wore on, with Crawley playing the role Roy might – in a parallel universe – have filled instead, it was evident the two sides were playing the same sport in different ways, and none more so than the top three. During the final innings of the series, Usman Khawaja reached 56, matching Crawley's series tally, but from 1,246 balls to Crawley's 548.

By then, Pope had undergone shoulder surgery, cheerfully posting a picture of himself on social media from his hospital bed on the first day of the Old Trafford Test: 'Surgery a success.' Pope was the unfulfilled talent, a player who looked all at sea on his first Ashes tour, in 2021–22, but later batted at No 3 for the first time in his professional career. Stokes later promoted him to vice-captain, as a bridge between the younger and older players. Lees was the grinder, unable to shake off the mentality he had forged with Durham, only to transform himself into a stroke-maker in an attempt to fit in. (His growing confidence was epitomised by a sledging row with Virat Kohli, of which more later.) Duckett was the lost soul, a player who had talent but was dropped by England during a tour of India in 2016–17, when he struggled to fit their vision of how a Test batsman should look. The message from Alastair Cook, then the captain, was 'play safe and build an innings', but against the skill of Indian off-spinner Ravichandran Ashwin this was easier said than done. It didn't help his cause when, in perhaps the definitive example of how not to win friends and influence people, he threw up on Bayliss during an internal flight.

Duckett then found himself in trouble on a night out in a Perth bar in 2017–18, when he and his England Lions teammates were in town to shadow the Ashes tourists. As the evening grew lively, he was spotted by security pouring a vodka and lemonade over the head of Jimmy Anderson. Revisiting the incident during a radio interview shortly before the 2023 Ashes, he said: 'In a funny way, I think it would have been applauded in this environment. I have never really spoken about it, but it was a ridiculous situation that got blown out of proportion.'

Back then, Duckett's problem was that the incident occurred not long after Jonny Bairstow had greeted Cameron Bancroft, the Western Australia and Test opener, with a playful headbutt in a bar. This became a massive issue during the first Test at Brisbane, where it was leaked to the Australian media and portrayed as a violent incident. And it happened only weeks after Stokes had been arrested for the fight in Bristol that prevented him from travelling. The Duckett–Anderson high jinks added to the impression that England were lads on a stag trip, not serious athletes playing professional sport.

But England never lost sight of Duckett's gifts, and McCullum brought him into the squad for the Oval Test against South Africa after Bairstow broke his leg playing golf. He didn't play there – Brook made his debut instead – but Duckett was named for the winter tour of Pakistan. McCullum can relate to players who have landed themselves in off-field scrapes, but he also liked Duckett's positivity with the bat.

Then there is Crawley. No other player has enjoyed so much backing from McCullum and Stokes or embodied their batting philosophy of living in the moment and committing to a method. 'It started with "just go out and express yourself, go out and bat however you want to,"' says Crawley. 'It's funny: we all took that to mean batting quite aggressively, which is how it has all happened. There wasn't really any chat when we started to score quickly: it was "just go and be yourself and do whatever you want to do". As an opening batsman, it is a good approach. We talk about absorbing pressure and putting it back on opponents, and it is a good chance at the start of the innings to seize the initiative. Baz was quite keen on that, especially when we play away, funnily enough.

'I have always been an aggressive player, and previously I felt I had to rein myself in a bit. My talent was not allowed to come out as much, and I couldn't show people my full array of shots. I didn't feel that pressure when I started in the England side, but as I got more into my Test career I felt I was playing for my place, and had to play a certain way. So it was very nice to be liberated when Baz and Stokes came in.'

Crawley shot to prominence in the Covid summer of 2020, scoring 267 against Pakistan at the Ageas Bowl – the second-highest maiden century by an Englishman, after Reginald 'Tip' Foster, whose debut Test against Australia at Sydney in 1903–04 had brought him a score of 287. Only two younger England players – Crawley was 22 years 200 days – had made a Test double-century: Len Hutton and David Gower.

But with success came expectation. Eight Tests in 2021 produced one half-century and an average below 11. After scores of 27 and 6 in the first Test against India at Trent Bridge in August that summer, he was dropped. Crawley was a passenger at the start of the 2021–22 Ashes tour, and it was only when the series was over as a contest that he showed off what he could do. At Sydney, he reeled off a crisp 77 that left Australians wondering why he had not been in the team from the start, ahead of the shot-shy Haseeb Hameed and the quirky Burns. It was as if he had settled on a form of Bazball by himself, months before the official version came along.

'That was when I first started emerging from my shell,' he says. 'They were coming at us hard, and I was sitting on the bench for those first two games, thinking: *you have to put some pressure on them here, otherwise they are just going to get you.* When I got my chance, that was what I was trying to do. Then Baz comes along a few months later and tells us to do pretty much that. I certainly played well that day in Sydney: it's the template of how I want to play, and at the time my favourite innings for England. I was just moving in the moment, which is what Baz talks about very well – being in the present, being where your feet are. I've done it well a couple of times since, and it's something we're always chasing.'

Consistency is the Crawley conundrum: during the Ashes, he passed 50 three times in a series for the first time, including his destructive 189 at Old Trafford. Just after the double-century against Pakistan, the former England captain Ted Dexter had likened him to a right-handed Graeme Pollock, the South African batting legend. But his average in the Bazball era heading into the Ashes was 27, with one century – that 122 in Rawalpindi.

Mark Ramprakash, writing in the *Guardian*, said he could not remember a player enjoying so much selectorial faith, 'not only in the England side but in any cricket team'. Mark Butcher, who – like Ramprakash – never received the same leniency from the selectors, at one point described the retention of Crawley as 'cruel'. As he struggled against South Africa, Butcher thought the experience was doing him more harm than good. 'You cannot keep failing and not have it affect you mentally,' he said on Sky. 'He is 24 years old, so it is not terminal for him to be left out now and come back a better player.'

It was said that Kevin Pietersen was a player of great innings rather than a great batsman. This was a dig at his flashiness, and his perceived preference for style over substance. It was unfair, but it stuck. Crawley is a notch down: a player of great shots, rather than one who regularly converts them into great innings – despite Old Trafford. Pietersen often copped criticism for getting out to the kind of strokes played as a matter of course under Bazball. Famously, he was shouted at by batting coach Graham Gooch after he was caught at long-on trying to hit Nathan Lyon out of the WACA in 2013–14. Pietersen sees something of himself in Crawley, though he had a far better defence. 'The only way they can continue is if the backroom staff led by Brendon and Ben give players that trust in knowing they will play for a very long time,' he said in an interview with the *Daily Telegraph*. 'They are doing that by sticking with Zak Crawley, which I think is magnificent.'

There was a clamour to drop Crawley after the New Zealand tour in February 2023, when he averaged 14. Following the Rawalpindi century, his remaining nine Test innings of the winter had yielded a top score of 50. His colleagues talk about how McCullum would try to lift him after each failure, sitting next to him in the dressing-room to offer reassurance and encouragement, sometimes with a cigar in hand. Crawley says they have 'exaggerated' the detail about the cigar, but McCullum will 'sit there and make you feel good after a bad day. He will say: "Don't change a thing, stick with it." He never thinks I'm struggling, even when I have felt I'm in a rough patch. He has always commented on my impact in the game, even if I have only got 25. He bigs you up. He says: "I know you want the scores, but don't underestimate the impact." That is what we are about – the little impacts that contribute to a team performance, rather than chasing individual stats, or boosting your average and run tally. It is about how we can win a game.'

It is hard to argue, at least until the Ashes, that Crawley was not fortunate to stay in the team, but he was picked over Lees for the tours of Pakistan and New Zealand because attack came naturally to him. Lees always looked as if he was striving for it, as if standing on tiptoes trying to reach a tin of beans on the top shelf. At times, he was able to grasp it; at others, it was just out of reach. When he made his Test debut, on the Caribbean tour, he walked into a team that was in bits, with the Joe Root era on the verge of collapse. But he batted so slowly – including 30 off 138 balls on a dead pitch in Barbados – that spectators' thoughts strayed to rum punches on the beach. With a strike-rate of 27 across six innings, he might have been channelling the ghost of Trevor Bailey. After that experience, which left Lees with a series average of 21, McCullum and Stokes deserve credit for giving him a chance: it would have been easy to banish him to county cricket.

'I was quite a positive player, but then for a few years the county wickets were conducive to seam, so batters just found a way to survive and get through,' he says. 'I became more of an accumulator. At the time of my England debut, I was in the mindset of playing on really challenging wickets, and I took that into the West Indies series. After that old style of Test cricket, to be given the freedom to play however you want was refreshing, not just for Test cricket but the whole county game as well. The Bazball culture was just a mindset shift. It is looking for the positive option. It is non-English. The other thing I felt batting under that regime was I was always thinking about the team.'

Lees was nearly 29, with a decade in the county game behind him, when he made his Test debut – a late age at which to adapt. He had also moved from Yorkshire to Durham, making life harder for himself by playing on difficult surfaces up at Chester-le-Street. With more of the championship taking place in April than previously, it was a tough time to be an opener. His reticence on Test debut, after he had worked so hard to get there, was understandable. But he embraced change. In the home summer, he upped his game, scoring at 50 per 100 balls against New Zealand, 83 in the one-off Test against India, and 53 against a strong South African pace attack. With Crawley, he twice broke the record for England's fastest century opening stand – off 19.5 overs against India at Edgbaston, and off 17.2 against South Africa at The Oval.

Edgbaston was his finest Test, his 56 off 65 balls in the second innings an exhibition of strokeplay unimaginable in Barbados, setting England on their way to their record chase of 378. But Lees would not have approached it so aggressively if not for the team's change in attitude. He even felt confident enough to say he was trying to emulate the former Australian opener Matthew Hayden.

'I was just trying to take bowlers on, and during the Edgbaston stand I was trying to make a big dent in the score and give confidence to the run-chase,' he says. 'It was the same at The Oval against South Africa. It was in the forefront of our mind. Looking back now, I had opportunities in the first four or five games that summer to make a big hundred. That is my one regret: I was batting nicely on good wickets but didn't quite do it. That is the difference between county and Test cricket. If you don't make it worthwhile when you get in, it is the difference between averaging 25 and 45 in Tests. In county cricket, you get another couple of chances to make those big scores.'

Edgbaston was where Lees locked horns with Kohli, the world's richest and most famous cricketer, an Indian icon married to Bollywood superstar Anushka Sharma. Lees, the Durham nudger, felt emboldened to bite back when Kohli sledged him from slip. According to Lees, he was 'carrying on for quite a while. Because I was an inexperienced international, he was trying to use his weight. It was pretty poor cricket chat. He was just carrying on in a fashion he can do sometimes. He had been getting under people's skin in the field when he was batting. I'm not fussed about someone's position in the game. We are all equal out on the pitch. I just wasn't going to put up with someone trying to intimidate me. It was as simple as that. He is an incredible player, but I thought he was just being a bit of an idiot.'

Lees finally had enough and said to Kohli: 'I've had two kids since you last scored a century.' He had noticed the detail in the media: Kohli's previous international hundred in any format had come in November 2019 during a Test against Bangladesh (he would not break his drought until September 2022, during a dead T20 match against Afghanistan in the Asia Cup).

'There was a lot of noise around that,' says Lees. 'He is only human, and I knew it must be playing on his mind and was the thing that would probably wind him up the most. Once I had spoken to him, he saw a bit of red mist, especially when we came out after tea. He is a competitor. He wants to win. I will never understand the weight of a billion people on my shoulders, but you can be competitive without losing your cool. I knew I had got to him. The biggest shame for me was I reached 56 and then got run out. The ultimate reply would have been to get an unbeaten hundred and win the game, but I didn't get the chance.'

Lees, though, had given England's chase a turbocharged start. And, with Kohli fuming, a series that had started a year earlier and finally finished in a 2–2 draw instead felt like another staging post in their brave new world. India flew home, tail between legs.

Lees was dropped after the Oval Test against South Africa, the first regular member of the side to be left out. It was crushing: 'I had showed signs I could play at that level, but I didn't get enough runs. When you are looking for good-faith decisions, or it is 50-50 and it does not go your way, then you are disappointed. I don't think it was unfair. The only thing was, we had changed how we wanted to play and we did it on seamer-friendly wickets, particularly against South Africa. So it was disappointing I did not get a series away from home on those Pakistan wickets. They were proved right with the decision to use Ben [Duckett]. He played beautifully. I don't have any qualms. My intention now is to get back into the mix and have another crack at it.' By the end of the Ashes, his four-day stats for Durham in 2023 showed he had been true to his word: 1,152 runs, including four hundreds, at an average of 72 and with a strike-rate of nearly 74. At that stage, he was the leading run-scorer in the country.

He might look at Duckett, who played four Tests in Bangladesh and India in 2016–17, and never gave up hope – despite his off-field misdemeanours. He moved from Northamptonshire to Nottinghamshire, seeking to catch the selectors' eye at a bigger club, and averaged 56 in the 2020 Bob Willis Trophy (which replaced the championship for a year because of Covid). Via the white-ball teams, he started to creep back into the England set-up. He was more mature, too, with a serious girlfriend and a settled life off the field. If he wanted to play Test cricket again, he recognised he would have to be more dedicated. When he was picked for the Twenty20 series in Pakistan in October 2022, and batted well on the spin-friendly tracks, he was chosen for the Test tour that followed.

'I watched the Test team that summer, and it was pretty clear how they wanted to play their cricket,' says Duckett. 'It was almost lucky that I was in such good form and the

England side wanted to play that brand, which was the way I play too. Four years ago, I probably wouldn't have been selected, because that wasn't the way England were playing. I think Stokesy and McCullum believed I could do that in the international arena as well, so the timing was perfect.

'Before the first Test in Pakistan, McCullum pulled me aside and said: "Don't worry too much about this game – you're going to get a good run." In my small time with England before, that's something I'd never been told. Every single game it felt like I was fighting to stay in the team – every single game. Hearing those words really took the pressure off and allowed me to go out and enjoy playing for England, as opposed to being nervous and worrying about putting in a performance that was going to keep me in the side for the next match.'

Duckett started superbly. The pitch in Rawalpindi was made for his dabs and sweeps, cuts and pulls, and a quick outfield ensured he got full value for his strokes. An innings of 107 off 110 balls, after he had spent most of the night visiting the bathroom because of the bug that had swept through the camp, immediately justified his recall. And he had played within himself: aggressive, yes, but not reckless or uncontrolled.

'I'd have had to be horrifically ill to miss out,' he says. 'We had Keats [Lancashire opener Keaton Jennings] there. If I miss that first game, who knows – I might not play any of the others. Everything could look very different now. It's going to take a lot for me to miss a game for England. The whole day is a bit of a blur – the build-up and how I was feeling, and how emotionally exhausted I was after I got out. But I remember sitting in the dressing-room at the end of the day's play, and [assistant coach] Paul Collingwood read through a list of about 25 records we had broken, which was pretty special. There had been no plan to go out and do all that. It was more a case of let's just ease our way into the series. But everything that day went to plan.'

That evening, Crawley and Duckett wrote their names on the honours board at the Pindi Stadium in felt-tipped pen, two of the day's four centurions along with Pope and Brook – another England record. The openers sat next to each other in the press conference, Duckett looking a little dazed, Crawley loving the moment.

Crawley had taken 14 off the first over of the Test, from Naseem Shah – the first sign that something special was brewing. 'I didn't have a number in mind for that first over,' he says, 'but I wanted to show them they could not just bowl in that area and get away with it on that wicket. Six an over didn't feel like we were taking many risks.'

If Duckett had butterflies, who could blame him? In his first England stint, he had smashed a fifty in Dhaka, before becoming the first of ten wickets to fall in a session as England lost a Test to Bangladesh for the first time. Then came his nightmare at the hands of Ashwin. In what would be his last Test innings for six years, he was told to go out and block for a draw at Visakhapatnam. He lasted a quarter of an hour before making a mess of a sweep and falling for a 16-ball duck.

Back then, there were recriminations for getting out to aggressive strokes. But there were no such problems under Stokes and McCullum. Duckett's desire to feel bat on ball fits the Bazball mantra, though it can leave him vulnerable in the fifth-stump channel against the new ball. He plays at deliveries other left-handers would normally leave and, after he made 182 against Ireland at Lord's in the one-off game before the 2023 Ashes, one stat suggested he had shouldered arms only eight times in six Tests. His strike-rate under McCullum at that point was 97. His tendency to play at everything was not missed by the Australians. When he let two go by at Lord's, Cummins needled him: 'What about that percentage, mate?' Duckett carried on playing his own way: in all, he left only 3.5 per cent of the 321 balls he faced from Australia's seamers.

The hundred in Rawalpindi was an instant confidence boost, but it was what happened next that stuck with Duckett. 'In the second innings of that Test I got a first-baller – poked one straight to second slip. I feel like most coaches would say to an opening batter: "Yeah, you should leave that, or let one go." But Baz was saying: "You were so unlucky there – a metre either side and it's four runs." And I was thinking *I've never heard a coach tell me that before,* to potentially poke even harder at a ball on fifth stump. Straight away I was thinking, *this environment is so different to anything I've ever been a part of.* I've just nicked off first ball, and he's saying that to me. There was another moment. In the second Test in New Zealand at Wellington, it was nipping around loads with the new ball, and I asked Baz what he'd have done. He said: "I'd have batted outside leg stump and run at every other ball."'

There is an endearing honesty to Duckett. Professional sportsmen rarely admit a weakness, but he gladly accepts the Bazball approach covers up deficiencies. He admitted after the Pakistan Test series, where he scored 357 runs at 71, that he had still not put 'Ashwin to bed', and that his defence was not good enough for him to play any other way. 'If I'm looking to survive then I'm pretty useless. My way of surviving is to put the bowlers under pressure and look to score.'

Crawley and Duckett complement each other naturally. One is 6ft 5in and strong off the front foot and down the ground; the other is 5ft 7in – 'not so tall', in Crawley's words – and prefers to hang back and score square of the wicket.

One is a right-hander, the other a left-hander, so the bowlers have to adjust both their length and their line. By the end of the Ashes, they averaged 48 together after 21 innings; by way of comparison, the average partnership between Alastair Cook and Andrew Strauss was just under 41. Crawley and Duckett were helped by their stand of 233 in Rawalpindi, where they had 174 by lunch – breaking a national record set in 1938. In that game, they also set a record for England's quickest century opening stand (13.5 overs), smashing the marks set by Crawley and Lees in the summer.

Runs flowed all day. At No 3 was Pope, who would make his first hundred overseas, off 90 balls. From the start of their alliance, McCullum and Stokes had a long list of problems to solve – and high up was the question of who would bat at first drop.

It had been nearly a decade since the retirement of Jonathan Trott, but England had never found a long-term solution to the No 3 conundrum. Gary Ballance flowered briefly, scoring four hundreds and averaging 46, before he was found out by pace; his career faded into obscurity and worse, when the Yorkshire racism scandal unfolded. Joe Denly had been the favoured pick of former national selector Ed Smith, but was rendered almost mute at the crease under Chris Silverwood. He would have enjoyed the Bazball culture but was too old by the time it came along. Dawid Malan was dumped after the Ashes tour, having begun promisingly with 82 at Brisbane and 80 at Adelaide. And since Root averaged 39 at No 3, a full 11 below his career mark, why blunt your best force?

England had to find someone else. Pope had been picked out as the next Root, a southern version who dominated county attacks and age-group teams at Surrey. He was selected by Smith at the age of 20, batting at No 4 against India, but it was too early, and under Root he was in and out of the side. He looked scarred by his first Ashes experience in Australia, a lost child among the carnage, and averaged 11 in six innings. And though he was retained in the squad for the West Indies trip, Dan Lawrence made the starting XI ahead of him. Stokes is a fan of Lawrence, believing he has the cricket brain to captain England one day, but a hamstring injury ruled him out at the start of the Bazball era, handing Pope a way back. He knew, though, that it would mean a change of role. He had never batted at No 3 – not even for Surrey – and Stokes was impressed that Pope called him to request the opportunity.

As Key said at the time: 'The bet is that with the talent they have, this environment and these coaches can get the best out of one of our most talented cricketers. Ollie Pope is one of those who, if we can unlock him – which I think they can – there's a seriously good Test cricketer there.'

Pope takes up the story. 'I saw Rooty was moving back to No 4, and I thought No 3 was probably the one spot that was going to be available. I just thought I'd say to Stokesy: "Do you want me to go and bat No 3 for Surrey this week, and give myself a chance of being selected there?" But with the mindset he has, he wasn't too fussed where you're batting. Because if you're scoring runs and playing well, it doesn't matter – it's just a ball coming down at you.'

In 15 Tests, until his injury at Lord's, Pope averaged 45 in his new position, earning the vice-captaincy for the start of the 2023 summer. That, though, included a double-century against Ireland, who had the weakest attack to arrive in England since Bangladesh toured in their early days as a Test nation. It was help-yourself time. For Pope, the problem has been pace, and Australia cracked open those old insecurities. He was heavily criticised for the pull shot that sparked England's collapse in the first innings at Lord's. In the dressing-room, though, there was only support.

'Stokesy's always backed me as a player, and he made me believe in myself that I am a No 3,' says Pope. 'I kind of knew it in my mind, and I put in a lot of hard work. But even in those tough times in the 2021–22 Ashes, he's really driven that forward, and he's always been vocal about how much he backs me. Those things really help you to get the best out of yourself, and not worry too much about the end result, or being dropped.'

Pope has often advanced down the pitch to fast bowlers in a bid to disrupt their lengths. It can look frenetic, but McCullum wants him to take the initiative: for him, the No 3 is supposed to be the aggressor. Bayliss, an Australian ingrained with the belief that your best player fills that position, had looked for the same quality when he was England coach, but never found it. Pope is relaxed about dancing down the pitch. 'You know that if you get out early, you're not going to get a telling-off. In the past, everyone might have said: "What's he doing there?" But the way we play in England, on some tough wickets at times, it's a good way of applying a bit of pressure on the bowler. It doesn't matter if I'm not scoring, but it might lead to me getting a good cut shot or pull shot away.'

Pope scored 145 in his second Test at No 3, against New Zealand at Trent Bridge, then that hundred in Rawalpindi, but he missed out on flat pitches for the rest of the Pakistan tour. Even so, his strike-rate has been nearly 78, where previously it had been 50. And he has struck nine sixes at No 3 – where he generally faces the new ball – which is seven more than Root managed in 34 more innings in the same position.

'The hundred at Trent Bridge felt like a relief,' says Pope. 'It was good to prove to myself that I could do it at No 3, and against a good attack as well. Cricket's a simple game that is made complicated sometimes, especially when you're out of touch. Baz is good at keeping things real, so you're not over-thinking things. It's not about technique, but about staying in the environment, playing for your team.'

England put so much faith in Pope that, when his Surrey teammate and friend Ben Foakes was ill in Pakistan, they made him wicketkeeper at Rawalpindi, and again at Multan so they could pick an extra bowler – even though Foakes was by now available. It wasn't the first time Pope had kept wicket in a Test: at Hamilton in November 2019, Jos Buttler suffered a back spasm in the gym the day before the game, leaving Pope with the gloves in only his fourth Test; he kept competently, and made 75. And, before Foakes returned at Karachi, Pope more than pulled his weight behind the stumps. 'I don't think I clanged too many,' he says, though he did have to borrow Foakes's gloves. 'Yeah, that was the only awkward bit.'

With Pope keeping wicket at Multan for nearly 63 overs in Pakistan's first innings, England rejigged the batting order for their second, as they looked to build quickly on a 79-run lead. Will Jacks, who had taken a six-for on his debut at Rawalpindi, had never batted at No 3 in first-class cricket, and had gone in at seven or eight in his first three Test innings, scoring a total of 85 runs off 86 balls and hitting five sixes.

'I was literally just sat in my chair after we walked off,' Jacks says. 'I had a towel over my head, enjoying a drink. Baz walked up behind me and tapped me on the shoulder. I looked up. He said: "You're batting at three, boss." I said: "What?" He said: "Yeah, you're going in at three." I said: "OK, cool." So I ran downstairs, had a little bite to eat and got my pads on. It did not pay off.' Jacks was out for 4, bowled trying to sweep a googly from Abrar Ahmed. 'I was trying to be positive, putting the bowler under pressure, so Baz was happy with that. He said "no regrets", and said I did the right thing for the team.'

Jacks doesn't quite see it that way. 'I tried to play a massive slog-sweep fourth ball. I'll be honest, I do slightly regret that, because I've only played two Tests and you don't know when your next Test innings is going to be. I had a chat with Stokesy and Baz when they let me know I wasn't going to play in the third Test. I said: "Thinking back now, I would rather have given myself ten balls to get going." Stokesy said: "No. I'm happy with that. I'd much rather you did that than pat it around and get 15 off 40." I guess that tells you everything you need to know.'

Strike-rates, fours and sixes were not the currency of the top three before the Bazball era. The aggression is risky, but entertaining. It does not guarantee consistency, but England had been toppling over easily against the new ball for years. At least now they were getting their retaliation in first. It feels unlikely that, even after the McCullum era, top orders will go back to nudging and nurdling. Of all the areas of change, it is perhaps here that Bazball will have its lasting effect. 'Scoring quickly is a way of putting pressure back on,' says Crawley. 'That is how sides feel pressure the most. It is about picking when to do it.' And that first day at Rawalpindi will always be part of history.

The 2023 Ashes
Third Test, Headingley

What does it feel like to bowl 95mph, to have a full house roar you to the crease, to see your pace flash up on the big screen? 'Woohoo,' replied Mark Wood.

At Headingley, Ben Stokes finally had his wish. He had always said he wanted to take on Australia with a group of eight fast bowlers to choose from, only for Jofra Archer and Olly Stone – two of the three quickest – to fall injured by the wayside. Wood was England's only other fast-and-nasty, which meant Stokes at last had express pace with the ball to match the breakneck speed of his team's batting. At 2–0 down, just when he needed a pick-me-up, he could hit Australia with lightning pace.

Wood had not been ready for the first two Tests, because an elbow injury in his right arm was still grumbling – a worry, since surgery the previous year was supposed to have fixed it, and England knew what had happened to Archer when chronic pain in the same joint refused to heal. But in his first spell on day one, Wood reached 96.5mph and averaged 92. He was back, and the Australians had the bruises to prove it.

'There was one ball that Marnus [Labuschagne] played, and after it he had a sort of wry, awkward smile on his face,' wrote

Ollie Robinson on Wisden.com. 'He was trying to give off the persona that everything's fine, when it's really not. And even Uzzie [Usman Khawaja], who plays pace really well and has been in such good form, even he struggled with the pace at times. He went from having this quiet persona at the crease to suddenly smiling and joking, trying to give off the feelgood vibes that he was fine. Us bowlers were saying that if we'd been batting out there, we might just have kicked our poles over.'

Robinson also revealed that, just minutes before the players took the field for the national anthems, Wood was on all fours in the dressing-room, barking like a dog, straining at an imaginary leash. 'There's a dog in here, lads,' he told teammates. Robinson observed: 'You think he's drunk half the time, yet he doesn't touch a drop.' Stokes asked Wood if he was ready to bowl 'thunderbolts'. To everyone else, more earthily, he suggested: 'Let's beat these c****.'

This was a rollicking Test match, another Headingley Ashes classic, with England winning by three wickets late on the fourth afternoon. Wood's five for 34, Stokes's crisis-averting 80, Chris Woakes's triumphant return with bat and ball, and Harry Brook's nerveless 75 all dragged England over the line. They batted with more control than at Lord's – Bazball with brains – and beat an Australian side that at one stage in their second innings had a hand on the urn, only for Labuschagne and Steve Smith to gift Moeen Ali their wickets and let England back in.

The pre-match talk was all about the Lord's stumping, the row following the teams north up the M1 from St John's Wood. 'I think it's time for everyone to move on,' said Root. 'Let's concentrate on this game.' Fat chance. Almost every question at his press conference, two days before the Test, brought up the incident, and he called on home fans to behave responsibly; Australian scare stories included a suggestion that extra security had been called in to protect the players' families from abuse. Cummins denied this was the case. 'Support England,' said Root. 'That's the most important thing. It should never go beyond that.' And it didn't. The Australians copped the usual chanting, but Headingley's notorious Western Terrace was relatively calm, all things considered. Knowing what was at stake, everyone was too tense about the cricket.

Stokes declined to tell supporters how to behave, but mentioned the earfuls he had received in Australia. He did, though, allude to events at Lord's: 'I don't think we can be any more galvanised than we are.' Cummins looked tense, replying with one-word answers, and insisting his team would not shy away from a repeat of Bairstow's dismissal, should the situation arise; as the questions mounted, the Australian press officer rolled his eyes. Headingley was not a happy place for Cummins. This was his first visit since Stokes smashed him for the winning boundary in 2019. 'I've seen it about a thousand times in the last four years,' he said. 'I actually haven't been out on the field yet – I've just walked through the changing-room. And the first thing you think of is 2019.'

England made changes that were enforced as well as tactical. With Ollie Pope ruled out, Brook would bat at No 3 for the first time in a Test. England knew it was a gamble: he averaged 21 in 14 innings there for Yorkshire, but they were determined to keep Root at No 4. They also opted not to pick Dan Lawrence because, with Stokes handicapped by his knee, they wanted the extra bowler – a balance they would stick with. In came Wood, Woakes – for his first Test of the Bazball era – and Moeen Ali; following Pope out of the team were Jimmy Anderson, rested after two ineffectual Tests, and Josh Tongue, Wood's fast-bowling deputy. Nathan Lyon's injury at least spared him the need to relive his own Headingley meltdown in 2019; Todd Murphy, a 22-year-old off-spinner from Victoria who had performed well in India earlier in the year, took his place. Mitchell Marsh, meanwhile, was a late inclusion after Cameron Green pulled up with a minor hamstring strain.

Stokes won another toss, and within five balls Stuart Broad had knocked over David Warner for the 16th time, the pitch already showing signs of the pace and carry missing at Edgbaston and Lord's. Stokes was itching to hurl Wood into the fray. He had not played any red-ball cricket since the Karachi Test in December, but was raring to go after weeks building up his 'loads' in the nets. He began with a 91mph loosener, reeled off three maidens and, when Labuschagne eventually escaped the strike, flattened Khawaja's leg stump with a 94.6mph yorker. Just like that, the mood of the series changed.

Woakes removed Labuschagne, and Broad snared Smith to make it 85 for four, but England were still making mistakes. Bairstow contrived to drop Head down the leg side on 9 off Wood, though the costliest error came soon after lunch, when Root at slip missed Marsh, on 12, off Woakes. Marsh revelled on a pitch that perhaps reminded him of home, in Western Australia, pulverising England with blistering drives and pulls, and scoring 113 in the session. His fifty, brought up with a pulled six off Wood, took 59 deliveries; another six, off Moeen, took him to 99, before a tapped single brought up a 102-ball century, the second-fastest for Australia in England, behind Victor Trumper (95 balls) at Old Trafford in 1902.

By now, Robinson had walked off with a back spasm, in effect ending his series. But Woakes dismissed Marsh in the last over before tea to end a 155-run stand with Head, who had 39. It was a crucial intervention. After the break, Wood terrorised Australia's lower order with four wickets in 14 balls: Starc was bowled through the gate, Cummins pinned leg-before for a duck, Carey caught at cover the ball after being hit on the head, and Murphy bowled, dragging on a drive. Australia collapsed from 240 for four to 263 all out, leaving Wood with his first five-for in a home Test, eight injury-hit years after his debut. Since then, he had played 29 times out of a possible 109.

'I haven't done that well in this country, so before the game there were a few nerves flying around,' he said, resisting the urge to bark. 'I've felt for a while I have a point to prove here – all my good stuff has happened away from home. So to be able to finally do it at home was a massive relief. My mam and dad were here, and to be able to raise the ball to them… it was the first time they've seen me get five wickets, so a pretty special moment. I was chomping at the bit a couple of games ago. To finally get in now, I'm really, really happy.'

Even so, England's muddled thinking at Lord's continued in the first half of their reply. They were three down by stumps, with Brook making just 3 in his first innings in his new position before fiddling at Cummins. Root departed second ball next morning, and Bairstow edged an ambitious drive. Moeen and Woakes both fell in the leg trap before lunch, paying the price as they failed to commit to hook shots. Stokes was still there, on 27, but England were 142 for seven, trailing by 121. Insiders described it as their worst session of the series: 3–0 looked on the cards.

As the crowd drifted away to the bars and food stands, Wood – pads on – walked down the dressing-room steps and across the outfield. He was accompanied by England's assistant coach Paul Collingwood, and heading for the indoor school. There, he spent the break taking on bouncers. When Wood immediately pulled Starc into the crowd after the interval, he became the first player to hit his first ball of an Ashes Test for six since Ian Botham at Edgbaston in 1985. The next two deliveries disappeared for four and six, before Wood pulled Cummins for six more. He soon fell for 24 off eight, but England's counter-thrust was on. 'He actually said to me: "Do you reckon I should go and do some pull shots in the nets?"' said Moeen. 'I was like, "yeah why not?" I didn't expect him to go out and hit the first ball out of the ground.'

Stokes now revisited his Lord's mayhem, lashing Starc for three fours in an over, and Murphy for five sixes in 14 balls. In all, England's final three wickets had added 95 in 62 after the break. Cummins finished with six wickets, and Smith with five catches, but Australia's lead was just 26. England were back in it, but parity was as difficult to retain as it had been to regain.

At 68 for one – Warner again falling cheaply to Broad – Australia were cruising: 94 ahead with nine wickets in hand, and England handicapped by the loss of Robinson. Labuschagne, with a Test average of 53, was at the crease. Smith (59) and Head (46) were in next. England were sinking, more so when Bairstow missed a tough leg-side catch off Labuschagne. But Stokes kept trying to manufacture a chance. With a fielder placed on the boundary straight down the ground, and mid-on and mid-off in catching positions, Labuschagne – no great sweeper – had nowhere to go against Moeen. Instead, he slogged towards the longest boundary, square of the wicket on the leg side, and holed out for 33. Moments later, Smith lamely picked out short midwicket – Moeen's 200th Test victim. Among England spinners, only Derek Underwood and Graeme Swann had got there before him. When the bustling Woakes nipped out Khawaja, the match had turned again.

Rain delayed the start of the third day until 4.45 p.m., with Australia 116 for four, and Head and Marsh, their two most aggressive players, in situ. The gloomy conditions were tailor-made for Woakes, who dismissed Marsh, caught off the underside of his glove as he tried to leave the ball, and then bowled Carey, playing on as he shouldered arms. Wood polished off Starc, Brook holding a sprawling chance as he ran back from short leg while Bairstow, whose catch it might have been, hesitated. Wood again removed Cummins cheaply. Australia were 170 for eight, their lead not yet 200.

But still there, on 34 off 82, was Head, who – like Stokes – was obliged to lead the tailend resistance. He did so in style, as England persisted with a bouncer tactic that had previously seemed more effective early in his innings, less so when he was set. At times, they had all nine fielders on the boundary, but Head kept taking them on, stoically supported by Murphy. The last two wickets added 54 in seven overs, with Head last out for 77.

England's target was 251, smaller than the four chases they had knocked off in the summer of 2022, but similar to the one they had stumbled over in Wellington. Broad said they would be approaching it like a one-day innings – one of his more uncanny observations, since victory came from the last ball of the 50th over. Still, English nerves needed settling, and Ben Duckett and Zak Crawley negotiated a tense 25 minutes before the close, trimming 27 off the equation. 'The thought of winning the Test, chasing down a score, and keeping yourself in the series always fills this team with excitement,' said Woakes that night, little realising he would play a crucial hand next day himself.

The 2019 epic had ended on a Sunday, too, but surely this would be a little more comfortable. England needed a further 224, which hardly required someone to dress up as Superman. Before a run had been added to their overnight score, Moeen came closest, offering to bat at No 3 and allow Brook to move back to No 5 – a selfless suggestion after Brook's first-innings struggles.

'I didn't go directly to Baz initially,' says Moeen. 'I asked a few of the players what they thought. A lot of them said it made perfect sense. Baz must have got wind of it. We spoke and he said: "What do you think about three?" I said: "If it comes off great, if it doesn't, we haven't lost anything." I felt good in the first innings with the bat. Red ball is more of a mental thing – you need rhythm in your batting. I felt I was getting closer to the pace of Test cricket. But I also thought Brooky was more effective at five, and that means Bluey [Bairstow] is more effective at seven. Without trying to sound like a big team player, it was more about them than myself, really. If I come off, great. If I don't come off, then if I can delay them coming in as much as I can, it will be better for the team.

'Definitely it made Australia think. I would rather them think: "Oh, we have Root, Brook, Stokes and Bairstow coming in." It sounds better than "Root, Stokes, Bairstow and, oh, Ali as well." It was best for the team at the time, and I am past that stage where I want a good average. I have no interest in that at all. I don't think that is what cricket should be about anyway. There are a couple of players in the series who average 55, and it becomes a burden.'

Duckett did not last long next morning, and Crawley failed to capitalise on some crisp shot-making, caught behind for 44 aiming one of his no-holds-barred drives at Marsh. On the one hand, Moeen's promotion did not work: b Starc 5.

On the other, it reinvigorated Brook. When Root fell to Cummins for the third innings in a row, England were still 120 short, and starting to worry. And when Starc had Stokes strangled down the leg side in the second over after lunch, then ended Bairstow's miserable Test by bowling him off the edge for 5, they were 171 for six. Australia were four wickets away from their first Ashes win on English soil in a generation.

But Cummins was reluctant to bowl Murphy, conscious that one big over could change the momentum, so it was down to Australia's three frontline seamers to bring it home. Cummins, Starc and Scott Boland, however, were starting to show signs of fading, and Brook played positively but not recklessly, proving he had learned from Lord's by resisting the short ball until he felt in. Woakes struggled at first, flapping at the bouncer, but Australia soon decided to go after him outside off stump: at a crucial moment in the series, they were standing off. Brook reached a 67-ball half-century, and was steering England to victory when he was surprised by a Starc bouncer, holing out for 75. He had ticked off 1,000 runs in his tenth Test, from a record 1,058 balls. His strike-rate was 94. It had been a remarkable first year as a Test cricketer, though he would have traded some of those numbers to finish off the chase on his home ground.

With 21 needed, it was down to Woakes and Wood, the two friends who share a car at away Tests, and had been called in to rescue England's Ashes hopes. As he had two days earlier, Wood took on the bouncer, smashing Cummins for six and bringing Headingley to its feet. He then drove Starc for four: seven needed. Stokes was unable to watch – for once, England's strongman captain could not bear the strain. Wood got away with a top edge that Carey insisted on chasing when he should have left it to Boland at fine third man, before Woakes ended it all with a four off Starc through point, struck from the end at which Stokes had walloped the winning runs four years earlier. Woakes had made 32 in 75 minutes of cliff-hanging cricket, to go with his six wickets; Wood finished with seven, plus 40 runs in the game off 16 balls, including four sixes. They had been inspired selections. England were alive.

Speaking a week later, after a restorative break in Ibiza, Brook says: 'I thought we were going to cruise it, to be honest, but then everything changed when Rooty got out, followed by Stokesy and Jonny. I hadn't been looking at the total – I was just trying to bat. But when those three got out, I had to knuckle down and look at the score a bit more. It is a bit different when you have Stokes at the other end. He has done it so many times, and it is a lot more comfortable chasing with him.'

Stokes was in the unaccustomed position of having to watch others finish the job: 'I'm not gonna lie. I was a bit nervous at the end. I walked about 2k around the Headingley dressing-room in the last half hour. I didn't actually watch the last 20 runs being scored. It's a completely different place when you can't do anything, you can't influence the game any more, you're left watching and hoping things are going to go your way. Because of where the series was at before this game started, the whole performance with bat, ball, in the field... it was an unbelievable effort from everybody.'

Cummins was asked if momentum had turned. 'Not really,' he said. Why not? '2–1.' But neither his bravado, nor the scoreline, could disguise the unfolding reality: England now looked the stronger team.

ENGLAND v AUSTRALIA (3rd Test)

At Headingley, Leeds, on 6, 7, 8, 9 July 2023.
Toss: England. Result: **ENGLAND** won by three wickets.
Debuts: None.

AUSTRALIA

D.A.Warner	c Crawley b Broad	4	(2)	c Crawley b Broad		1
U.T.Khawaja	b Wood	13	(1)	c Bairstow b Woakes		43
M.Labuschagne	c Root b Woakes	21		c Brook b Ali		33
S.P.D.Smith	c Bairstow b Broad	22		c Duckett b Ali		2
T.M.Head	c Root b Woakes	39		c Duckett b Broad		77
M.R.Marsh	c Crawley b Woakes	118		c Bairstow b Woakes		28
† A.T.Carey	c Woakes b Wood	8		b Woakes		5
M.A.Starc	b Wood	2		c Brook b Wood		16
* P.J.Cummins	lbw b Wood	0		c Bairstow b Wood		1
T.R.Murphy	b Wood	13		lbw b Broad		11
S.M.Boland	not out	0		not out		0
Extras	(B 10, LB 10, NB 3)	23		(B 5, LB 2)		7
Total	**(60.4 overs)**	**263**		**(67.1 overs)**		**224**

ENGLAND

Z.Crawley	c Warner b Marsh	33		c Carey b Marsh		44
B.M.Duckett	c Carey b Cummins	2		lbw b Starc		23
H.C.Brook	c Smith b Cummins	3	(5)	c Cummins b Starc		75
J.E.Root	c Warner b Cummins	19		c Carey b Cummins		21
† J.M.Bairstow	c Smith b Starc	12	(7)	b Starc		5
* B.A.Stokes	c Smith b Murphy	80		c Carey b Starc		13
M.M.Ali	c Smith b Cummins	21	(3)	b Starc		5
C.R.Woakes	c Carey b Starc	10		not out		32
M.A.Wood	c Marsh b Cummins	24		not out		16
S.C.J.Broad	c Smith b Cummins	7				
O.E.Robinson	not out	5				
Extras	(B 4, LB 3, NB 9, W 5)	21		(B 7, LB 7, NB 5, W 1)		20
Total	**(52.3 overs)**	**237**		**(7 wkts; 50 overs)**		**254**

ENGLAND	O	M	R	W		O	M	R	W
Broad	11.4	0	58	2		14.1	3	45	3
Robinson	11.2	2	38	0					
Wood	11.4	4	34	5		17	2	66	2
Woakes	17	1	73	3	(2)	18	0	68	3
Ali	9	1	40	0		17	3	34	2
Root					(4)	1	0	4	0
AUSTRALIA									
Starc	14	3	59	2	(2)	16	0	78	5
Cummins	18	1	91	6	(1)	15	0	77	1
Boland	10	0	35	0		11	1	49	0
Marsh	3	1	9	1		6	0	23	1
Murphy	7.3	0	36	1		2	0	13	0

FALL OF WICKETS

	A	E	A	E
Wkt	*1st*	*1st*	*2nd*	*2nd*
1st	4	18	11	42
2nd	42	22	68	60
3rd	61	65	72	93
4th	85	68	90	131
5th	240	87	131	161
6th	245	131	139	171
7th	249	142	168	230
8th	249	167	170	-
9th	254	199	211	-
10th	263	237	224	-

Umpires: H.D.P.K.Dharmasena (*Sri Lanka*) and N.N.Menon (*India*).
Referee: R.S.Madugalle (*Sri Lanka*).   Player of the Match: M.A.Wood.
Close of Play – Day 1: E(1) 68-3; Day 2: A(2) 116-4; Day 3: E(2) 27-0.

8

Strong Yorkshire…

On the fourth morning of the second Test against New Zealand at Trent Bridge, Joe Root was terrified – his word, not ours. He had 'got a few runs the day before' – Root-speak for 163 not out, backing up his unbeaten 115 to secure victory at Lord's eight days earlier. Now, from the first ball of the day's third over, he switched his stance – chest on, facing down the pitch – as Tim Southee released the ball. It was on a good length around off stump. Up in the commentary box, Mike Atherton – who during his career would probably have defended the delivery with a high left elbow – was agog as Root, left elbow closer to midriff, reverse-scooped Southee for six. 'Unbelievable!' said Atherton, before repeating himself, the emphasis on the first syllable. Earlier that morning, Root had told Sky Sports' Ian Ward that he was looking to take batting to new areas. Over the rope at third man, propelled by a vertical bat, ticked that box.

As much as any stroke in the summer of 2022, it heralded the new dawn. England had been relatively restrained at Lord's, scoring at 3.29 runs an over in the first innings and 3.53 in the second. But the sight of Root, the epitome of red-ball orthodoxy, dipping into the white-ball playbook at a crucial moment of an important Test, confirmed change was afoot.

But why terrified? 'Because it was premeditated,' he says. Yet as with so much of Bazball, this was no scattergun attack. 'They'd set a field which meant it was going to be hard to score through the off side, so it was clear he was going to bowl wide. I knew bowled and lbw were out of the game. The only place I was going to get caught was gully or slip. It felt quite a safe shot. I managed to get it pretty good, and ended up changing the field, which made life easier for me. There was method behind what I was trying to do. A few of the guys enjoyed it. Leesy was like: "What's 'e doin'?" But, as a senior player, you want to put that message forward. That was my way of showing I was fully involved in what we were trying to do.'

Root is sitting on the white benches in front of the Lord's pavilion, looking out at the ground that has brought him five of his 30 Test hundreds, plus a World Cup winner's medal. It is over a year since he gave up the captaincy, exhausted by the demands of leading England here, there and everywhere, and mindful of the effect his job was having on his young family. 'I loved it for the time I did it, but it got to a point where they did not have their husband or dad,' he says quietly. 'It was time for someone else to have that honour, time for the team to have a new voice and a new direction.'

He does not sound bitter, though there is regret. Why wouldn't there be? Few references to the new era are complete without a comparison with the old: every bouquet tossed to Stokes implies a brickbat hurled at Root. And if he spent his first year under Stokes revelling in his return to the rank and file, it also gave him time to reflect on the end of his own reign, an England-record 64 Tests in charge. There was plenty of success: home and away wins against South Africa, a 4–1 walloping of India, a 3–0 triumph in Sri Lanka. But 15 Ashes Tests brought two victories, ten defeats and no urn. Now, even after his liberation, there is wistfulness.

'When players say "I've had a great career, I wouldn't change anything," I always think that's a load of crap. I'd have changed a load of things. I still loved it and treasure the way it's been. But the amount of knowledge you gain, the things you see – clearly you'd do things differently. I've seen things go right, I've seen things go wrong, I've made mistakes, I've not been strong enough in certain areas, and I like to think I'd be able to help. There are so many things I had to deal with over those five years, on and off the field, that, if I had my time again, I'd have done very differently. I'd have been a little bit stronger about how we looked to play the game. If you look at how we started under me, here against South Africa, we were more aggressive.'

He gestures towards the outfield, recalling his first Test as captain, in July 2017. Root made 190 from 234 balls against a South African attack including Morne Morkel, Vernon Philander and Kagiso Rabada, and England raced to 458 at 4.34 an over, setting up a big win. In five more years under his leadership, England would score more quickly in their first innings only once – against India at Lord's in 2018. The South Africa game proved a tantalising glimpse of his team's promise. Root had hoped for more.

'I wanted us to be a little bit closer to how we played in white-ball cricket. Trevor [Bayliss] was a perfect foil and was a brilliant coach for the group. But maybe I needed someone a little stronger to help reinforce all the messages and make sure, if things didn't quite go according to plan, that I didn't waver from how we wanted to do things. With Silvers [Chris Silverwood] coming in, there was a change in approach with the way he saw the team moving forward. Whether, looking back, I'd have liked to have gone a slightly different way... it's easy to say with hindsight. I think I'd have liked to be a little bit stronger with my views on the game. But, again, we wouldn't be where we are now without the journey we've been on...'

It's one of cricket's oldest clichés, and – for those born south of Sheffield, west of Huddersfield or north of Middlesbrough – one of its most irritating. For large chunks of Test cricket's ancient history, it has also been untrue. But the idea that a strong Yorkshire means a strong England has been repeated so often, by one county in particular, that it has seeped into the collective conscience. To argue with it is futile, rarely more so than during the first few months of the Bazball era.

Between that first Test against New Zealand in June 2022, and the second Test against them at Wellington the following February, two-thirds of England's 18 hundreds were scored by Root (born in Sheffield), Jonny Bairstow (Bradford) and Harry Brook (Keighley). In that period, Root averaged 62, Bairstow 75 and Brook 80. And if Bairstow and Brook were the most outrageous early standard-bearers for England's new style, striking at 96 and 98 per 100 balls, then Root was no slouch: his strike-rate of 75 was around 20 higher than his career figure.

And it was Root who had to make the biggest adjustment. Not every former England captain had done this successfully – that's if they hadn't retired first. In his first Test after standing down, in 2003, Nasser Hussain dropped South Africa's Graeme Smith on 8 at Lord's, then watched him make 259. The man who replaced him, Michael Vaughan, was unimpressed. Vaughan, meanwhile, never played another Test after stepping down five years later; neither did Andrew Strauss after he quit, in 2012. Alastair Cook played on for 18 months after relinquishing the captaincy in early 2017 – but, according to Root, 'he was almost like Frodo after the ring went in the volcano, carrying a heavy burden still'.

Root, on the other hand, was an ex-England captain at the age of 31, with several years – if he chose – still ahead of him as a Test cricketer. It is testament to his close friendship with Stokes that the final phase of his career began so smoothly. Root is easy to manage, it's true: ego-free, popular, collegiate. Even when he was struggling towards the end of his tenure, no teammate would hear a word against him. And Stokes's loyalty to Root ensured the favour would be unquestioningly repaid. Even better, Root is enthused by the prospect: 'It feels like the most exciting and enjoyable part of my career is still to come, which I don't think many former captains can say.'

It helped that his first Test back in the ranks brought him a match-winning century, as England completed a chase of 277 against New Zealand at Lord's – the first fourth-innings hundred of his career, taking him past 10,000 Test runs. When Root walked off after pulling the winning four off Southee, Cook – the only other Englishman with more Test runs – was waiting for him in the Long Room with a bottle of champagne.

But Root was just warming up. Next came 176 in Nottingham, and the reverse-scoop off Southee, followed by an unbeaten 86 to make light work of a target of 296 at Headingley. And, having made one fourth-innings century, Root quickly made another: 142 not out in the remarkable seven-wicket win over India at Edgbaston. Because Bairstow was doing astonishing things at the other end, and because

Joe Root edges Kyle Mayers to John Campbell for 5 as England head for defeat against West Indies in Grenada in March 2022. Within three weeks, he has stepped down as Test captain.

Ben Stokes, wearing the bucket hat that became a symbol of England's new relaxed approach, head coach Brendon McCullum and Rob Key, the ECB's managing director of men's cricket, are all smiles.

Matthew Potts and Ben Stokes each make their feelings known after Potts takes the wicket of New Zealand captain Kane Williamson with his fifth ball as a Test cricketer, at Lord's in June 2022.

Joe Root joins the Bazball party, reverse-ramping New Zealand's Tim Southee over third man for six during the second Test at Trent Bridge.

India captain Virat Kohli advises Jonny Bairstow to put a sock in it during a tetchy exchange at Edgbaston; wicketkeeper Rishabh Pant looks on. But Bairstow has the last laugh, scoring a pair of hundreds as England chase down a national-record 387 for three.

Ben Duckett celebrates becoming the second of England's four centurions on a remarkable first day of the Pakistan tour at Rawalpindi in December 2022. His opening partner, Zak Crawley, has already got there; Ollie Pope and Harry Brook join them later, as England reach stumps on 506 for four from 75 overs.

With minutes to go before the sun sets on the final evening at Rawalpindi, Jack Leach pins Pakistan's Naseem Shah leg-before, and England have won a dramatic Test by 74 runs.

Leg-spinner Rehan Ahmed, the ultimate Bazball pick, having played just three first-class games prior to the third Test in Karachi, leads England off after his five for 48 leaves them on course for a clean sweep.

Harry Brook plays arguably the shot of the winter, easing Tim Southee over long-off for six during the first Test against New Zealand at Mount Maunganui in February 2023. England win by 267 runs, their tenth victory in 11 Bazball Tests.

Jimmy Anderson is caught behind down the leg side off Neil Wagner, and – agonisingly – England have lost the second Test at Wellington by one run, having asked New Zealand to follow on.

Zak Crawley gets the 2023 Ashes off to a breathtaking start, launching Pat Cummins's first ball at Edgbaston through the covers, and setting up a day in which England eventually declare on 393 for eight.

Ben Stokes can't quite cling on to a tough chance offered by Nathan Lyon during the tense closing stages at Edgbaston. Australia, with only two wickets in hand, still need 37 – but get over the line. Stokes later describes the drop as his only regret of the series.

Moeen Ali's unexpected return to Test cricket, following an injury to Jack Leach, is interrupted after one game by a painful blister on his spinning finger. The problem is solved when a fan writes to him to suggest a gel made from Manuka honey.

All hell is about to break loose, as Australia's wicketkeeper Alex Carey stumps his England counterpart Jonny Bairstow on the final day of the second Test at Lord's. Bairstow, wrongly, believed the ball was dead – but that doesn't stop furious MCC members shouting abuse at the tourists as they walk off for lunch.

Ben Stokes, egged on by a febrile Lord's, hits Cameron Green for a third successive six to bring up his century as he continues his pursuit of an improbable target of 371.

Stuart Broad becomes, in his own words, a 'facetious prat' as he goads the Australians following Bairstow's stumping, shouting 'in' every time he touches his bat behind the crease. He adds 108 for the seventh wicket with Stokes, but can't prevent England from going 2–0 down.

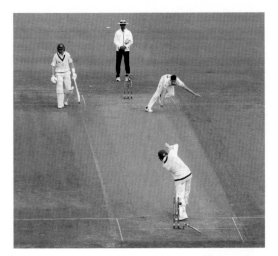

Almost immovable during the first two Tests, Australian opener Usman Khawaja is bowled on the first morning at Headingley by a delivery from Mark Wood timed at 94.6mph. Before the day is out, Wood has his first Test five-for in England.

Chris Woakes cuts Mitchell Starc for the winning four, and celebrates with Wood, his close friend and car buddy. Both men are playing their first game of the series, and England have cut the deficit to 2–1.

After facing criticism for his glovework at Edgbaston and Lord's, Jonny Bairstow holds the pose after a superb one-handed take to see off Mitchell Marsh on the first evening of the fourth Test at Old Trafford. Two days later, Bairstow smashes 99 not out from 81 balls.

Stuart Broad, with his long-time new-ball partner Jimmy Anderson, receives a guard of honour from Australia's fielders on the fourth day at The Oval, the morning after announcing that this Test, his 167th, will be his last.

Broad signs off in style with the match-winning wicket of Alex Carey, caught behind by Jonny Bairstow, as England complete a 49-run win, leaving the Ashes series all square at 2–2.

The two captains, Ben Stokes – holding the tankard given to each player by Brendon McCullum – and Pat Cummins await the presentations at The Oval.

Brook later shone in Pakistan, it was easy to forget how regal Root was in the first four Bazball Tests: 569 runs at 113, all made with an age-defying smile.

Above all, he saw parallels in the Lord's win with the start made by England's new-look white-ball team in 2015, when their home series against New Zealand (captain: Brendon McCullum) began at Edgbaston with a score of 408 for nine, of which Root made 104 off 78 balls. 'When you send such a strong message about how you want to do things, it was important we got off to a good start,' he says. 'It happened with the white-ball team. We made a statement in that first ODI, and it happened in that first Test match, which was an important moment for the group. It meant it was not just empty words: we backed it up with a performance and got over the line. I will always treasure playing a big part in that.'

When McCullum took over, he didn't need to say much to Root: 'He tried to just let me get on with it. He respected the time I had as captain, and wanted to make sure that transition was as smooth as it could be. In terms of batting, it was just: "Go and do what you have been doing." It was good that he tried to encourage me to help bring through the younger batters, and have a bit more of an active role in that. As captain, naturally, they would be a bit more stand-offish with me – they wouldn't come and talk to me about things, because they felt it was a vulnerable position to lay yourself bare with someone who might affect selection, though that's not how I saw it at the time. But over the last 12 months, guys have been a little bit more forthcoming, which has been nice.'

Root also grasped that the key to playing under the new coach was to 'solve problems'. He explains: 'If he's bowling in an area, find a way of getting him to bowl somewhere else.

If that means coming down the wicket, and getting outside off stump, then do that. If it means taking a risk early, there's a reason you're doing it. You're not stupid: you've played the game long enough to understand. By giving that different mindset on batting, on individual skill, guys were able to feel freer and express themselves more.'

In Pakistan, Root faced two balls as a left-hander against the leg-breaks of Zahid Mahmood, even if he should have been caught off the first by a diving Naseem Shah at what was now square leg (but moments earlier had been point). As with Southee, the innovation was the product of ruthless logic, though this time the ball was pitching a yard outside leg stump.

'It didn't feel like that much of a risk. I couldn't get bowled or lbw because he was bowling so wide, and I'd cover it with my pad. Caught was the only way I was going to get out. I backed myself to miss the field, even though I didn't. The fellow was on debut, and clearly quite nervous – Brooky had taken him to the cleaners first innings. I felt it was a way to put pressure on him, trying to get the field where you want it. It might look maverick at times, but there's a reason you do it. It wasn't an ego-driven thing, or to try to get an Instagram post. It was about trying to find a way of solving the problem.'

At the same time, was Root trying *too* hard? After all, by the time he resigned as captain, he had problem-solved his way to nearly 10,000 Test runs at an average close to 50. Why gild the lily? After plundering the attacks of New Zealand and India, he tailed off against South Africa (averaging 11) and Pakistan (25). When he was twice caught playing reverse-bat shots – a scoop and a sweep – for 14 and 57, in the first Test against New Zealand at Mount Maunganui, critics wondered whether he was sacrificing his reliability on the altar of gimmickry, even if McCullum kept encouraging him to play the stroke. Root knew they had a point. He knew he was in danger of over-reaching.

'I was so desperate to buy into what we were trying to do, I went away from the stuff I'd done really well,' he says. 'I knew it was important that we all tried to go towards our goal, which was to entertain and see how high the ceiling was. I probably went too far on that spectrum, instead of understanding how the message might apply more to the guys around me than it necessarily did to me. You saw guys scoring the way they were, and you want to be able to play that way as well. The realisation over time that my role within the team might be quite similar to what it has previously been actually fits with what we're trying to do. Going through that has been beneficial and helpful.'

In the second Test at Wellington, Root trusted his instincts. Despite the characterisation of Bazball in some quarters as mindless slogging, this was actually one of its central tenets: the idea that you should be the most positive form of yourself, not a pastiche of someone else. And if that sounded like a line from a self-help manual, it seemed to help Root. After 100 balls, he had 36, with a lone boundary; not until he got to 88 did he pull out a reverse-scoop; and by the time he brought up three figures, he had hit just seven fours. Next morning, he reverse-ramped Southee's fourth ball for six, and finished with 153 not out, deprived of something even bigger because Stokes declared England's first innings on 435 for eight. By then, he and Brook had added 302 at five an over, having joined forces at 21 for three. Root followed up with 95 during a chase that fell one run short. He had sampled the most extreme elements of Bazball and decided which bits worked for him – or at least when best to do what.

So it was a shame he suffered a costly aberration during that Wellington chase. England had reached 80 for three in pursuit of 258 to complete a 2–0 win. One of those three wickets was nightwatchman Ollie Robinson, so their position was slightly better than it seemed. But Ollie Pope back-cut Neil Wagner to second slip, where Tom Latham held a superb catch, changing the mood in an instant. England needed to take a deep breath. Instead, Root dabbed the next ball into the gully, and set off for a single that moved from optimistic to lunatic in the moment Michael Bracewell swooped from third slip and arrowed a return into the gloves of Tom Blundell. At this point, Brook – yet to face a ball – was not even in the frame. As Root realised his misjudgement, Brook kept running, all the way to the pavilion. Had Root stayed put, or Brook sent him back, England would surely have gone on to become the first visiting team to win a Test series in New Zealand for six years. The live ball-by-ball commentary on ESPNcricinfo captured the moment by doing what many have done in the new era, and assessing its worth by the success or otherwise of its latest deed: 'Bazball on its uppers.'

For Brook, it was a return to earth after a blistering century in the first innings, taking him to 809 runs from his first nine Test knocks at an average of almost 90 and a strike-rate of 98. These were absurd figures for someone who had only just turned 24, and who, in five seasons of first-class cricket with Yorkshire before the previous summer, had averaged 13, 25, 21, 43 and 37. But he had worked on his trigger movement, a step across to off stump at the point of delivery that allowed him to leave anything outside his right eyeline.

In 2021, he had also had the good sense to flourish in a match for Northern Superchargers in the first season of The Hundred: one of the teammates watching him hit Welsh Fire for 62 off 31 balls was Stokes. Seeds were being sown. The following summer he was a different player, averaging 107 for a Yorkshire side struggling in division one of the county championship. And because he was now in and around the Test squad, though as yet uncapped, he knew he had to pay attention to stand any chance of getting noticed. 'I tried to take everything up to Yorkshire that Baz and Stokesy were saying about how they wanted us to play, and play that way in county cricket,' he says. He also thrashed 140 for England Lions in a non-first-class game against the South African tourists. When Bairstow broke his leg, Brook earned a Test debut at The Oval.

The news came via a call from the coach. 'I answered the phone and said: "Hi, McCullum." I was so used to seeing his name in the papers as "McCullum", and I didn't feel I knew him well enough to be on first-name terms. He was very nice and made me feel as though I'm unstoppable. He is very good at making you feel confident.' Initially, at least, Stokes chose another method of making Brook feel at home, singing his praises during a pre-match media huddle, then – with a grin – calling him 'a bit dumb'. He later apologised to Brook, but with an explanation: 'I used to get called dumb as well when I was younger, so I'm just getting my own back.'

During a chaotic week in Kennington, he also had his first taster of Stokes's aggression, after the first two days were lost to rain and the death of the Queen. 'Stokesy came up and said: "We have three days here – we are 100 per cent going to make a result." I can't remember too much about batting. I played a nice forward defensive in the first few balls, which felt good.'

That last remark is unlikely to prove Brook's epitaph. He fell for 12, pulling the giant left-armer Marco Jansen to fine leg, and encouraging experts to note a potential weakness against the short ball that would crop up again when the Australians arrived a year later. But England won the Test, and the series, and they liked the cut of Brook's jib. In Pakistan, he embarked on a dreamy first tour.

It was England's first Test series there in 17 years, but Brook was no stranger to the conditions. He had flourished for Lahore Qalandars in the T20 Pakistan Super League earlier in 2022, at one point hitting 102 not out from 49 balls in front of his new home crowd; an unbeaten 41 off 22 balls helped Lahore to victory in the final. On his next trip to Pakistan, for England's seven-match T20 series in the autumn, he put his local knowledge to good use, scoring 238 runs at 79 with a strike-rate of 163. By the time he returned for the three-match Test series in December, he was undaunted: 'I knew all their bowlers, and I knew what the pitches were going to do. It felt comfortable for me starting my Test career there.'

The extent to which England's younger generation of batsmen are not as fazed by foreign conditions as their predecessors, thanks in part to the non-stop T20 franchise circuit, is another part of the Bazball story. So is the T20 format itself. Because Root has never been a natural 20-over player, his challenge has been to work out how to adapt to the new ways. For Brook, by contrast, the new ways are simply a fact of life: existing in parallel with the orthodoxy of his red-ball Yorkshire upbringing has been a white-ball world offering fame and fortune for the gifted and the inventive.

In Pakistan, he batted as if he had been waiting for Bazball all his life. He began as one of four first-day centurions in Rawalpindi, where he became the first England player to hit six fours in a Test over, off Zahid Mahmood, the leg-spinner who was fast turning into a punchline for the cruellest jokes. It felt almost incidental that Brook's 80-ball hundred was the third-fastest for England, behind Bairstow (77 against New

Zealand at Trent Bridge a few months earlier), and Gilbert Jessop (76 against Australia at The Oval in 1902). Time and again in the coming weeks, Jessop would crop up in despatches as batsmen threatened his record. Brook says he was on his mind during the second innings, when he followed 153 from 116 balls with 87 off 65. Had he not been bowled by Naseem Shah trying to hit his ninth six of the match, he would surely have beaten his 120-year-old record. As it was, Brook had to settle for taking 27 off an over from occasional slow left-armer Saud Shakil – breaking the England record he had equalled in the first innings. That had been held by Ian Botham. Barely out of Test nappies, Brook was mixing it with some of English cricket's most evocative names.

In the second Test at Multan, he fell cheaply to Pakistan's new mystery spinner Abrar Ahmed on a chaotic first morning. England lunched on 180 for five (Abrar 13-0-70-5), which was some going even after the session was extended by half an hour because of Friday prayers. But, in an early sign he was a quick learner, Brook was not happy after skying one to mid-off, a stroke he describes as 'crap' and a 'give-away wicket'. After a chat with Martin Speight, the former Sussex cricketer who had coached him at Sedbergh School, Brook decided to 'knuckle down second innings', when he made 108 from 149 balls. Then, at Karachi, he made 111, overcoming his part in the run-out of Stokes, who briefly looked as if he wanted to throttle his young partner before offering a thumbs up. Brook finished the series with 468 runs, the most by an England player in Pakistan, beating David Gower's 449 in 1983–84: more cricketing royalty erased from the record books. And he had grown in confidence. At one point, Brook was at the non-striker's end when Stokes missed three in a row. 'What's happened there?' he asked his captain. 'Do you not watch the ball?'

By now, the sceptics who had wondered whether Bazball could work in Pakistan were tweaking their argument. The Pakistani pitches, they said, were flatter than expected (which was partly true, although Multan offered turn). No, a better test would come on the more seamer-friendly surfaces of New Zealand, especially with the first of the two Tests taking place with a pink ball under lights, at Mount Maunganui. Brook responded with 89 off 81 balls in the first innings, having at one stage poked Jessop's ghost when he reached 76 off 56 by launching Southee for six over long-off. The shot went viral on social media, encouraging comparisons with Kevin Pietersen, though Brook doesn't even describe it as his favourite shot of the winter.

'I played another one over the top off Matt Henry at Wellington which went for four,' he says, before explaining the psychology of the stroke. 'It asserts dominance on the bowlers. You don't get hit back over your head often, especially by someone who has just started his career. It sent a message to everyone in the world – not just from me, but from the whole team. We are going to come for you and take the game to you and play how we want to play.'

These clarion calls sounded very un-English. For a long time, gallows humour had been the default setting, the better to deal with inevitable disappointment. Unbridled confidence was unsettling – for opponents and possibly even for England fans. It helped that Brook was matching word with deed. He added 54 off 41 in the second innings, taking the player of the match award as England completed victory by 276 runs: a tenth win out of 11 was their best sequence since 2004.

During the game, Stokes had finally broken McCullum's Test record of 107 sixes, hoisting Scott Kuggeleijn to leg and earning a round of applause from his coach. Next ball, he celebrated with six more, though it needed Wagner to step on the fine-leg rope as he tried to catch him. Later, Stokes reflected briefly on his achievement, while predicting the identity of the man who might one day take the record off him. 'When it went, it was like I picked Brendon up off my shoulder and dropped him,' said Stokes. 'He said "well done" to me, and I just said: "Brooky will probably break it in the next 20 games the way he is going." At that point, Brook had 15 sixes from five Tests. In the next game, at Wellington, he added five more during an incandescent 186 off 176 balls that ought to have ensured against defeat. Then came Root's dodgy call as England stumbled in the chase.

Run-outs can breed resentment: Geoff Boycott never forgave Botham for deliberately sabotaging him when England needed to set up a declaration at Christchurch in 1977–78. But the Root–Brook farrago is unlikely to become so much as an aside on the after-dinner circuit. More than eight years separate them, their Test debuts a decade apart. Brook played with Root at Yorkshire from an early age and used to boast to friends of bowling to him in the nets. If the dynamic sounds vaguely master-servant, it has evolved to master-apprentice, and perhaps beyond – to something approaching equality. Even before Brook was picked for England, Root was saying he was the next big thing; Brook repays the compliment by saying Root is 'willing to help everybody, with batting or in life'. There is no insecurity in the older man, and in the younger only admiration.

'To have someone in your team sat next to you who has done it in every country against every attack... He knows it all,' says Brook. 'Seaming, swinging, spin, reverse-swing – he has faced it all. You can have little conversations with him, which in the changing-room people wouldn't notice,

BAZBALL

but they make a big difference. He's one of the best to have played the game.'

For both men, the story evolved once more during the Ashes. On an adrenaline-fuelled first day at Edgbaston, Root got the crowd going with a reverse-scoop for six off Scott Boland in the first over after tea to bring up England's 250 and was soon celebrating a century – interrupted only by another Stokes declaration. Root then tried to play the same shot off Pat Cummins's first ball of the fourth morning. He missed, before succeeding in the next over, off the hapless Boland. Again, he was applying the logic that had allowed him to attack Southee a year earlier in Nottingham, even if his adventure sparked criticism when he was stumped off Nathan Lyon for 46. Root went quiet after that, but finished strongly. He made an accomplished 84 in the fourth Test at Old Trafford, where he was denied an apparently inevitable hundred only by a ball from Josh Hazlewood that barely rose above ankle height. And he reached 91 at The Oval before his defences were breached by another pea-shooter, from off-spinner Todd Murphy. One more reverse-scoop for six, off Mitchell Marsh, took his Bazball tally with the stroke to 71 runs off 26 attempts, that one dismissal at Mount Maunganui, and countless changes of field.

Brook was going through his own readjustment, having struggled to live up to his £1.35 million fee during his first season at the IPL with Sunrisers Hyderabad. He didn't help himself when he reacted to his one big innings – 100 not out off 55 balls against Kolkata Knight Riders – by suggesting he had 'shut up' the 'keyboard warriors'. It would be his only score above 27 in 11 IPL innings. Back in England, he did his best to play down the significance of the Ashes, telling *Wisden Cricket Monthly* it represented 'just another game'. His logic was very

196

Bazball: 'The same ball coming down at me. Just another human bowling a little round leather thing at another human. And I've got to hit it with a bit of wood. That's it, really.'

In the first innings at Edgbaston, though, his problem was not using that bit of wood: he was bowled by Lyon for 32 when the ball ballooned off his pad, then bounced behind him as he stood there shouldering arms, and on to the stumps via his back leg. 'I lost the ball,' he says. 'I thought Labuschagne was going to catch it at short leg. I couldn't do anything – it was horrendous. You see it but don't have time to move. You just watch it hitting the stumps.' In the second innings, like Root, he fell to Lyon for 46, pulling him low to midwicket.

But at Lord's the story returned to his perceived naivety against the short ball. His teammates flailed, too, as Australia turned the game round with a barrage of bouncers on the second afternoon, though Brook's ugly dismissal for 50 on the third morning – slapping a short one from Starc to Cummins at cover – went down especially badly. When the cameras panned to Boycott in the posh seats, he had his head in his hands. But Brook says the bounce was uneven, which made ducking the short ball a hazardous business. 'I was just trying to score as many runs as we could,' he says. 'Later, we bowled plenty of bouncers at them and I reckon we scored double or triple amount of runs they scored. The lads said we got stick in the media, but I think we played it better than they did.'

Brook was averaging 42 in his first Ashes series, but the sense that Australia weren't seeing the best of him was compounded by a beauty from Cummins in the second innings at Lord's, which cleaned him up for 4. Then, promoted to No 3 at Headingley because of Pope's injury, he nibbled at Cummins and was caught in the slips for 3. More than the bouncer mishap at Lord's, it was these two dismissals that played on

Brook's mind. 'I was a bit annoyed, because I felt I was a bit tentative,' he says. 'I got stuck on the crease at Lord's, then I nicked off at Headingley, which I've done very rarely since triggering.'

Moeen Ali's offer to bat at No 3 allowed Brook to return to his preferred slot at No 5, away from Cummins's new-ball probing. If that turned Ali into something between a sacrificial lamb and a laboratory guinea pig, it played to Brook's, and the team's, strengths. In the second innings at Headingley, as England chased 251, he made an accomplished 75, losing Root, Stokes and Bairstow on the way, before adding 59 for the seventh wicket with Chris Woakes, who soon completed the job with Mark Wood.

'Mo came up to me a few times and said: "I'll go to three next innings. I will go and try and smack it,"' says Brook. 'I wasn't sure if he was serious. Then Baz came up to me the morning of the run chase and said: "Right, Mo is going to three, you're at five." No discussion about it. Nothing. It could have been a match-winning decision from Mo. To be that unselfish was unbelievable. I'd only found out a day or two before that I was potentially going to three. It was a little bit like: "Oh God." I have batted at five for the last four or five years now, and I just feel more comfortable there. Mo's decision could have been the difference in the game.'

At Old Trafford, Brook added a cautious 61, his tenth score of 50 or more in just his 18th Test innings; Bradman got there in 19. At The Oval, after admitting he had been too reckless at times earlier in the series, he made a more assured 85. And by now he'd got over the Wellington run-out. Hadn't he? 'He didn't even say sorry,' says Brook. 'He said: "You should have turned me back." Yes, cheers Rooty.'

9

'That's Marc with a C!'

It was a bright May morning at The Oval, the day after Ben Foakes had been dropped by England. The decision had been coming: Jonny Bairstow was available again after recovering from his broken leg, and Harry Brook had thrived as his replacement in Pakistan and New Zealand. Foakes had been left out before – notably at Multan, where Ollie Pope was preferred behind the stumps, allowing England to play an extra bowler in Mark Wood. And the plan had worked: on the final day of that second Test, Wood made the match-winning breakthroughs, his pace besting the blandness of the pitch. But none of this consoled Foakes ahead of an Ashes summer that would have brought his skills to a wider audience. Wandering over for a chat, he promised to talk more once the disappointment had waned, then headed for the nets. Perhaps the feel of bat on ball would provide solace.

No cricketer is as vulnerable as the wicketkeeper – there's room for only one, after all – and no country argues about wicketkeeping like England. In the blue corner are the aesthetes, the lovers of glovework for glovework's sake, the fans of Alan Knott, Jack Russell, Chris Read, Ben Foakes. In the red corner are the pragmatists, who prefer the safety valve of a run-maker at No 7, and never mind the odd missed stumping. They prefer Alec Stewart, Matt Prior, Jonny Bairstow. Those in the blue corner also drop catches, of course, just as those in the red take blinders. But the debate has shed much of its nuance. These two groups may support the same team, but they are otherwise irreconcilable, for ever totting up the runs that are accumulated on one side of the stumps and those that are squandered on the other – as if a mathematical answer will emerge to what remains a question of temperament.

By his own admission, Foakes is no natural Bazballer. Of those who played regularly under McCullum in 2022, only Alex Lees had a lower strike-rate than his 48 – perfectly respectable, but well behind most of his teammates, and exactly half Bairstow's 96 that year. Over coffee in Karachi in December, Foakes suggested with a chuckle that he was not 'Bazball-compliant', which was partly true and typically self-deprecating. Still, it must have been nice to hear Ben Stokes call him the best wicketkeeper in the world after he helped beat New Zealand at Lord's several months earlier? Foakes pauses. 'I don't know. That sort of stuff I take as tongue-in-cheek. It's a lovely compliment, but I find it hard to process.' Something is stopping him from embracing the bromides and ego-boosts that occasionally fuel the Bazball discourse.

In the aftermath of Foakes's omission, that comment by Stokes must have been even harder to process – not least because he had finally begun to feel at home. After an assured Test century on debut against Sri Lanka at Galle in November 2018, he had claimed the player of the series award as England won 3–0. He then appeared twice in the Caribbean in early 2019, but injuries and selectorial whim meant he would play no more Test cricket for two years. Then, after three difficult matches in India, there was another gap, of 12 months. He needed to feel supported – and Stokes seemed ready to step in.

Did that make this Ashes axing especially tough to take? 'Yeah, definitely. This is by far the best environment I've been involved with over the five or six years I've played for England. It does make it difficult. It's the most I've ever felt valued by an England team – the first time I've felt a member of it, rather than popping in. To feel that way, and then get dropped, makes it more of a hammer blow.'

Even if he scored at only a run every other ball, Foakes embodied one of Bazball's core tenets: he understood the principle of absorbing pressure, as he did so well in the company of Stokes against South Africa at Old Trafford, where England had slipped to 147 for five in reply to 151. As a middle-order batsman for Surrey, Foakes is used to building an innings. At No 7 in the Test team, he had often been left with the tail, unsure whether to stick or twist. That day, though, Stokes was batting as calmly as he had done at any stage of his captaincy, which meant Foakes could proceed at his own tempo.

'For me, Bazball is not necessarily whacking fours or sixes every ball,' he says. 'I'm not someone who does that anyway, so it would be stupid batting. But it's about being positive. In the past, if an off-spinner is on and I haven't faced many balls, I'd think: *I can't run down here and whip one.* Whereas now, if I'm thinking it, just do it. If it's a strength of yours, let's do it, rather than err on the cautious side. That's the message I take: do what you do, but be brave in doing it.'

At one point during their partnership in Manchester, Stokes and Foakes each had 41, and were scoring at an almost old-school tempo. Like Zak Crawley, who had earlier made 38 in two-and-a-half hours – an innings valued more highly in the dressing-room than by many in the crowd or the press box – they were paying respect to South Africa's fast bowlers, playing the long game, waiting to cash in. It was as if they were saying: this, too, is Bazball! By the time Stokes reached three figures, Foakes had 62 – and was relaxed about the discrepancy. Later, in his own good time, he was celebrating a well-crafted second Test century.

'I crept up the gears, but Stokesy flew up them, and put the pressure back on,' he says. 'We complemented each other really well as we got deeper into the game, then into a position where we were odds-on favourite to win.' They added 173 in nearly 54 overs. Of England's 28 century stands in the Bazball era so far, this was the slowest – at 3.22 an over. (Bairstow, for what it's worth, has been involved in the two quickest.)

But their rate of progress didn't bother Foakes and, because he was committing to his natural game, it didn't bother England. At the other end, Stokes was quietly supportive. Both players were clear about their plan, of being more aggressive against whichever spinner was turning the ball in to them: the left-handed Stokes took on slow left-armer Keshav Maharaj, the right-handed Foakes tackled the off-breaks of Simon Harmer. 'I was seeking a bit of reassurance, because I wasn't slogging Harmer into the stands,' says Foakes. 'It was more: are you happy with the way I'm playing? I was getting clear messages back from him that he was good with what I was doing. I'd run an idea past him, and he'd just say "yes" – if it was a positive option.'

His insecurity was understandable. 'When I first came into the set-up, I was wary of my style of play clashing with the expectations of what was happening. You wonder how you'll fit in, how to expand your game. But with this regime, if you're willing to be open and practise, they're happy.'

To talk to Foakes is to encounter a rare instance of a player who understands Bazball's potential benefits, but wrestles with some of its implications. He has always been a thoughtful, industrious cricketer, turning himself in his early teens from a fast bowler – he is 6ft 2in – into a wicketkeeper because no one else in Essex age-group cricket fancied the job. Or, as he puts it: 'I was the only one stupid enough to try.' Above all, he is used to feedback from experts.

But McCullum, a former keeper himself, sees things differently: his decision to streamline the dressing-room involved dispensing with the services of James Foster as England's wicketkeeping coach. Foster's predecessor had been another ex-England keeper, Bruce French, who had been a confidant as well as a technician. After leaving the job in November 2020, he told the *Daily Telegraph*: 'When I talk to the keepers today, it is crucial to have someone who has been a top-line keeper and had these feelings. Yes, there are technical things you need to know, but you have to know how a keeper is feeling. I go and watch a game of cricket, and someone will score a hundred and I won't notice because I am watching the keeper. People say to me later: "Did you see that shot?" And I reply: "Not really – but I saw a good keeper."'

Foakes felt the absence of a kindred spirit. 'That was probably one of the things I found difficult at the start. When I began with England 12 years ago, it was all about specialist coaches. I had always grown up with that, at Essex and the Lions and then Stewie [Surrey director of cricket Alec Stewart]. I did a lot of work with Bruce French, and always had someone to bounce off and talk to. Training was high intensity: I was always being pushed by the coach.

'Baz is less about specialist coaching, more about "back yourself, rock up, do your job". It was one of the things I found a little bit different from what I was used to, and I had to adapt to it. But it can stop me from overthinking and delving too much into the technical. At Old Trafford, the ball was shooting through low, and I felt like I lost my rhythm behind the stumps. I asked Baz: "What do you reckon, is there anything different?" He just said: "You're catching the ball well, boss, you're doing well." That's his approach. That's why he was as free as a player and was as good as he was, because he had that mindset and never really delved into things. He was just quite present at doing what he does: whatever happens, happens. I tried not to be as regimented as I had been.'

Foakes's observation strikes a chord with Sam Billings, who replaced him as a Covid substitute on the fourth morning of the Headingley Test against New Zealand, then kept his place against India at Edgbaston. 'When I played those Tests, the thing I was most nervous about was the wicketkeeping,' says Billings. 'Normally, it's batting, and how many runs you score. But straight away I was going into the Test match thinking, *I don't want to drop one here or make a mistake because it will be plastered everywhere, and people will say you should pick your best keeper* – all that garbage.

'There was one that wobbled on me at Edgbaston, and I parried it to slip, where Rooty caught it. It was Virat Kohli, too. I watched the replay at tea, and was gutted, because I'd kept so well up to that point and felt I hadn't done myself justice. Baz came up and put his arm round me: "What's the matter? You've kept unbelievably. You haven't dropped a ball all day, and it hasn't cost the team anything, so don't worry about it." That's what Baz does. He shuts out all the noise. "Everyone in here knows how well you've done, and that's what's important."'

Foakes kept chipping in whenever he got the chance. After the Old Trafford hundred, he made 64 on his recall in Karachi, then 38 and 51 in the win over New Zealand at Mount Maunganui. At Wellington, he almost retrieved a lost cause as England dipped to 215 for eight in pursuit of 258. Marshalling the strike with growing skill, he had taken them to within seven of victory when he top-edged a hook off New Zealand captain Tim Southee and was brilliantly caught at fine leg for 35 by a sprawling Neil Wagner. Three overs later, Wagner had Jimmy Anderson caught behind down the leg side. England had lost by one run.

Yet the mood was of mutual celebration. McCullum walked grinning on to the field, and Southee joked with Anderson that 'you guys owed us one' – a reference to the 2019 World Cup final. But Foakes wasn't drinking the Kool-Aid. 'I was just disappointed, to be honest with you. I fully get there's a bigger picture: it was an incredible Test match, and it was great to be part of it. But when you're the guy who's out there batting… I was really happy with the way I handled the situation. To get so close – I was very disappointed.'

One thing was clear: because of the pace at which England's innings were progressing, it wasn't just the bowlers who were denied the breather they craved. Only four times in the Bazball era have England batted for longer than 90 overs, or the equivalent of a day: they made 539 in 128.2 overs against New Zealand at Trent Bridge, 415 for nine declared in 106.4 against South Africa at Old Trafford, 657 off 101 against Pakistan at Rawalpindi, and 592 off 107.4 against Australia, again at Old Trafford. Otherwise, there was no rest at the wicket.

'That was the first thing I noticed,' says Foakes. 'Because we bat so fast, you're in the field the whole time. You have to be prepared to be tired a lot. I think it was at Wellington: I looked up and felt like we were winning the game, but you've fielded for double the time and they've got fewer runs. It's crazy. You definitely have to be fitter than you otherwise would be.'

This phenomenon peaked at Rawalpindi, where England totalled 921 runs off 136.5 overs, and Pakistan 847 off 252. England's second-innings 264 for seven lasted just 35.5 overs, which meant they spent all but one and a bit of the game's last 11 sessions in the field. It was back-breaking work. No wonder even the seasoned Anderson declared the victory England's best ever.

For Foakes, life as a Bazball wicketkeeper demanded focus as well as fitness. 'You do think there are going to be chances. Ordinarily in red-ball stuff you go through dull phases where the batting team might be on top and you've got one slip in. But this team are always on the attack, so you feel you're in the game. Regardless of what is happening, you feel like you're dominating the opposition. You're not saying: "Well played, we'll spread the field, and if you nick it there's only one slip." Instead it's: "You're playing well, but we're going to get you out next ball."'

Foakes began the new season in strong form for Surrey, scoring 76 and 103 not out against Lancashire at Old Trafford, then 124 as they chased down a record-breaking 501 against Kent at Canterbury. But by then he knew his fate: when England named their squad for the one-off Test against Ireland and the first two Tests against Australia, he wasn't in it. Was he told England simply had to find a way to reintegrate Bairstow?

'Yeah, essentially. I think I wanted a bit more understanding of the reasons – what I need to do to get back in, and to be around squads. One thing I've always found is that I've been put in the keeper mould only. My numbers from the past few years have been very good for a batter. I guess I'm wary of whether it's a perception thing, or is this something I need to change in my game or play a certain style of cricket or try to improve? But what I got back was just "Jonny's been that good he needs to come back in", which is understandable.'

Those last three words sound like a generous concession, but the aesthetes in the blue corner were irritated. Foakes had been an integral part of Bazball and was a calming presence behind the stumps. The dressing-room, though, were mainly red. Billings, for one, is adamant the decision to replace him with Bairstow was correct. 'Ultimately, everyone can talk about Foakesy, who is a fantastic player,' he says. 'But who would the Aussies want coming at No 7 in a Test match, Jonny Bairstow or Ben Foakes? It's a no-brainer. Jonny's one of the best players in the world. If you get guys like him playing well, the upside is phenomenal. That's the whole attitude: it's looking at the upside of players, not the downside, and that's a really un-English thing to do, because we are inherently sceptical and cynical.'

It's a conclusion with which Bairstow, unprompted, agrees. He, too, is at The Oval, though later in the summer – two days before the final Test of an Ashes series in which he has been a prominent subplot. He has scored runs, dropped catches, taken screamers, sparked a culture war by wandering out of his crease, and spoken with magnificent fury. So much has happened since the summer of 2022 that it is easy to forget he was Bazball's first poster boy; it is also easy to forget that, back then, before the emergence of Brook, there was room in the side for both Bairstow and Foakes.

Bazball's strength, Bairstow believes, has been its resilience. 'It's easy to do it for one or two games,' he says. 'But to carry on doing it, to stay on the front foot when it potentially doesn't go right, it's not very English. We're generally quite a negative nation. It's a very un-English way of playing the game. It's against the trend of Test cricket. It's questioning people that have played in the past, who then say: "Oh no, we can't be doing that!"'

As we chat on the seats just below the home side's dressing-room, others come and go, including McCullum and David Saker, the fast-bowling coach. Bairstow assures them he's talking only about the previous summer, not the Ashes. They both laugh, because they know Jonny, a veteran approaching his 95th Test who speaks with the candour of a newcomer. The laugh says: *you'll be talking about the Ashes soon enough…*

First, though, 2022. After five Tests at No 6 or 7 in Australia and the Caribbean, where he hit centuries in Sydney and Antigua, Bairstow was playing for Punjab Kings at the IPL when he took a call from McCullum: 'You're batting at five. We want you to go out and whack it. Can't wait to catch up with you.' Bairstow places an imaginary phone on its receiver. 'The clarity was really helpful.'

He had often been regarded by teammates as a destructive player who needed handling a bit differently. It was too simplistic to ascribe everything to the tragic suicide of his father, David, when Jonny was eight. Equally, there was no doubt he craved reassurance. To have become, like David, a wicketkeeper for Yorkshire and England, added to the poignancy of his story, but it also left him more vulnerable to the ebb and flow of selection than a bowler or a batsman. And before Foakes, there had been Jos Buttler, the choice of former national selector Ed Smith. By the time McCullum arrived, Buttler had drifted away from Test cricket, having managed only two centuries from 100 innings – a scandalous return for a player of his talent. But his rivalry with Bairstow added to England's wicketkeeping psychodrama.

'We've all known for years how good Jonny is,' says Billings. 'It's just about him realising that, and also feeling loved enough in the environment and in a place where he knows he's going to be playing and be the main guy. Too many times he's had that head-to-head with Jos and wrestled so much with that. There's been a huge amount of resentment in terms of that dynamic. Baz and Stokesy have just grabbed Jonny and made him into a phenomenal player.'

Stokes had long grasped how to make him tick, and had often batted well with him, not least during a stand of 399 in 57 overs against South Africa at Cape Town in 2015–16. Stokes made the quickest double-century in English history, Bairstow an emotional first Test hundred, looking to the skies as he thought of his dad. It was Bazball in the days when McCullum was still playing for New Zealand. Stokes also knew, in the words of one insider, that Bairstow sometimes needed 'an arm round him *and* a kick up the arse'. As Mike Brearley pointed out in his North London study: 'Empathy has to be combined with a willingness to confront. It starts with empathy to be able to get to that point.'

Above all, Stokes knew Bairstow needed to feel wanted. After the Lord's win against New Zealand, he praised him in the press conference for an innings of 16, which seemed strange at the time, but later made sense. Earlier in the game, Bairstow had returned despondent to the dressing-room, having been bowled aiming a big shot in possibly the last over of a long spell from fast bowler Kyle Jamieson. Convention said Bairstow should have seen him off. But Stokes was having none of it. 'If you're in that position again, do it again,' he told him. 'That's exactly what I want to see from you. It's all about putting pressure back on opponents. If you're in the same situation next week, I want you to do the same thing.' And next week, in Nottingham, that's exactly what Bairstow did.

'At Lord's, I went about it the same way, but it just didn't come off,' says Bairstow. 'Trent Bridge was next. I didn't get many in the first innings, but the mindset hadn't changed.' He embarks on a string of mixed metaphors, mirroring the chaos wrought by his batting. 'It just needed someone to take the bull by the horns and unleash everything we've seen over the last 12 months. The capabilities have always been there. It's about taking the harness off, unbuckling the seat belt and letting it fly. And then it was like a snowball effect. Can we bat this way? Yes, we can, so we'll go again and go again and go again. It had that ripple effect throughout the group.'

So it was that, on the last afternoon of the second Test, Jonny Bairstow became Bazball's first standard-bearer. Set 299 to wrap up the series with a game to spare, England had reached tea on 139 for four. Bairstow, after scores of 1, 16 and 8, had 43. The first thought of the old regime would have been to ensure against defeat, guarantee at least a share of the series, and start again five days later at Headingley. But the chat during the interval was simple: England were going for it. If 160 runs in a session sounded a lot, the irregular shape of the Trent Bridge boundaries offered some tempting areas, especially towards Bridgford Road, a short cross-batted thrash from the Pavilion End.

In the dressing-room, Bairstow chose a novel method of pumping himself up. Thinking he was alone, he addressed a mirror with gusto. 'Jonathan Marc Bairstow!' he roared. 'This is your day, your chance to show what you can do.' But the Trent Bridge dressing-room is L-shaped, and spacious enough for a lone teammate to be sitting unnoticed round the corner. Finally, Bairstow spotted him. 'That's Marc with a C!' he boomed, and marched off to slay New Zealand.

Out in the middle, Stokes noticed 'those Jonny eyes', and offered some advice. Bairstow remembers it: '"It's a short boundary, so hit it up." There was no negative thought about trying to contain and hit the ball down. Just hit it into the stand because that's probably the safer option anyway.' The final session was carnage, with Bairstow blasting 93 runs from 44 balls, including seven sixes as New Zealand repeatedly dropped short. Stokes played a virtuoso second fiddle – 75 from 70, with four sixes of his own – and the remaining runs came at ten an over. With Trent Bridge throwing open the gates for free, and Bairstow blazing away in the sunshine, the atmosphere was more like a carnival than a Test match. It chimed perfectly with England's desire to entertain. For the first time since 2005, the summer Michael Vaughan's team regained the Ashes after 16 years in Australian hands, cricket was beginning to feel like the people's sport again.

Cock of the walk, Bairstow held a barbeque at his home in North Leeds before the final Test at Headingley. Those present say he was the perfect host, buying in the best cuts of meat, and supplying cigars and whisky into the small hours. Even so, traces of insecurity remained. After his heroics in Nottingham, Bairstow surprised McCullum by asking how he should bat from now on. 'I've never heard a bloke get 130 off 90 balls a week before, then ask his head coach: "How should I go out and play?"' said McCullum. 'I told him: "Go and get your Sudoku book, come and sit next to me, and shut up. Whatever you did last week, go out and do it again."'

Bairstow obliged, though not before a stumble or two. On the second day at Headingley, England were in trouble at 55 for six in reply to New Zealand's 329. Bairstow was holding the fort on his home ground, but if Wagner – a left-arm seamer – had reviewed an lbw shout against debutant Jamie Overton, it would soon have been 63 for seven. Quite possibly, the game would have been done. The New Zealanders, though, had lost a review in Wagner's previous over after the ball pitched outside leg stump. Now, they didn't even discuss using DRS. It would have revealed three reds. 'It was close,' says Overton. 'At the time, I thought I had hit it, but looking back at replays I got nowhere near. I must have hit my pad at the same time, so it must have sounded like I'd hit the ball. They thought I'd hit it as well.'

Good teams need luck, and England were receiving their share. At Lord's, Stokes had been bowled on the charge by Colin de Grandhomme, only for replays to reveal a no-ball. Had he not overstepped, England would have been 75 for five in pursuit of 277, and project Bazball heading for an underwhelming start. Two overs later, de Grandhomme hobbled out of the series with a heel injury, making the chase a little easier; Stokes went on to make a vital 54. 'No matter what my wife gets for my birthday, it probably won't be as good as that,' he said. 'A huge bit of luck – sometimes you need it. I don't think he oversteps the mark that often. Lord's and drama seems to follow me around, doesn't it?'

Back at Headingley, Bairstow and Overton cashed in on New Zealand's misjudgement. 'I was just trying to get through the first 25 to 30 balls,' says Overton. 'Having Jonny at the other end, scoring the way he did, took the pressure off me because I didn't need to score quickly.' They ended up adding 241 – an England record for the seventh wicket. Overton finally fell on the third morning for 97, having resumed on 89 and struggled to relocate his rhythm. But Bairstow went on to 162 off 157 balls, with 24 punishing fours. In the second innings, he thumped an unbeaten 71 off 44 as England breezed a chase of 296 inside 55 overs. That was a total of 233 runs off 201 balls, for only once out.

On he went. Against India, he kept England in the game with a first-innings century after they had slipped to 83 for five in reply to 416. With him for the first part of the recovery was Billings, who had his own take on the Jonny eyes. 'You can't talk to him when he gets into that mood, because he's glazed over,' he says. Billings adopts a Yorkshire accent: 'He is "Jonathan Marc Bairstow". He gets into this trance. I've played with Jonny a long time now, and you just keep pumping his tyres up: "How well are you hitting that?" He's just never happy, is he?'

India's cause may not have been helped when Kohli engaged Bairstow in tetchy conversation, prompting the umpires to intervene. 'There was a bit of banter flying around,' says Billings. 'I was chuckling away. The worst decision you can possibly make is to chirp Jonny Bairstow. He went redder and redder, as if he was saying: "I'm going to show him." Which he absolutely did. I love a chirp, but there are certain players where you think: *just don't do it!* It wasn't one of Virat's best moments.' When Bairstow walked back to the dressing-room after supervising England's second-innings pursuit of 378 with another century, he was still drawing sustenance from Kohli's sledging. 'When will they fucking learn?'

Root had completed victory with a mishit reverse-sweep for a single, bringing his partnership with Bairstow to an unbroken 269, the highest fourth-wicket stand in the fourth innings of a Test. As if bearing in mind McCullum's injunction to reconnect with the youngster who first fell in love with cricket, Bairstow and Root had spent time in the middle reminiscing about a Second XI game for Yorkshire at Oakham in 2009, when they were chasing 402 to beat Leicestershire. Both were teenagers, yet from the depths of 44 for three they added an unbeaten 358. 'We were chuckling about that in the middle,' says Bairstow. 'We said: "Let's do what we did there and have a bit of fun."'

It was fun, too, to finish on the winning side after the spat with Kohli, who had started to needle Bairstow on the second evening during a testing spell from Jasprit Bumrah and Mohammed Shami. He finished the day on 12 off 47 balls. 'Little bit faster than Southee, eh?' said Kohli, emphasising his seamers' speed. Next morning, he instructed Bairstow: 'Shut up. Just stand and bat.' Bairstow made a blabbering motion with his gloves; Kohli put his finger to his lips, a gesture – joked England – that made him look as if he was picking his nose.

Bairstow plays down the Edgbaston repartee, while also suggesting it spurred him on. 'There wasn't really much said. I get on well with Virat. He plays the game tough. He's the ultimate competitor, and he's got 1.4 billion people watching his every move. If it was the other way, he'd be copping it. But, yeah, that sparked something – I don't know what it was. It was very nice to draw that series after the previous year, when we'd played in completely contrasting fashion and been a bit submissive to India. To go out and play in a way that was dominating, and knock off 378 for three, was very pleasing.'

By the end of the Test, Bairstow had made 589 from 578 balls in five innings, with 75 fours and 13 sixes. It was one of the purplest patches in the history of batting. He was Bazball's shining light. 'I am very proud of that,' he says. 'I'm also proud of the way the lads have carried on playing in that manner.'

During our chat, Bairstow gestures a couple of times to his ankle, but almost imperceptibly, as if he'd rather not engage with the memory. After beginning the series against South Africa with scores of 0, 18 and 49, he broke his left leg in freakish fashion, slipping in a tee-box at Pannal Golf Club near Harrogate. The injury was horrific enough without a prankster recording a WhatsApp voice note in which he falsely claimed to have witnessed the real cause: a sliding tackle by Stokes as Bairstow lined up a putt on the 18th. The message went viral, successfully hooking in to events outside the Bristol nightclub five years earlier.

Back in the real world, Bairstow was in despair. He had just equalled the England record of six Test centuries in a calendar year, and there were still four matches to go. Not yet 33, he was in the form of his life. Of all the moments to break a leg. As his teammates headed for Pakistan, Bairstow embarked on a dark and lonely winter of rehab, wondering at times if he would ever walk again, let alone return to cricket. Surely it wasn't all going to end with a whimper?

Not until late April did he play again, hitting 97 off 88 balls and 57 off 61 in a Second XI game for Yorkshire against Nottinghamshire at Headingley. Two championship matches followed, plus a T20 game. By the time he was picked at Foakes's expense against Ireland, Bairstow was still adapting to his injury. He held six catches against the Irish, but didn't get to bat, as England raced to 524 for four in 82.4 overs. It all meant he was slightly undercooked by the time of the first Ashes Test at Edgbaston on 16 June. But, as he would point out later, he hadn't exactly been keeping wicket much in recent times anyway: between the end of the 2019 Ashes and the Ireland game, he had worn the gloves in only one Test, against India at The Oval in 2021, and then only because Buttler was on paternity leave.

When Bairstow began the 2023 Ashes with a run-a-ball 78, helping to turn England's perilous 176 for five into 393 for eight, it was widely agreed Foakes would have struggled to match him. But the simmering resentment of Foakes's supporters turned to outright anger next day when Bairstow fluffed two important chances off the spinners: Cameron Green on 0 (a missed stumping off Moeen Ali) and Alex Carey on 26 (a dropped catch off Root). Green went on to make 38 and Carey 66, so the damage was 78 runs, the same as Bairstow's contribution with the bat. By the time he dropped Carey in the first over of the third morning, this time off Anderson, the debate was in full flow.

It went quieter at Lord's, where the focus switched to Bairstow's stumping by Carey. But at Headingley the debate reared its head again. On the first morning, Bairstow dropped Steve Smith down the leg side from an inside edge off Ollie Robinson. No matter that it was a half-chance: supporters of Foakes agreed their man would have swallowed it. Five overs later, Bairstow dropped Travis Head off Mark Wood, another leg-side chance but far easier.

With any luck, Bairstow – still smarting from Lord's – was staying off social media. Because at roughly the moment he was out early on the second morning at Headingley, Australian rugby league team Canberra Raiders were trolling him thousands of miles away, celebrating a try against St George Illawarra Dragons by re-enacting his Lord's misadventure with a rugby ball, and redeploying the try line as the crease. The role of Bairstow, ambling to his doom, was played by Elliott Whitehead, born – like Bairstow – in Bradford. Later in the day, he shelled another chance down the leg side as Labuschagne failed to control a pull off Wood. When Labuschagne slog-swept his next delivery, off Moeen, to deep midwicket, Bairstow's cry of 'catch it, catch it!' hung in the air as surely as the ball. Fortunately for him and England, Brook held on.

By now, critics were totting up Bairstow's cost to the side – an equation not helped by the fact that his batting was falling away. After his opening bid of 78, he had made 20, 16, 10 and 12. And everything he did was under the microscope. When Smith chipped Moeen to midwicket in the over after Labuschagne's demise, Bairstow chirped: 'See ya, Smudge.' Fuming about his dismissal, Smith shot back: 'What was that, mate?' Bairstow replied: 'I said: "Cheers, see you later."' It wouldn't have made even the tamest book of Ashes Sledges, but that was not the point. On 7News in Australia, the headline read: 'England villain Jonny Bairstow strikes again with fiery Steve Smith sledge.' As some wondered whether Smith would ever recover, Bairstow remained a marked man: 7News regarded him as 'England's No 1 villain', even though he had yet to say a word on the stumping.

The discussion about whether he should have the gloves was not going away. Even Geoffrey Boycott, who had played a big part in his upbringing after the death of his dad, an old Yorkshire teammate, called for Jonny to be dropped. 'It is very sad, and outwardly he may show he is upbeat and full of exuberance,' wrote Boycott in his *Telegraph* column, 'but when you fail on the big stage in the full glare of publicity there is nowhere to hide, and deep down it affects your confidence. Someone needs to be brave for him and take him out of the limelight.'

Before the fourth Test at Old Trafford, Bairstow's team-mates went out of their way to make him feel loved. Broad even went public with his conviction that a big performance was brewing. So it proved. Bairstow took a superb one-handed catch low to his right to dismiss Mitchell Marsh off Chris Woakes, then smashed an unbeaten 99, with ten fours and four sixes, as England ran Australia ragged: 592 was their highest Ashes total in a home Test since 1985. That evening, his blood still pumping, he pointed out during a combative series of media appearances how hard he had worked to recover from his injury: 'I have nine pins, a plate and a wire running through my ankle.' How he'd 'not played in months and not kept properly in three years'. And how journalists might struggle to write a piece after a sabbatical from the press box: 'Three years off, a bit of touch-typing without a delete button, and see how that pops up.'

Many felt this simply confirmed that he should not have been keeping wicket. Looking back on his comments to the media a few days earlier, he says: 'I just think that when there's a lack of understanding about what has happened, without actually speaking to that person and gaining an understanding of the ins and outs of what's gone on, to then have an opinion... it was more that side of things. Also, we know I've not done *that* for a period of time.' He mimes a pair of gloves. 'So all of a sudden, it's like, what? You're expected to just...' He tails off.

Isn't he used to this by now, the scrutiny, the questions about Buttler and Foakes, the debate about his best position in the batting order? 'I've averaged 38 or 39 at five, six, seven and eight, whatever it is. It doesn't matter where I bat. I've kept and batted at five, six and seven. There aren't many who have kept and batted at five for a period of time. Kumar Sangakkara was one, but maybe not for long. Quinton de Kock did it for a bit. Adam Gilchrist never moved from seven. Alex Carey's at seven. No one goes to five or six. From that side of things, I'm just pleased to be playing. People will have their opinions: that's always going to be there. My job is to go out and play the game. But some of the abuse you cop at times, it doesn't just have an effect on you – it affects your family, and I'm really close to mine.' One headline on the back page of the *Daily Mail* especially bothered him. Taken from an interview with the veteran Australian broadcaster Jim Maxwell, it declared: 'Bairstow's overweight.' England were furious.

By 'pleased to be playing', he's referring, of course, to the fracture. 'Like I said last week in Manchester, my ankle was bad. Very bad. There was a big chance I wasn't going to be sat here now.' Professor James Calder, the orthopaedic surgeon who operated on him, told *The Times*: 'I had severe reservations that he was going to play in the Ashes, and even whether the injury was compatible with playing professional cricket. He was adamant I was wrong and was destined to prove me wrong.'

Calder's description of Bairstow's injury explains why he was sceptical. 'He had a severe lower-leg fracture dislocation. Multiple bones were broken in his leg and his ankle, as well as ligaments, and it was like putting Humpty Dumpty back together again. He had to have plates, pins, keyhole surgery and ligament stabilisation. Jonny was just incredibly stoical and matter-of-fact, and saying: "We're in this situation, what are the timelines and the guidance, and how do I get to play in the Ashes?" He was very focused and incredibly professional about it.'

Bairstow adds: 'That's also what I'm referencing, the times people are not aware of – when it was horrible, when you're up through the night unable to sleep because of your ankle.

The painful bits of the experience that I wouldn't wish on anyone. My close family and friends who have been there through thick and thin, and tried to remain as level as possible – they know how tough international cricket is, how mentally demanding the schedule is.'

He drifts ahead to the post-Ashes fixture list. There's The Hundred, then white-ball matches against New Zealand, followed by a World Cup and a five-Test series in India, possibly even the IPL: 'You play all that, and you've got 24 weeks in India this winter.' Bairstow has just become a dad, to baby Edward. Perspectives can change quickly. But there is no escaping the pleasure he derives from his dressing-room confrères; he's 'proud to be back around the guys'.

How, after all this, does he assess his Ashes? 'I've been delighted. I've put a couple of catches down, but there are also some that have touched my finger ends that people have said are chances. You're just not going to get them. I can't change the fact I'm 6ft 1, not 6ft 4. Do you understand what I mean? There are certain things that are in your power. I'm well aware there are a couple I have put down. That's fine. There are also a few I've taken that others wouldn't take.

'There have been a couple of interesting bits along the way. I could have potentially scored a bit more. That's the game. But to get back out there playing Test cricket after the last however many months is something I'm hugely proud of. We've become very tight-knit. It takes a lot of resilience and hard work to do that and to get back to where I was last summer, because it could have been quite easy just to fall off a cliff.'

Four days later, he pummels 78 to finish the Ashes with 322 runs at an average of 40. Among English wicketkeepers, only Alec Stewart and Alan Knott have scored more in a series against Australia, and they had six Tests to Bairstow's five. Two days after that, he does for Marsh again, this time off Moeen – a reflex catch to his right after the ball rebounds off inside edge and pad. It feels like a by-product of his growing confidence, on both sides of the stumps. Bit by bit, less has been heard about Foakes, though his time will surely come again.

Bairstow is a fascinating mix of warmth and defiance, grit and suspicion. Criticism both wounds and fuels him. Perhaps more than anyone, he has ridden the wave set in motion by McCullum and Stokes. He is central to its story. More than that, he *needs* to be central. He isn't perfect and has never claimed to be. But as the Ashes approaches its climax and he looks out across The Oval, it is hard to imagine Bazball without him.

The 2023 Ashes
Fourth Test, Old Trafford

Zak Crawley is sheltering from heavy rain under the overhang of the roof to the players' dressing-rooms and media centre. Large puddles have formed on the outfield, and a gaggle of noisy Australian fans are the only spectators left at Old Trafford, braving a soaking to congratulate their team on retaining the Ashes. No matter that it feels slightly hollow: Australia have drawn the fourth Test only because heavy rain prevented all but 30 overs on the final two days, denying England victory, and the series a winner-takes-all decider at The Oval. It would have captured not just two nations, but the world of cricket. The Manchester weather has done it again.

At 214 for five in their second innings, Australia were still 61 short of avoiding an innings defeat, after England hammered 592 at 5.49 an over. Only once had a Test innings produced more runs, more quickly – England themselves, seven months earlier, at Rawalpindi. And when the Test was abandoned at 5.24 p.m. on a grey, cold Sunday evening – more like late September than the height of summer – the Australians knew they had escaped a hiding. 'There's no point denying it,' Cameron Green said later. 'We got out of jail.' For the first time in 17 Tests under the new regime, England had to settle for a draw.

At least Crawley had a sunny disposition, having played the innings of the series, 189 from 182 balls, to give the Australians a Bazballing of the most brutal kind, and justify England's unshakable faith in his potential. 'I feel I'm as good a player as I have ever been,' he said. 'I feel good about my game – I've just got to build on it. I can kick on now. Fast bowling suits my game. The Australian attack is a quick attack, and I think a bit less when they're faster.'

Australia had been shredded, and shortly before three o'clock on the third afternoon they staggered off the field. It was curious to think that the two most lethal onslaughts their Test attack had ever suffered had both involved Brendon McCullum: Christchurch in February 2016, when he signed off from Test cricket with his world-record 54-ball hundred for New Zealand; and now this.

Six of England's top seven passed 50 – they had not had six half-centurions in a Test innings since 1965–66 – and at the height of the carnage, a third-wicket stand of 206 between Crawley and Joe Root had come at better than a run a ball. Crawley had reached his hundred from 93, the second-fastest Test century at Old Trafford, after Ian Botham got there in 86 against Australia in 1981. And he went on to the highest score by an England opener in a home Ashes Test since Graham Gooch made 196 at The Oval in 1985. That was also the last time England had made a larger total at home against Australia.

Further vindication for McCullum and Stokes came from another player who had been under pressure but appeared to be protected by the coach and captain: Jonny Bairstow thrashed a storming, angry 99 not out from 81 balls as all the keeping errors and the stumping row fell from his shoulders. At lunch on the third day, he had reached 41 off 39, with England already 506 for eight, a lead of 189, and many wondering about a declaration.

But Bairstow laid into the bowling with such ferocity, and Stokes was enjoying the show so much – at one point banging on the dressing-room window and shouting 'wow, that's huge' as a monstrous six disappeared over midwicket – that he allowed the innings to continue. Bairstow was denied a rip-roaring century only when Jimmy Anderson was leg-before to Green, ending a last-wicket stand of 66 in 49 balls, of which Anderson made 5.

Stokes's decision not to declare would become a talking point as the weather closed in, but the sight of the Australians dazed by the assault showed where the power now lay. All three of their fast bowlers – Mitchell Starc, Pat Cummins and Josh Hazlewood – conceded more than 100, at around five an over. Still, had Stokes lacked ruthlessness? Perhaps, but the incessant rain meant it probably made no difference. He also wanted to bat only once: arguably, Bairstow's pyrotechnics improved that prospect.

'We did literally everything we possibly could, and Mother Cricket didn't help us,' said Stokes. 'We can't change that. It's a tough pill to swallow, knowing that's the reason we sit here with a draw. But we were completely and utterly dominant. It's a shame, but oh well...'

That was it: the great comeback had been interrupted, and England had lost the chance to become only the second team to win a Test series from 2–0 down. 'In the first two games we played some brilliant cricket, but we also played some cricket we knew we could have been better at,' said Stokes. 'But in this game I can't actually look back and think we could have been better. We were pretty much perfect throughout the whole game when we played.' Those last three words hung in the air.

Four years earlier, Australia had retained the Ashes with victory at Old Trafford, and celebrated hard. Not this time. 'It's a bit of a strange one,' said Cummins. 'As a group [we're] proud that we've retained the Ashes, but it's off the back of not our greatest week.'

Stuart Broad had become the second seamer, after Anderson, to reach 600 Test wickets, when he dismissed Travis Head from the James Anderson End – also taking him past Ian Botham's England record of 148 Test wickets against Australia. But otherwise he had a quiet game. Anderson had been recalled on his home ground in place of Ollie Robinson, but managed just one wicket. Instead, as at Headingley, it was the rejuvenated Chris Woakes, with his first Ashes five-for, and the rapid Mark Wood, who dictated terms to Australia.

Woakes had been the star of Australia's first-innings 317, not enough on a decent pitch after Stokes had won yet another toss. Several batsmen made starts but lacked the form or concentration to go on. Warner had hit 32 after rushing out of the traps, but edged Woakes just when he threatened to make the score his team needed. Marnus Labuschagne inched his way into some nick with a painstaking 51, his first half-century of the series, while Steve Smith missed a Wood thunderbolt and was hit in front for 41. Head fell in the leg trap to give Broad his big moment, Root gobbling up a good catch running in off the fine-leg boundary. But it was Woakes's wickets of Green, Mitchell Marsh and Alex Carey that dragged things back for England.

After his Headingley hundred, Marsh had looked ominous again, but on 51 he edged behind. Bairstow took a remarkable, instinctive grab to his right, and – still on his backside – held a starfish pose with a huge grin while brandishing the ball above his head. After three difficult Tests, it was the boost he needed. The confidence would flow into his batting.

Broad's magnificent series even stretched into the paranormal, telling Crawley on the first day that he fancied him to make 150. 'A few people did,' said Crawley, 'which I don't normally like – it puts you under a bit of pressure.' But he didn't look under pressure as he freewheeled his way to one of the great Ashes innings for England. He had threatened to go big in each of the first three Tests, with scores of 61, 48 and 44, but this time he stayed in, and grew in stature. While a few came off the inside edge in the first session, when Crawley overturned an lbw decision on 20, his timing and placement in the afternoon were magnificent. Between lunch and tea, England scored 178 in 25 overs, with Crawley alone making 106, and Moeen Ali, still at No 3, contributing his first Test half-century since 2019. In doing so, he became the fourth England player – after Botham, Flintoff and Broad – to achieve the Test double of 3,000 runs and 200 wickets.

Root reverse-scooped his way past 50 soon after tea, as England flew past Australia's 317 in the 55th over, and appeared to be steaming towards a century when he was bowled by a grubber from Hazlewood on 84. Moments earlier, Crawley had chopped on against Green, bringing to an end four-and-a-half hours of mayhem. 'I do doubt myself at times,' he said, 'but I have to say "keep being me". That is the way I play. I am quite streaky, but then I go on a run. They [Stokes and McCullum] tell me to go out and have an impact at the top of the order. Sometimes I am going to have streaks of low scores, because I'm taking a punt, but thankfully today it came off.'

England were 384 for four overnight after some watchful deceleration by Harry Brook. Next day, he reached his third 50 of the series. Stokes made a half-century too, but as Bairstow crashed 58 off 42 balls after lunch, everyone was studying the weather forecast, with competing apps delivering different verdicts. Forget England v Australia: this was AccuWeather v the Met Office.

England knew rain was coming, just not how much. When the ninth wicket fell, Anderson came out to play probably his last Test innings at Old Trafford. He wore a couple of bouncers, and a message was sent out: England would declare in two overs. But Bairstow hit those two overs for 20 to move into the 80s, and Stokes did not want to deny him an Ashes hundred. Bairstow flat-batted each of Starc, Cummins and Hazlewood for sixes over square leg, the crowd roaring him on. Stealing byes to Carey – who, unlike at Lord's, was unable to locate the stumps – he farmed the strike. On 98, he pushed to long-off and set off for two, but could manage only one. Australia had bowled 17 short balls at Anderson. Finally, they pitched one up. He missed it, apologising to Bairstow on their way off and promising to buy him a beer. But Bairstow wore a huge grin. After all he had been through, he seemed not to care that he had just made his second Test 99 at Old Trafford.

'Everyone thinks I play better when people go at me,' he said. 'It gets a bit tiresome, to be honest with you. I've played a lot of cricket now and to be keep being told that you're rubbish... Well, if I was that rubbish, I wouldn't have played 94 games.' He hit out at critics of his glovework, for not taking account of his horrific leg injury. 'I'm still only ten months post-operation right now. There's times when there's aches and pains and people are saying you're limping. Well, yeah, I am at times, because there's a lot going on in the ankle, and other bits that people won't understand.'

With a big lead in their back pockets, England hunted victory. Anderson had good bowling conditions and knew every blade of grass, but Australia blunted the new ball, and again England had to be patient. With the score on 32, Wood had Usman Khawaja caught behind; at 54, Woakes removed Warner, chopping on. Wood was not quite as fast as at

Headingley, but he was fast enough, and found shape through the air too. He had Smith gloving down the leg side – his 100th Test wicket – then went after Head with the bouncer: plainly uncomfortable, he flinched to Duckett at a floating slip.

This was a big innings for Labuschagne, who had not lived up to his reputation, pulled this way and that by England, and raging in his own head about his technique. This time he muddled through, reaching the close on 44, with Australia 113 for four, still 162 behind. That evening, Hazlewood – who had picked up an expensive five-for – cheerfully admitted his side were hoping for the rain that was forecast over the weekend. It was a reasonable wish, though it was branded un-Australian by many, evidence that the series was shifting on its axis.

In the event, the clouds cleared long enough on the fourth day to allow a restart at 2.45 p.m., and 30 overs to be bowled in all. With the light fading, and Labuschagne and Marsh holding on grimly, Stokes was told by the umpires he could bowl only his spinners, which meant Moeen and Root. England had just had the ball changed, but Anderson sent down only four deliveries with it before the umpires stepped in, having spotted Wood marking his run-up. Labuschagne went after Root to move into the 90s. He edged a skilful arm-ball through Crawley's grasp at slip, but in the next over, off Moeen, he reached his hundred – only his second abroad, to go with nine at home. England looked out of ideas, until Labuschagne, aiming a cut, edged Root on 111. Bairstow took the catch on the rebound, and called for a review after umpire Nitin Menon said not out. But rain fell at tea, and the players never returned.

'It's always a privilege to score a Test hundred,' said Labuschagne. 'But it's still a bit bittersweet with the circumstances of the game.' Marcus Trescothick, England's assistant coach, spoke for the team, and possibly the country:

'In the dressing-room everyone has a different weather app open on their phones, and they are all saying pretty much the same thing about tomorrow – rain. But if we get a decent amount of time to force victory, we can still do it.'

Initially, the forecast for Sunday had been better than Saturday, and the players emerged briefly when it was announced play would start at 1 p.m. But the rain returned during the early lunch break, and never stopped. England tried to make out all was well, enjoying a kickabout on the outfield while drenched fans used rolled-up newspapers as bats for a quick game in the stands. The DJ played 'Here Comes the Sun' by the Beatles. As Stokes stared glumly through the dressing-room window, 'Why Does It Always Rain on Me?' by Travis would have been more pertinent. Later, he reflected on what victory might have meant. 'It would have elevated everything that the series has already done for Test cricket, especially in England,' he said. 'But I think what we've managed to do, up until today anyway, has already done wonders for cricket in England. We'll still have the support that we have done throughout the series next week.'

Half-baked suggestions about how to extend play, including the introduction of reserve days, were proposed in the aftermath, which did little to discourage stereotypes about whingeing Poms. Richard Thompson, the ECB chair, promised to raise the matter at the next ICC meeting. In the end, though, the British summer was the winner. 'Even when it was still pouring down, Baz was like "don't worry, we will get out there,"' said Crawley. 'I didn't believe it, but I think he did.' For once, Bazball's positivity was misplaced. But England still had a long unbeaten home record against Australia to protect. Manchester might have been a damp squib, but The Oval mattered hugely – to both sides.

ENGLAND v AUSTRALIA (4th Test)

At Old Trafford, Manchester, on 19, 20, 21, 22, 23 (*no play*) July 2023.
Toss: England. Result: **MATCH DRAWN**.
Debuts: None.

AUSTRALIA

D.A.Warner	c Bairstow b Woakes	32	(2)	b Woakes	28
U.T.Khawaja	lbw b Broad	3	(1)	c Bairstow b Wood	18
M.Labuschagne	lbw b Ali	51		c Bairstow b Root	111
S.P.D.Smith	lbw b Wood	41		c Bairstow b Wood	17
T.M.Head	c Root b Broad	48		c Duckett b Wood	1
M.R.Marsh	c Bairstow b Woakes	51		not out	31
C.D.Green	lbw b Woakes	16		not out	3
† A.T.Carey	c Bairstow b Woakes	20			
M.A.Starc	not out	36			
* P.J.Cummins	c Stokes b Anderson	1			
J.R.Hazlewood	c Duckett b Woakes	4			
Extras	(B 8, LB 3, NB 3)	14		(B 1, LB 2, NB 1, W 1)	5
Total	**(90.2 overs)**	**317**		**(5 wkts; 71 overs)**	**214**

ENGLAND

Z.Crawley	b Green	189
B.M.Duckett	c Carey b Starc	1
M.M.Ali	c Khawaja b Starc	54
J.E.Root	b Hazlewood	84
H.C.Brook	c Starc b Hazlewood	61
* B.A.Stokes	b Cummins	51
† J.M.Bairstow	not out	99
C.R.Woakes	c Carey b Hazlewood	0
M.A.Wood	b Hazlewood	6
S.C.J.Broad	c and b Hazlewood	7
J.M.Anderson	lbw b Green	5
Extras	(B 15, LB 9, NB 11)	35
Total	**(107.4 overs)**	**592**

ENGLAND	O	M	R	W		O	M	R	W
Broad	14	0	68	2	(2)	12	2	47	0
Anderson	20	4	51	1	(1)	17	5	30	0
Woakes	22.2	4	62	5	(5)	12	5	31	1
Wood	17	5	60	1		11	0	27	3
Ali	17	1	65	1	(3)	13	2	44	0
Root						6	1	32	1
AUSTRALIA									
Starc	25	0	137	2					
Hazlewood	27	2	126	5					
Cummins	23	0	129	1					
Green	15.4	1	64	2					
Head	7	0	52	0					
Marsh	9	0	57	0					
Labuschagne	1	0	3	0					

FALL OF WICKETS

Wkt	A 1st	E 1st	A 2nd
1st	15	9	32
2nd	61	130	54
3rd	120	336	97
4th	183	351	108
5th	189	437	211
6th	254	474	-
7th	255	486	-
8th	294	506	-
9th	299	526	-
10th	317	592	-

Umpires: N.N.Menon (*India*) and J.S.Wilson (*West Indies*).
Referee: R.S.Madugalle (*Sri Lanka*).   Player of the Match: Z.Crawley.
Close of Play – Day 1: A(1) 299-8; Day 2: E(1) 384-4; Day 3: A(2) 113-4; Day 4: A(2) 214-5.

10

Old dogs, new tricks

When Multan's city smog combines with smoke from stubble-burning after the Punjab crop harvest, breathing can be difficult. It is no place to be an England fast bowler, trying to gulp in lungfuls of air to power the legs while attempting to extract something – anything – out of a lifeless surface.

Mark Wood is playing his first Test under Brendon McCullum and Ben Stokes, the second of England's historic tour of Pakistan. At the end of day one, with dusk falling, he is despondent, after leaking runs and struggling for control. He had heard plenty about the positivity pulsing through the team, and sampled it briefly when he joined the squad at The Oval a few months earlier as he stepped up his recovery from elbow surgery. He wondered back then whether the no-fear, no-consequence environment had been overhyped. Now, he was about to find out if it was true.

'That first spell, I bowled four overs for 20,' he says. 'So that's five an over, and in a Test match you'd think, *well, that's not that great*. I came back in, and Baz was all over me: "Wow, that was so fast! Can you imagine what the tailenders are thinking? If you bowl like that again, you're going to end up with four or five wickets." Automatically, I was like, *bloody hell, that was awesome.*'

England's players all have a similar story, but this vignette boils down Bazball for bowling. Much has been made of the batting, the strike-rates, the sixes and the reverse-ramps, but it is bowlers who win Test matches and, for 25 innings in a row leading into the Ashes, England took all ten wickets. (The sequence, their best since the late 1970s, ended with Australia's second innings at Edgbaston.) At that point, England's bowlers under McCullum and Stokes averaged 28 per wicket, 12 lower than their opponents. It has been an easily overlooked part of their success.

'We just crack on – we don't need that pat on the back, and we know what we have to do,' says Ollie Robinson, who made a name for himself at Multan by becoming the first to bowl Pakistan captain Babar Azam twice in a Test. The second dismissal, jagging back dramatically as a startled Babar shouldered arms, came soon after Jimmy Anderson had bowled Mohammad Rizwan with a peach, and shortly before Wood himself knocked back Abdullah Shafique's off stump with another: three contenders for ball of the series in the space of an hour after lunch on the third day in the most unforgiving conditions imaginable. The deliveries by Robinson and Anderson relied on movement off the seam, and possibly a crack. But Wood's was all about miles per hour, which explains McCullum's upbeat assessment: pace, as he knows, often equals wickets. The impact Wood made on the 2023 Ashes after being drafted in for the third Test at Headingley, where he was clocked at 96.5mph, underlined the point. Who cares if he briefly went for five an over that day in Multan?

For a long time in English cricket, the preference was for 'bowling dry' – being patient and probing away, inducing error by building dots. It was the strategy implemented so successfully by Andy Flower and Andrew Strauss during the 2010–11 Ashes, when a below-par Australian side lacked the discipline to cope and suffered three innings defeats. It remains England's only series victory in Australia since 1986–87. In 2011, the same approach took them to the top of the Test rankings after a 4–0 home win against India. It was efficient rather than thrilling, leading Strauss to admit to the *Daily Mirror* during the 2023 Ashes: 'In my time we were lucky to get to No 1 in the world, and it felt like we achieved everything we wanted to, but there was something slightly missing, I think. And it was that excitement. That feeling of pioneering and trying new things. If I had my time again maybe I would do things differently.' Stokes's team, he said, were 'a lot more entertaining than the way my team did it'. If Strauss was being a little harsh on himself and his team's achievements, then nobody embodied the method better than Anderson, the master of swing and seam. Now, he too has mixed feelings about the past.

'I feel like bowling dry might have held a few individuals back, although I don't know if it held the team back,' he says. 'I was fortunate I could be patient and bowl on the same spot. It made me better, more accurate. There are bowlers out there it didn't suit. Maybe there are players who could have played more, but didn't because of the way we bowled.

'My job was to create pressure and keep an eye on the run-rate, which was always a big thing for us in Test cricket – we wanted, for example, to keep it at 2.7 an over. We had various stats thrown in, so bowling three maidens in a row raised your chance of creating a wicket-taking opportunity. All these things were... not necessarily on the negative side, but in the back of my mind was not going for runs, and that meant bowling upwards of 20 overs an innings to get your wickets. The change has been, scrap all that: just focus on getting 20 wickets.'

Remarkably, Anderson has been tighter under the new regime, conceding 2.59 an over – down by 0.19 an over. He has bowled to six slips (in the first Test against New Zealand at Lord's) and he has bowled a period of bouncers (against India at Edgbaston). At Rawalpindi, he happily gave up the new ball because it served the team's cause: Joe Root's suggestion that England go short to Pakistan's top order in the second innings reaped instant rewards. Not until the 2023 Ashes, when he turned 41 on the penultimate day of the series, did he threaten to look his age, though he was still the second-most economical bowler on either side, behind Robinson. And, despite the retirement of his old buddy Stuart Broad, who rode off into the sunset after taking Australia's last two wickets at The Oval, Anderson was determined to carry on. He has been the old dog – pedigree, of course – learning new tricks.

He tells a story from the India Test. 'I went over to Stokesy and said: "Look, the ball's not doing anything, I don't feel threatening over the wicket." [Cheteshwar] Pujara was batting, so I came round the wicket and bowled bouncers for a bit. I hit him and unsettled him. That's normally left to someone else, like Woody or Broady, or someone who's a bit quicker. But everyone feels they've got to be able to try different things to help the team get the wickets. Rather than me go, "why don't we get Woody on to bowl round the wicket?" you can actually put yourself on. It's a bit of a shift. Ben's got that sixth sense about making something happen. Sometimes he can bowl someone for two overs, then take him off – it just doesn't feel right, so let's go with someone else.'

In Broad's case, being coaxed to bowl fuller, with more attacking fields, cost him runs – 3.43 an over, compared with 2.96 beforehand. But his strike-rate dropped: a wicket every 46 balls, nearly ten fewer than previously. And, after surprising himself by playing all five matches in the Ashes, he was England's leading wicket-taker with 22, taking him past 600 in all. The sight of the Baggy Green lit his fire like nothing else. His retirement, announced on the third evening of the final Test, was not entirely unexpected, but his performances showed he still had more to offer.

So why now? A man with a sense of occasion, Broad knew an Ashes Test at The Oval – so often the scene of farewells – would be the perfect sign-off. 'At about 8.30 last night I made the call,' he told Sky on the Oval outfield. 'Something inside me wanted to finish playing at the top level. And England versus Australia at The Oval in one of the most entertaining, fun Ashes I can remember, seems an appropriate time.' Not out overnight as England's second innings neared its conclusion, he walked out next morning to a guard of honour from Australia, and even made an unexpected impression. 'My God, Broady,' said Mitchell Marsh. 'Your hair looks amazing.' The following evening, he was dismissing Todd Murphy and Alex Carey to wrap up a 49-run win and grab a share of the series. The choreography was uncanny.

Persuading a pair of vastly experienced bowlers to be bolder was easier for Stokes than for previous captains. He had their respect, as did McCullum, but they also owed their place to him, since he had made their return a pre-condition of accepting the job. When they were dropped for the West Indies tour, the cricketing obituaries were written. But England's woeful performance in the Caribbean, and the new regime's change in mindset – pick the best team for the game in front of you, don't overplan the future – ensured their return. Without it ever being said, both knew they had no choice but to buy in to Stokes's tactics.

'It felt like a new start for me,' says Anderson. 'When you are left out, I felt – and Stuart felt the same – that it could be the end of your career, and you're not sure you're ever going to play again. Then that phone call comes from the new coach, who says: "We're going to pick our strongest team, and you're in our strongest team."'

McCullum quickly decided that, with Anderson and Broad around, he did not need a bowling coach complicating the mix, so Jon Lewis was moved on, eventually taking charge of England's women. McCullum wanted the players to take responsibility: the presence of England's two highest wicket-takers, he felt, should be enough. Anderson and Broad had to set an example to younger bowlers by not complaining about tactics if they were conceding runs. McCullum got the response he was after, and that brought the senior bowlers closer to colleagues, notably Robinson.

Broad explains: 'Rob Key told me that when he called him about the captaincy, Stokesy's first line was: "I'm having Broad and Anderson back." Good clarity. When you hear that, it leaves you wanting to run through a brick wall for him as friend and player. Jimmy would do the same. It helped us change our mentality a bit from thinking about economy-rates all the time. When you go for four, as long as it is a shot that could bring a wicket, it is perfectly fine. Stokesy and Baz have brought an element of entertainment and fun to training and matches. When you're 37 and 41, fun is what you are after.

'Baz wants to entertain the people who watch us, because results will then look after themselves. The first two or three games you think: *how long can it last?* But we've shown it's sustainable. It is pretty cool. Now you are seeing county cricketers trying it. Jimmy has been energised. He has loved everything about it.'

In Robinson, Anderson especially saw a troubled character, with a good cricket brain, who had been maligned for his fitness. Like Stokes, Anderson sympathised with Robinson when Lewis publicly called out his attitude in Australia. Others had come and gone without being fully accepted into the Branderson inner circle. But Robinson, closely involved in plans, now feels wanted. As Anderson says: 'At the start of his career, he's had a few people criticise him and tell him to get fitter and whatever else. Maybe they've handled him slightly poorly. Whereas here, all he gets is love and positive reinforcement. Because of that he's worked harder at his fitness. You've got to treat everyone differently.'

Robinson himself sees the benefit of feeling part of a group. Speaking before Broad's retirement, he said: 'We're the Three Amigos, really. We do everything together. Every day, it's "what are we doing after training?" If we finish early, it's me, Jimmy and Broady getting an Uber back to the hotel. Little things where we're so close outside cricket, and maybe people don't realise.'

Robinson knew Anderson respected his bowling from almost their first meeting around the England squad. 'First or second day, he said something and I took the royal piss out of him. He laughed but everyone else went silent – as if no one should take the mick out of Jimmy Anderson. But I did, and he enjoyed the fact that I'd treated him as a normal person. Since then, we have always had a bit of banter. We've got good honesty in our group. On the last Ashes tour at Adelaide, we came out on the third evening under lights and bowled really poorly. Next morning, we had an honest chat. I singled out the two older guys – they agreed, but didn't like it. Because we have that working relationship, we can tell each other where we think we've gone wrong, which makes the bowlers – and the team – better.

'When we're training, we're always trying to up-skill, and show off our skills to each other. Jimmy was world-class already – he doesn't need to get much better. But it's helped me to spend time with them and see how they go about their business. Before Pakistan, I was trying to learn a leg-cutter. Jimmy and Broady each bowl it slightly different, so I was going between their actions and releases, and trying to nail it. Jimmy's wobble seam is something I've worked closely with him on, talking about finger pressure and release points, which not all bowlers have. Some just chuck it down and hope for the best. With Jimmy, we've both got that technical side we like exploring. It's really helped my game.'

Robinson was not selected for the first five Tests of the McCullum era. There was a hangover from the 2021–22 winter, and he was still struggling for fitness, picking up early-season niggles that added to the narrative he did not look after his body. He was at a crossroads. His talent was not in doubt – his nine Tests before McCullum had brought 39 wickets at 21 in a losing side – but two paths lay ahead: a comfortable life in county cricket, where he is too good for most batsmen, or lots of hard work but with the rewards of an England career and a lucrative central contract. He chose hard work.

'That's probably fair, and I also didn't have a choice,' he says. 'I had an honest conversation with Stokesy, who told me where he wanted me to be. He told me at the start of the 2022 summer: "You'll be in my team." So I thought, *OK,*

I'll play a couple of games. Then, in April and May, before the New Zealand series, I hadn't played a lot of cricket, and I was struggling with a back issue. He rang me and said: "You're not in." He told me why – he was brutally honest. He said: "You haven't played enough, you haven't backed up enough." I think the penny dropped then.

'You have to be at the top of your game to get in the team. That was the moment for me when I felt I can't keep coasting, I can't keep relying on my skill, I have to put something else in to be a world-class cricketer and be as good as I can be for a long time. Those words from Stokesy, and the support he's given me since then, have been immense. He's spoken to me about his fitness journey, and he's turned himself into an animal. I used that to help me. I owe a lot to Rob Key, McCullum and Stokesy. They've played a big part in turning me into the cricketer I am today.'

Was Lewis harsh in Hobart, where Robinson pulled up injured after declaring himself fit to play? 'Maybe. It's easy to say that to someone when you're getting beat 4–0. You probably haven't given your best performance, but the black and white stats were that I was averaging 25 in Australia in my first Ashes series. Although people jumped on the bandwagon and slated me, I didn't have a horrendous tour. I got injured in one game, and that makes you look like you're not equipped for Test cricket. But playing your first Ashes series in Australia is harder than you think, and maybe I wasn't quite ready. But when I saw the likes of Pat Cummins and Mitchell Starc running in and delivering over after over, it gave me a lot of drive and showed me a lesson in where I need to be.'

The 2023 Ashes were another reminder that the lessons never stop. Robinson played in the first three Tests, but a nine-over spell of bouncers at Lord's – which brought him figures of two for 7 – proved draining, and at Headingley he suffered a back spasm, ruling him out of the last two games. His series haul of ten wickets at 28 was pretty good, and left him with a lower average than both Cummins and Josh Hazlewood. But stringing together back-to-back Tests again appeared difficult, a surprise after his endeavours in Pakistan.

Despite this slight setback, one of the qualities Anderson and Broad like about Robinson's personality – and it goes unsaid – is his innate stroppiness. He has that angry, narky side fast bowlers need if they are to power long spells on hot days when there is nothing in the surface. Just ask Australian opener Usman Khawaja. Robinson's send-off in the first innings at Edgbaston after Khawaja had made 141 was not classy, and he earned a rebuke from the match referee, but it confirmed his new role as sledger-in-chief.

'If someone's going at a teammate, I will come in and back them up,' he says, even if the Khawaja incident stemmed from frustration rather than two-way banter. 'I've been pushed to do that more. We're a tighter-knit unit now, and if anyone goes at one of the lads in the team, we all have that freedom to get stuck in. Against India two summers ago at Lord's, I came in and Mohammed Siraj had just got Sam Curran out first ball. I got hit in the chest first up, and all 11 Indian players swarmed round me. That's been used as an example where, because I had got stuck into their batters, their whole team got stuck into me, and if that happens to anyone in our XI now, we have that freedom to support each other – whereas before it was a little bit more individual, a bit more caring about yourself.

'I always have a go at bowlers who are bowling bouncers at the tail. I say: "Oh, you're ramping it up for the tail, are you? Shame you didn't do that for the top six after they banged you everywhere." You get into them for being weak, or brave for doing it against the tail instead of the batters. It's little things like that: get under their skin, change their game, give us a little bit of an edge.'

Robinson took over Broad's mantle as public enemy No 1 among Australians, and continued to annoy them with his outspoken column on the Wisden website. His claim that England felt as if they had won at Edgbaston went down badly with the army of ex-Aussie pros in the media. Matthew Hayden, the former opener, was so irritated he introduced a new entry into cricket's lexicon, accusing Robinson of bowling 'nude nuts' and having a 'mouth from the south'. This was not lost on England fans of a certain generation who had grown up watching their heroes get a regular earful from the Australians.

Even within the dynamics of England's dressing-room, Robinson can stand up for himself when necessary. While many praise Stokes for his empathy, there is a fear factor too: players are intimidated by his physical presence. Is it difficult to say no to him? 'It is hard,' says Anderson. 'I think he and I have been all right, but I know he and Broady have had a couple of ding dongs, because Broady is the most stubborn person I have met. Stokesy is like: "No, we are going with this for a bit. If it doesn't work it is my fault, and I will take the brunt of it, but we are going with it." And then Broady gets hit for four and looks straight at him.'

Robinson has confronted Stokes and lived to tell the tale. 'It's not that everyone's scared of Stokesy, but he's got that edge to him,' he says. 'We had a spat at The Oval against South Africa, who were having a little partnership. I bowled a four-over spell, and thought I was going to get a wicket. Then it was drinks. Stokesy said: "Take a break there." I wasn't overly happy, and told him. He said: "Robbo, stop being so selfish, it's not all about you." My comeback was: "I just want to win the game for the team," which he didn't expect. After we won, we had a chat in the changing-room, and he mentioned the incident. Everyone went silent – there was a bit of tension. But he said he loved the fact I questioned it, and wanted a win for the team, not for myself.'

As acknowledged by every member of the attack, it helps that Stokes is an all-rounder. He knows how it feels to produce draining spells, and has the scars to prove it, though his troublesome left knee limited him to 29 overs during the Ashes. It may also explain why Stokes is so good tactically: he has an instinct for the meaningful bowling change, sensing what the batsman least wants. For almost all his career, Anderson has played under batsmen; few bowlers become captain at any level of professional cricket, and at Old Trafford – where the Australian attack took a hammering – Cummins seemed to struggle with the two roles. Stokes understands the mental challenge, the battle with the batsmen, the loss of cool after a bad ball or a misfield. 'Using him as a sounding-board, and his experience with his body, has helped me a lot,' says Robinson. 'Sometimes you get bowling captains who are maybe a bit generous. Sometimes you get batting captains who expect the world after the batters get bowled out for 150. He's got a balance of being fair to both sides of it.'

Broad thinks hard when asked how Bazball changed his bowling. He echoes the thoughts of others about aggressive fields and forgetting about his economy-rate, which will bring a wry smile from some of his former captains and teammates. However, one change easy to overlook has been the physical effect. He bowled more short balls than usual, and the speed of England's batting meant little time for rest. Bowlers like to put their feet up, and watch the batsmen dig in. It was how England won the 2010–11 Ashes, with Alastair Cook grinding Australia down so the bowlers were fresh and raring to go.

Under McCullum and Stokes, there has been little time to sip a cup of tea or read the paper. Anderson loves cryptic crosswords and used to pop up to the media centre, or send one of the backroom team, to cut them out of the newspapers. That has stopped. With Stokes as captain, you have to be on your toes, ready for the unexpected.

'You just have to accept bowling's coming around quicker,' says Broad. 'When he was our bowling coach first time round, David Saker would say: "Give my guys two nights' sleep, and they'll win you the game." That's gone. You used to think, *I'll have two hours to chill out before I do any rehab.* Now it's get your boots off and straight into rehab. Especially when I bat eight – because four [wickets], you're pads on. It's changed. I don't mean that in a disrespectful way. At Edgbaston against Australia, I wasn't expecting that declaration – it was five minutes before, right, we're going to have a bowl. Are we? Oh shit, go and get my whites on. But that's Stokesy's greatest strength. He goes off his instincts. The change is preparing to bowl immediately. I'd argue we're probably getting more rest than we did in Australia in 2021–22.'

It can be challenging to manage players set in their ways, but experienced cricketers also know what to expect, and what is expected from them. Chris Woakes had won 45 caps, but none under McCullum and Stokes before the third Ashes Test at Headingley. He was able to fall back on his experience and slot in easily, making a match-winning contribution with bat and ball. He had always made good use of his skills of swing and seam – his average in home Tests of 21 is England's best since Fred Trueman – but bowling for Stokes still involved an adjustment.

'Towards the start of my Test career, it was more about how can we hold an end up?' he says. 'There has never been a mention of trying not to go for runs under Stokesy and Baz. There's not that negative mindset. It's all about how can we get the guy out and impact the game, moving it forward and not letting it stagnate? It's never going to be: come on let's tighten it up for a few overs.'

Woakes flourished on his recall, having played no Test cricket since the last match of the Root era, in Grenada, where an injured knee led to fears he might not play again. But he was committed to a comeback and pulled out of the 2023 IPL in a bid to be fit for the Ashes. He took six wickets at Headingley, where he also hit the winning runs, and followed that with his first Ashes five-for, at Old Trafford. And it was his breakthroughs on the final morning of the series at The Oval, despite bowling with a grade one tear in his thigh, that drove England to victory. He finished with 19 Australian wickets at 18, and the Compton–Miller Medal, for the player of the series. First awarded after the 2005 Ashes, it had previously been won by some of the greats of the game: Andrew Flintoff, Ricky Ponting, Andrew Strauss, Alastair Cook, Ian Bell, Mitchell Johnson, Joe Root, Steve Smith (twice) and Travis Head. The addition of Woakes had a nice ring to it.

Speaking after England levelled the series, he was still trying to process it all. 'The last three weeks have been a bit of a whirlwind,' he said. 'It's been amazing to be a part of. Just turning up at Headingley knowing I was going to play, and the belief in the dressing-room was we could win 3–2. In the past, we may have thrown the towel in, but that was never the case. The captain and the coach aren't interested in draws, so we knew they were going to be results games. And coming off the back of Headingley, we felt that we could go on and win. Were it not for the weather, maybe we would be standing here 3–2.

'I turned down the IPL for a number of reasons, one being the opportunity to be a part of this series. But at no point did I think I'd be stood here. That's not how far [ahead] your mind works. You don't think: *I can't wait to be player of the series in the Ashes.* You just want to be a part of it, contribute and hopefully win. To think that I'm stood here now… I think I need to let it sink in.'

It has also been a habit of the McCullum–Stokes era that debutants make an instant impression: Matt Potts took four for 13 against New Zealand at Lord's, Will Jacks six wickets with his off-breaks in Rawalpindi, Josh Tongue five for 66 at Lord's against Ireland. In between, at Karachi, Leicestershire's teenage leg-spinner Rehan Ahmed became not only England's youngest Test debutant, but the youngest of any nationality to claim a five-for in his first Test. Before that, Jamie Overton took just two wickets on debut at Headingley against New Zealand, but smacked a crucial 97. None held down a regular place, but they are picks for the future – particularly Ahmed, who is seen as a successor to Leach, and was called into the Ashes squad ahead of the second Test because of Moeen Ali's blistered spinning finger.

Tongue was plucked from county cricket, where his bowling average for the summer of 42 before the Ireland Test hardly marked him out as the country's in-form bowler. But his career record – 162 first-class wickets at 26 – was good. He had also laid down a marker in the winter for the Lions, taking eight wickets against Sri Lanka A on a flat one in Colombo. This left an impression on Key, who was always on the lookout for pace.

'I woke up to see a missed call from a New Zealand number I didn't recognise,' says Tongue. 'I thought maybe it was someone trying to sell me something. Then I had a message straight after saying: "Hi Josh, it's Baz McCullum here, can you give me a quick call?" I had a little feeling he was going to say I was in the squad for the Ireland game. I rang him back, and he told me the good news, which was a dream come true. I'd grown up wanting to play for England.'

Tongue is strolling around Old Trafford a couple of days after the end of the Ashes, preparing to play for Manchester Originals in The Hundred. It has been a summer that has changed his life. 'When I got to Lord's, it was a very welcoming group. I was told two days before the match that I was playing against Ireland. To make my debut at Lord's was an amazing feeling – I had never played in front of 30,000 people before. I didn't take a wicket in the first innings, but I knew I'd bowled well. Stokesy said at the end of the day: "Tonguey, you were unlucky not to take two or three wickets. Good pace, good aggression." That helped. In the second innings, getting two wickets in the first over calmed me down, because I had been searching for that first. Getting five in the end, and being on the honours board – words can't describe the feeling.'

Tongue sounds a little emotional. He had been on the sidelines with a mystery shoulder injury between June 2021 and August 2022, and had thought about 'pulling the pin' on his career, maybe becoming a coach. It was only when a third MRI scan discovered an impingement on an artery next to his rib that the problem was resolved. Two months after an injection of Botox, he was bowling again. And less than a year after that, he was England's battering ram in his only Ashes Test, at Lord's, sending down back-breaking bouncers on a slow pitch. Normally he bowls around 84mph for Worcestershire, but for England he touched 90; despite the added pressure, he felt relaxed.

'I like being the aggressor, and I knew they would use my pace against Ireland. They said: "We are going to go with short-pitched bowling." I said: "Definitely – let's do it." It carried into the Aussie Test as well. Baz and Stokesy said "just go out and enjoy the moment and entertain the crowd". That was great for me because I play my best cricket with a smile on my face. Against Australia was the first time I had bowled more than maybe a five-over spell. I was a bit tired, but the crowd got me through it. Playing in an Ashes Test, you want to get a wicket for your country, and the adrenaline kicked in as soon as that happened.'

Tongue bowled Khawaja, one of Australia's match-winners at Edgbaston, for 17 with a beauty on the stroke of lunch, and removed David Warner and Steve Smith twice each. Back in May, playing for Worcestershire at New Road, he had been the first bowler of the summer to dismiss Smith, trapping him leg-before for 30 during his stint with Sussex. Now, after Lord's, a Twitter meme did the rounds depicting Smith – one of the most prolific batsmen in Test history – as his bunny. Admittedly, Smith had made 110 by the time Tongue lured him into a loose drive in the first innings, but he then bounced him out in the second for 34. The whole thing was, he said, 'surreal'.

Despite taking as many wickets in one game as Anderson managed in the entire series, Tongue spent the rest of the Ashes as understudy to Wood. 'I said to myself before the series that even if I didn't play a single Test, just to be around this environment would be amazing. Even playing the one Test was so good. I knew I did well. I know it was not about me not performing. I'm happy.'

He remained with the squad and sat wide-eyed in the Oval dressing-room as McCullum, Stokes, Broad and Anderson addressed the group in the post-series wind-down. 'I'm a bit nervous talking to big groups so I didn't say anything, but I just feel so happy I was part of five Ashes squads. I was just trying to take it all in – being part of an Ashes and sat there at the end at The Oval? Dreams come true.' His strongest memory? 'I will always remember walking through the Long Room for the national anthem against Australia. I will never forget that moment for the rest of my life.'

Potts was left behind by Tongue and did not feature in the Ashes, but he was there at the start of the Bazball project, having bowled his way into the first squad of the new era with good performances in county cricket. But England base selection on character as well as numbers, and Stokes was impressed when Potts bowled through the pain of a side injury against Glamorgan at Chester-le-Street in May 2022, potentially jeopardising his England ambitions to help Durham to victory. He popped a couple of painkillers and took seven for 40.

'No one wants to bowl the hard overs,' says Potts. 'If you do, you're the kind of character Stokesy and Baz want. It's not easy. It's a mental thing – it hurts. That Glamorgan game, I was in pieces. I thought I'd torn my side off, ahead of potentially being picked in the Test squad. You try to put that out of your mind, but you're also thinking, *if I am injured, I'm going out with a bang, I'm going to win this game, because it might be my last for a while.* So, yeah, I convinced him then. I said to the physio: "Just chuck me some pills. I'm going out there." And Ben overheard it, and realised I was really sore, but I still went out and bowled seven overs on the trot.'

Overton also used county cricket to send England a message. The week before his selection, he bowled a lively spell to his twin brother, Craig, in a championship match between Surrey and Somerset. 'I had a conversation with Keysy, and he said he really loved me hitting Craig on the head,' says Jamie. 'He laughed, and said: "We've got to get this guy in now."'

When Potts arrived at Lord's on the Monday before his debut, having just about emerged in one piece after the Glamorgan game, he seemed unlikely to make the starting XI. But his good start to the season meant he was in rhythm and full of confidence. A sharp performance in the Nursery Ground nets earned him a first cap – just as Tongue would leapfrog Woakes before the Ireland game.

'There was a little chat at Lord's before I made my debut,' says Potts. 'I chuckle at it now, but it was a text message from Stokesy saying: "Can you come downstairs and have a chat?" I thought he probably wants to chat about dinner. I went downstairs and he said: "Are you ready to be a Test cricketer?" Which I thought was a silly question. I said: "You're bloody right I am."' And he was, dismissing Kane Williamson with his fifth ball in Test cricket. 'There's a great photo of Stokesy behind me. We're both jumping, and I think he was more happy than I was, which says a hell of a lot about his character.'

The demands on bowlers are not easy – mental as well as physical, with Stokes's attacking fields a challenge for players reared on the defensiveness of county cricket. 'I was sitting on four for 11, and we've got four slips and a gully,' says Potts. 'I'd be like, "what about an extra cover to give me a bit of protection?" He's like: "Nah, stop playing it safe. We're going for wickets. You're bowling well. We'll get that extra catcher in." Just that extra belief someone has in you allows you to relax. So I didn't feel under pressure at all. Obviously, my body had other ideas when I went off with cramp in both legs. But in my mind, I was completely relaxed. Cricket is a sport to be enjoyed.'

He took 20 wickets from five Tests before running out of puff and losing his place when Robinson returned. Potts struggled bowling to left-handers and was less effective when conditions were more benign, which is why he was left out of the Pakistan trip. He toured New Zealand without playing a match, then returned for the Ireland Test. And he remained in England's thinking: Stokes made sure he namechecked him after the Ashes.

'I was gutted to be left out,' says Potts. 'But the environment we've got, we hold each other in good standing. Yes, disappointed, but you do everything you can to support the playing group. I guess that comes with maturing. A younger me would have spat the dummy – I'm not afraid to say that. To be fair, I'd played against South Africa at Lord's and wasn't my best. They made a change, and we won the series.'

One of England's tactics has been to bowl bouncers at the tail. It does not always work, and requires pace to be fully effective, but it is about trying to bully the opposition. For Wood, it comes naturally: his transition under Stokes and McCullum has been smoother because his job has always been to take wickets. He is a shock bowler, not a cricketer to bring on when a captain wants to tease out a breakthrough. When he, like Woakes, joined the Ashes at Headingley, his impact was immediate: he picked up his first five-for in a home Test, and unsettled Australia like no other bowler. Even on the last day at The Oval, where he was struggling with a heel injury, he removed Marnus Labuschagne – his 14th and final wicket of a memorable three matches.

All those months earlier, back at Multan, the surface was a classic low, slow turner. Pakistan had lost their quickest bowler – Shaheen Shah Afridi – to injury and, after their defeat in the first Test, pitch preparation had been overseen by assistant coach Mohammad Yousuf. As the match wore on, the heavy roller sucked any life out of it and, at the start of the fourth day, Pakistan were 198 for four in pursuit of 355. For England, it was a nervous time. Wood was playing his first first-class match since the Antigua Test in March, but the heat, the air and the pitch meant he felt cooked. No matter: he was England's one genuine quick bowler. Stokes revved him up.

'He threw me the ball and said: "Come on, make something happen,"' says Wood. 'Even something like that, the confidence it gave me to think: *I'm going to do this for you, or I'm going to change the game.* It wasn't: "What do you think about this field or think about that?" It was: "Make something happen." Direct, to the point, not over-complicated, not too many methods. It's just who he is as a person.'

During two overs of bouncers before lunch, Wood removed Mohammad Nawaz for 45, breaking a sixth-wicket stand of 80, then Saud Shakil for 94, even if not everyone agreed with third umpire Joel Wilson's verdict that Ollie Pope had gathered the ball cleanly in his gloves as he swooped low to his right. It was not just pace and aggression: Stokes had brought up his leg-side catchers, and asked Wood to aim at the body.

'Stokesy made tiny changes to the field in Pakistan which made people play different,' says Wood. 'That spell from me with the bouncer, guys were ducking and defending. We brought men up, we put men on the corner, and said: "Go and play it." They did, and were caught down the leg side. I'm not saying that is rocket science, but what he did was change the field more than people think. He has an excellent cricket brain. It is a bit like chess: he is a step ahead. I know what move you want to make, I will change the field. If it doesn't work, we will change it back. How can we get a wicket and put this guy under pressure?

'At Rawalpindi, he had kept the field up, and I thought why doesn't he just push them back? But he wanted the speed of the game to move on because he knew we would need time at the end, otherwise it would be a draw. When you look back, you think, how did he know that? It would never have come into my mind. But he was far ahead of the game. For me, it is the little tweaks and intricacies he has done well.'

But Wood's work at Multan was not over. After lunch, tailender Abrar Ahmed hit four fours to hold England up. Stokes kept Wood on, to put a lid on the counter-attack and ensure a series-winning victory. 'He is hard to say no to, but because I know him so well, I can tell him if I'm not feeling it. I bombed Abrar a few times and he was squirting it. I was getting frustrated, and Stokesy could tell. He said: "If you change anything here, I'm taking you off. Keep bombing the shit out of this bloke until he has had enough." When you put it like that, I want to stay on. If he has an idea and that is the way he wants to play, it is hard to say no.

'But I don't want to put the emphasis on Baz and Stokesy all the time. Yes, they lead the team, but each player has to have their own internal values of why they love playing for England. Stokesy and Baz recognise that. It is not just them telling everybody how to play. You don't get to international standard by someone telling you what to do. There has to be a bit of feel, and I would say they get the feel right. Sometimes in the past we got that feeling wrong. I love Spoons [Chris Silverwood] to bits, and he was fantastic for my career, but in the Ashes in Australia we were not getting practice right – it was raining all the time, we could not get the facilities we wanted, people were unhappy. The feel was awful, but now it is totally different.

'That is not always on the coaches: it is on the individual. They have to be honest with themselves and buy in to what they are saying. But you need values you hold dear – why you charge in when it is hard, why you guts it out for the team with the bat when conditions are difficult. There has to be a marry-up of the two. It is not that Baz has come in and said: "This is all glory, Stokes is the Messiah." Yes, they have made a huge impact, but the individual has to do it as well.'

Wood has known Stokes longer than anyone in the England set-up. He has seen him endure highs and lows. As one of two non-golfers in the group (Ben Foakes is the other), and a teetotaller to boot, he has often ended an evening as Stokes's taxi driver. Has he seen a difference in his old mate?

'He has become a bit more diplomatic and grown up. I didn't think it was in his vocabulary to use some of the words he has. In the Durham academy days, he had an amazing cricket brain, but I didn't have him down as the brightest lad. But when he speaks as captain, he speaks intellectually. The thing I take the mickey out of him the most for is that he has developed a TV voice. When he is on the telly, I say: "Where are you from, mate?" He has this posh southern accent. He doesn't like that so I will stick to it as my go-to if he gets on my back.'

In the end, England scraped through against Australia with their oldest attack since Don Bradman's debut in 1928–29. While the batting appears settled for the Stokes era, with plenty of talent lurking underneath too, the seam-bowling personnel will evolve. Broad will now bowl bouncers of the verbal kind for Sky, Anderson is unsure how long he will carry on for, and Woakes and Wood constantly manage their bodies through the injuries that are a fast bowler's burden. If he can stay fit, Robinson should have a big future. Tongue and Potts made their mark at various points, and young bowlers can emerge quickly, as Surrey's Gus Atkinson proved later in the summer during the white-ball matches against New Zealand. The personnel will change but not the approach.

'England will continue to play this way,' says Anderson. 'It is just entrenched now. I feel the seeds are sown deeply. The future captain of England is in the squad now and will want to put his stamp on things for sure, but deep down there will be something from this era that will move forward.' Bowling to take 20 wickets is one of McCullum's go-to phrases. It sounds so simple, so obvious, but – somewhere along the line – it had become over-complicated. Bazball has stripped it back.

Fight and flight

Chennai's Leela Palace hotel overlooks the lagoon where the Bay of Bengal meets the Adyar river and offers sanctuary from a sprawling megacity of I I million. For the cricketers of Chennai Super Kings, its marbled walkways, upmarket restaurants and cafés are places to escape and relax away from the IPL's ubiquitous fans. In May 2023, it was also an unlikely setting for a spot of Ashes planning between two CSK teammates who, through unforeseen circumstances, would embrace warmly at The Oval two months later.

Moeen Ali had long given up Test cricket, applying his all-round skills to the world of franchise Twenty20 instead. Ben Stokes might have been CSK's big-money overseas star, but he was injured for most of the tournament and, when he returned to fitness, could not force his way back in the side. Instead, Moeen played the fuller part in their IPL-winning season. But Stokes had time to war-game the Ashes, chatting tactics with Moeen, a man with a lively cricket brain, a friend he could trust, and a deeply experienced Test player.

When Jack Leach was struck down by a back injury ten days after Stokes arrived home from the IPL, England's captain found himself without a spin bowler on the eve of the Ashes. He immediately thought back to the Leela Palace, and sent Moeen a one-word WhatsApp message: 'Ashes?' Nothing else needed to be said. It was a canny move. While Moeen, soon to turn 36, had not touched a red ball since his last Test, against India in September 2021, and turned down a similar approach for the Pakistan tour, Bazball was his kind of cricket. The fact that he now knew Stokes's thoughts inside out made his return to Test cricket all the smoother.

'I think the IPL really helped, because I spent a lot of time with Stokesy at Chennai speaking to him about what he was going to do with the team against Australia,' he says. 'I would say: "What are you going to do in this situation or that?" I was on the same wavelength as him. With me being retired, we were just chatting over tactics. Because of that, I would say I was probably filled in, and prepared for, the Ashes more than most of the other England players.'

Moeen saw his return as a one-off, a free pass to play the game differently, with less pressure and more enjoyment. After taking three wickets on the final day at The Oval, he immediately confirmed his re-retirement, even if it was overshadowed by Stuart Broad's own farewell. Moeen had been picked ahead of Rehan Ahmed and Will Jacks to protect them from the long-term damage of a potential mauling in a big series. 'Bazball, as people call it, was a huge attraction: Ben captain, McCullum coach. It does not get better than that for me.'

Life as a spin bowler in England is a tough gig. Just ask Moeen, who had to learn on the job as a Test cricketer because the county game had offered him so few opportunities. Spinners can go for weeks at the start of the season barely bowling a ball in the county championship. They play for captains who don't understand how to use them, rolling their eyes at the first four or six, and they bowl mostly on pitches that offer little encouragement. Young spinners are farmed out on loan, while medium-pacers are more highly prized, despite being ill-equipped for Test cricket. It is not surprising that only 22 per cent of championship overs between 2014 and 2022 were bowled by spinners. They have little margin for error. 'Your brain is made to protect yourself and be safe,' says Leach.

Then Stokes came along, with his bold, adventurous handling of spinners. And maybe he sees a little of himself in this maligned breed. He too has been an outsider, cast aside in his younger days by management for being too difficult to handle. It taught him compassion for those striving to impress. As a seamer, at least before his left knee packed in, he also recognises the value of a spinner at the other end, either to build a bowling partnership or to give the quicks a rest. And because he is a bowler too, his handling of other bowlers is gentler than that of his predecessors. He understands it does not always come off.

'It's like, this is a cricket match, let's relax,' says Leach. 'If you can bring that into it a bit more, it helps. He makes sure it is not fight-or-flight, so I'm not thinking that if I don't protect myself I'm going to get eaten by a bear – that I'm not worried about my place and trying to not stuff up rather than trying to do well. It's a difference in mindset. Not being a little bit safe would be the right way to put it.'

England have picked five specialist spin bowlers in the McCullum–Stokes era, plus Joe Root, who provided useful back-up during the Ashes. Leach was anointed No 1 straight away, and told he would have a long run in the side. Lancashire leg-spinner Matt Parkinson played one Test as a concussion substitute when Leach hit his head in the field in McCullum's first match, against New Zealand at Lord's – he was desperately chasing the ball to the boundary, trying to emulate his new coach's athleticism. Moeen was a break-emergency-glass pick for the Ashes when Leach was injured again, while Jacks and Ahmed were stabs in the dark for the tour of Pakistan, where England needed two spinners, plus Root. Each has a different story.

Leach is an orthodox left-armer brought up on county cricket's lone turning pitch, at Taunton, while Parkinson and Ahmed are still making their way as leggies (and Parkinson, for the moment, has dropped off England's radar altogether). Jacks had never contemplated any kind of career as a spinner, even at county level. But in 2022 Surrey decided they needed a frontline attack made up of seamers and a deeper batting line-up. Since he would be in the side for his batting anyway, they encouraged him to work on his off-breaks. A few months later he was taking a six-for in a Test match at Rawalpindi. Two games after that, at Karachi, Ahmed was the ultimate Bazball pick, becoming at 18 years and 126 days England's youngest Test cricketer; he had played three first-class games.

Slow bowling takes confidence, and a spinner cannot intimidate with pace. It requires guile, patience and a healthy dollop of self-belief, which Graeme Swann – England's best spinner since Derek Underwood – had in bucketfuls. But it is hard to be confident when you grow up in a system geared towards swing and seam. Plenty of spinners have been tried by England only briefly: Gareth Batty, James Tredwell, Simon Kerrigan, Zafar Ansari, Mason Crane.

Look at what was happening in county cricket during the Ashes. Parkinson had two loan spells from Lancashire to Durham, and announced he would be leaving Old Trafford at the end of the season for Kent. Off-spinner Dom Bess bowled in the nets before England played Australia at Headingley, having appeared in the most recent of his 14 Tests in March 2021 in India. But he was back on loan at his first club, Somerset, after failing to hold down a place at Yorkshire (by now, his CV also included a game on loan to Warwickshire). Leg-spinner Crane, who won his only Test cap at Sydney in 2017–18, was not even in Hampshire's T20 side, let alone playing championship cricket. Jacks was keeping specialist spinners Amar Virdi and Dan Moriarty – who was loaned to Yorkshire – out of the Surrey team. Ahmed took just five wickets in the first six rounds of the championship for Leicestershire, on fresh, early-summer pitches. It is partly why England plucked him out of county cricket so young: they do not trust the system to nurture him.

The numbers for spinners in the Bazball era are remarkably similar to those for the final year of Root's captaincy. Under Stokes, spinners have taken their wickets at an average of 38 and a strike-rate of 66, and have cost 3.47 an over. For the last 17 Tests under Root, which included three on some of the most turning tracks ever produced in India, they averaged 37 and conceded 3.06 an over, though their strike-rate – 72 – was higher. So spinners under Stokes have been slightly more expensive but have struck more often in less helpful conditions, which underlines one of his core messages: don't worry about runs, get me wickets.

The bravest pick was Ahmed. It helped that England were 2–0 up against Pakistan when he was selected in Karachi, the decision made almost as soon as victory was secured at Multan. Even before the series had begun, McCullum made it clear Ahmed was there to play, not just gain experience. 'He seems really confident in himself,' he said. 'I want to get to know him, and I want to try and help him out. Here he is. He's 18 and on an England tour to Pakistan, so there's some real opportunities there, and there'll be some challenges along the way, but it's our job to figure this out. We know he's not the finished product. He's a long way from that, but he's got something which is pretty kind of special.'

Ahmed, whose father, Naeem, was with him on tour, was told two days before the Karachi Test that he would break Brian Close's record as England's youngest Test cricketer. He was taking the place of James Anderson, who had made his debut more than a year before Ahmed was born. 'I was told if your dad is around, let him know you might be playing,' says Ahmed. 'The day before, Stokesy and Baz called me to their room. I didn't know what to expect. It could have been like, you're not playing. But they said I was in. I was like: "Oh wow, great!"'

It was a touching moment when Ahmed was awarded his cap by Nasser Hussain, with Naeem invited into the huddle by McCullum. A few years earlier, as a taxi driver working for an upmarket hotel in Bangalore, Naeem had driven McCullum and his family to the airport. He later moved to Nottingham and raised a family that included three cricket-mad boys. Ahmed joined Leicestershire and made his first-team debut aged 16 in a Royal London Cup 50-over match in July 2021. His younger brother, Farhan, aged just 15 and tipped to be the best of the sons, is an off-spinner who played for Nottinghamshire Second XI in May 2023 alongside his oldest brother, Raheem. Naeem, meanwhile, spent the Pakistan tour visiting family, and staying on in the hope of seeing his middle son play for England. He watched the game from the seats in front of the press box, punching the air when Rehan took his first Test wicket, Saud Shakil, caught at forward short leg. A few years earlier, Ahmed had bowled with Shane Warne in the nets at Lord's. Warne would have loved Bazball for its adventure and spirit, but picking a teenage leg-spinner would have topped the lot. And while Warne struggled on his Test debut, Ahmed flowered.

'I feel very privileged to have made my debut in such a team, because the nerves I had were just the nerves I put on myself,' he says. 'There were no extra nerves of "I need to impress this guy" or "I need to do this or do that". It was just the kind of nerves from a young guy who always wanted to play Test cricket – and it was finally happening. Seeing previous England teams, I don't think they would have picked me. I'm just so happy they did. I never expected to play before, but when Stokesy did become captain, and always took the positive option, I felt into it straight away: I really wanted to be part of this team. Whereas before, you keep your thoughts to yourself, because someone might think you were saying something silly like trying to hit the ball for six in a Test match. But here, everything in my head that I wanted to say, someone else said it for me. It was a great, great time.

'When I did get my first wicket, I bowled a full toss and it went for four, and I was like "oh no". And then just the reassurance from Stokesy: it doesn't matter, keep doing it. It made you feel like you're the best player in the world. Obviously I'm not. But it made me feel like I could get a wicket any ball.'

In the second innings, Ahmed picked up a five-wicket haul and put England in a match-winning position. It included Babar Azam, Mohammad Rizwan and Shakil again – all with Stokes's attacking fields, despite good players of spin facing a teenager. 'I quite enjoy that challenge,' he says. 'When you play county cricket, you go into a safe option of trying to settle yourself in. Whereas with England, from the first ball you try to get a wicket, and if you get hit, you get hit. The runs aren't the problem. It's more we want the wickets. Having everyone up on the leg side to Babar Azam, it was like what am I doing here? I was just smiling, because I never thought this would happen – I thought I'd have four people up on the fence.'

When he bowled a drag-down to Babar, his first thought was 'oh, there's four'. Instead, with the field up, Babar picked out Ollie Pope at midwicket. He then removed Rizwan and Shakil with googlies, which is almost his stock delivery while he works on adding more zip to his leg-break. After knocking over the tail, he led England off the field, casually tossing the match ball up in the air as if it were an everyday event. 'Walking off that day was a great feeling,' he says. 'I reckon it will be the best feeling I'll have on a cricket pitch.'

There was still time for one more surprise. McCullum told him he would bat at No 3, because Stokes wanted to wrap the game up in three days, with England set 167 to win and 22 overs left that afternoon. After Zak Crawley and Ben Duckett hit 87 in 11, Ahmed was sent out – England's first 'nighthawk', with their designated man for the job, Stuart Broad, watching at home while he helped change his new daughter Anabella's nappies.

'I was walking off after my five-for, so it couldn't get much better,' says Ahmed. 'Stokesy said: "Rehy, get your pads on." I looked at Popey, because he was batting three, and he said: "Yeah, hurry up, get 'em on, man." I was always going to try to run down and hit my first ball for six. I didn't get underneath it enough, but I got four, so that was fair enough.'

Ten off eight balls was a moderate start for the young hawk, but England had made him feel like a star, and that winter he made his debut in all three formats. He will get another chance at Test level, but for the time being England are content to let him develop on the franchise circuit. Even though he had a slow start to the 2023 season with Leicestershire, hardly a surprise given the early-season pitches, he was picked in an Ashes squad at Lord's, to cover for Moeen.

'It made me love red-ball cricket again, I'll be honest with you,' he says. 'I went on that tour thinking this is going to be the break of my career, I'm going to want to play more red-ball than white-ball, and that's exactly what's happened. White-ball cricket, I do enjoy it. But that Test cricket feeling – even being on the field at Lord's [he was twelfth man against Australia]. I loved it there. It's a different kind of thing. Everyone's always saying it's the hardest game, but I enjoy it the most as well. It's tit for tat – hard, but very enjoyable.'

Ahmed was a teenage leggie with the world at his feet. But Leach had endured an up-and-down career, and had been in and out of the side under Root. Stokes's management of him has been one of the smartest aspects of his captaincy – even if Leach's statistics are solid rather than spectacular. Until his back injury, he was the only bowler to play every game under Stokes, sending down more than 500 overs, and fulfilling the seemingly incompatible briefs of being more attacking while holding up an end. Leach's average (38), strike-rate (68) and economy-rate (3.33) were all higher than they were under Root – although that is partly explained by going on tours of Sri Lanka and India before Stokes took over. Numbers are only part of the story, anyway.

'I feel like I've thrived under him and know my role in the team more than ever,' says Leach. 'And that's not just as a player. It's also as a person, what I offer the dressing-room. Before – and this was no fault of anyone's – I felt like I had to be playing well to be myself, whereas Baz and Stokesy have said: "Offer the team your whole self as a person." I've loved how much it is about the team, and that takes me away from worrying about my own game. There are times, when we meet up, where I think it's as important we get back together as it is for our games to be spot on. I'd almost rather be 5 per cent less ready as an individual but feel connected with the others.'

Stokes has consistently backed Leach in public, recognising he sometimes needs a lift. There is a bond between them following their last-wicket stand against Australia at Headingley in 2019, and gratitude among the management that Leach rose off his sickbed in Rawalpindi, despite concerns over his health. He takes medication for Crohn's disease, and in New Zealand in 2019–20 was hospitalised with gastroenteritis, which developed into sepsis. His caution in Pakistan was sensible, but Stokes and McCullum both chatted to him the night before the first Test; without their intervention, he would probably have missed it.

'On the morning of the game, the doctor said: "Nah, you're no good,"' says Leach. 'They were a bit worried about Crohn's. I was desperate to play, but I didn't want to get two days into the game and be worse off, and then affect the team because I'm in hospital. I didn't know whether I was going to get better or worse. Stokesy came in and said: "Look, we could really do with you." I spoke to Baz, and he said it would be quite cool if we could get everyone playing, and it's just like we're all in a bad place and whatever happens, happens – who cares? It's more about everyone in it together. I was like, I just don't want to get worse.

'Stokesy said: "I don't want this to have a long-term effect with your Crohn's. I know it's difficult for you, but if you feel like you can play, then don't worry if you get worse during the

Test match. We'll try to do everything we can. If we bowl first today, you won't have to bowl much. We could do with you later in the game, potentially." And I was like: "I'm in." I feel like I'd run through a brick wall for him. So that was cool. And I am so happy I played.'

Despite a quiet match overall – Leach had figures of three for 246, the most he has conceded in a Test – he took the winning wicket in the final moments on day five. 'I remember being quite emotional afterwards, and Jimmy Anderson was the same. We couldn't believe we'd just won. To take that last wicket was epic – an amazing feeling.'

Stokes has handled spinners by attacking, rather than seeing them as a means to (holding) an end. He wants mid-off and mid-on up, preferring to chase wickets, not manage the run-rate. 'I've had times when someone's hit me over the top, and I was like "shall we put one back?"' says Leach. 'And he says: "No." I get hit over the top again, and he's at mid-off smiling and clapping. He's like, "this is the process we're going with and I'll live and die with it." That's a powerful thing, because as players we really start to trust it is the case. Stokesy and Baz are more worried about the style than the outcome. Naturally, the outcome then takes care of itself. That's another amazing thing: the less hard you try for that outcome, the more you can focus on the way you want to do it.

'They see things a bit differently from everyone else. They're less worried about themselves, and more worried about the state of Test cricket. When that becomes the focus, again it takes the pressure away from trying to win the game. We're competitors – we want to win. But the psychology is different.'

Leach worked with England's slow-bowling coach, Jeetan Patel, the former New Zealand off-spinner, on getting more over-spin. Regular Test appearances meant his confidence grew, and he became the first bowler under Stokes to take ten wickets in a match – at Headingley, no less, traditionally a seamers' stronghold. Stokes held his nerve, continually tempting the New Zealand batsmen to take Leach on, while keeping his fields up. One wicket was a fluke, when Henry Nicholls was caught at mid-off via a deflection off the bat of non-striker Daryl Mitchell. And Leach had another stroke of luck when Neil Wagner was caught between the legs of keeper Sam Billings. But it was the wicket of Mitchell for 109, caught by Stokes running round from mid-off just before lunch on day two, that gave Leach the most pleasure.

'Mitchell had hit me over the top a few times, and everything in me wanted to push the field back. I remember Ben saying: "Yeah, but then he won't try it." I thought, *yeah, I can't argue with that*. And then he did it, and Stokesy was the one under it. He had to run quite far – it was a good catch. He pointed back at me, and he was so over the moon that it worked. So was I.

'He was really investing in me as a bowler. After the first Test in New Zealand at Mount Maunganui, he said: "I want to bowl you in all different situations, because if you only bowl when it looks like it might spin, you'll only be good at that." The way Nathan Lyon has got good at bowling in different conditions is because he has done it in a four-man attack for quite a lot of his career. So Stokesy wants to put that trust in me, and understand you might have to go through a bit of shit before you do a good job consistently. You have to be put in those situations and know there's still going to be that scrutiny on the outside. But we don't listen to that.

'That was a big thing from Baz and the players: we don't care what the media say. And I thought, *that's good to hear*. Then you see him back it up with actions. As an individual you think, *well, if he doesn't care, why do I?* Baz says all he cared about when he played was people in his dressing-room and what they thought. Anything outside really didn't affect him. Suddenly you start to have confidence about what's in the room rather than listen to what's outside. And hopefully we drag the outside along with us with our more positive style.'

Stokes was devastated when Leach was ruled out of the Ashes after feeling back pain in the Ireland Test; it was later diagnosed as a stress fracture. He still went on the squad's team-bonding golf trip to Scotland as a non-playing guest, and was at Lord's addressing the group before training on the eve of the match.

Enter Moeen. He was sitting at home when his phone bleeped with the message from Stokes. Moeen scratched his head. He had no idea Leach was injured, and wondered whether Stokes was joking or offering him tickets. Then a news alert about Leach popped up on his phone. Suddenly Moeen was thinking about Test cricket again, nearly two years after his last match. Everything happened in a rush: he cancelled a family holiday to the Cotswolds and was allowed to miss training at Edgbaston so he could pick up his OBE from King Charles. It limited his preparation, but Moeen was thrilled. His only wish was that Bazball had come along earlier: 'If this had happened five years ago, it would have been a dream. It was always my type of cricket.'

He had spent most of his early county career for Worcestershire as a batsman who bowled a bit, but quickly learned off-spin, and was effective for several years. But he never looked totally happy playing for Root or Alastair Cook. They were both great players of spin themselves, but struggled to get the best out of the slow bowlers. The spinners would get together and chunter about a lack of support from the management, and how in particular there was no settled strategy for bowling outside Asia. By contrast, Moeen and leg-spinner Adil Rashid would regularly praise Eoin Morgan's white-ball captaincy: he gave them clear instructions, and would always back them, even on bad days.

'Out of the three Test captains – Stokesy, Rooty and Cooky – if you didn't know anything or watch any cricket and were asked who has the most patience when it comes to captaining spin, you would never say Stokesy first, because of the way he bats,' says Moeen. 'But he is really patient. Not to criticise the other two, but I never thought they captained spin well at all. Things like body language and not sticking to what you have planned – as a spinner, in particular a lone spinner, it can play on your mind. There is no way you can bowl that well. A lot of the body language when I was hit for four would be heads down, the hat comes off, sometimes kicking the turf. It was not just the captain, but also some of the senior players.

'I believe the way the leader leads affects how the players and management behave, and I have noticed a massive difference. When I was hit for four and six before, I could sense from the senior players they thought I was bowling shit, basically. Whereas now the captain comes up and says: "That's all right, we will get a wicket like that." I feel the other players are like that too because of the captain. Weirdly, I don't now feel like I have to bowl at two or three an over. I probably bowled better in terms of economy-rate after my return – not necessarily at Edgbaston, because I was just coming back, but at Headingley in Australia's second innings. It is such a weird thing. Even though we have this aggressive and positive mindset, there is time to be patient and soak it up. As a spinner, it has helped massively. I know people say Leachy's economy and average have gone up, but he has picked up more wickets and that is the main thing.'

Moeen had chatted to Stokes about a new fielding tactic for spinners. Against Australia, England stationed a man dead straight, a few metres in front of the sightscreen, while having wide mid-on and wide mid-off up. At Headingley, Australia struggled to score off Moeen, realising a shot down the ground was worth only one, while aiming aerially was fraught with danger if the ball turned. Partly because of the fields set, Moeen gobbled up Marnus Labuschagne and Steve Smith, both playing uncharacteristically poor shots across the line.

'Before I retired the first time, I would have men back,' he says. 'I would have cover back, a mid-on back, a deep square back, plus a short leg and slip. But now it is the most amazing field: I feel like batters are not sure whether to take it on or not. It is like I am tempting them with mid-on or mid-off up, but they have to get it right because of the man straight. Credit goes to Stokesy for that, because it never crossed my mind. With the way Australia play, they try to come down and hit as straight as they can. I just find it amazing he does these fields and hangs in there with it. I just then try to bowl my best ball. There is no frustration.'

Moeen's requirements were different from a young player still establishing a career, working on their own identity. He could give everything, because he had nothing to lose; as he said, he wasn't fussed about his average. But it was not an easy transition back to Test cricket. He bowled 33 first-innings overs at Edgbaston, his most in a Test innings since 48 at Sydney in 2017–18. It was no surprise a blister formed on his right index finger, an injury that had troubled him in Australia. Now, he was fined a percentage of his match fee for using a drying spray on his hands. He struggled through 14 overs in the second innings, and found it difficult to control the ball, sending down full tosses.

The blister prevented him playing at Lord's. It is an age-old problem for finger-spinners. The seam on the Dukes ball can rip off the top layer of skin: every time they bowl, it opens up again. There have been various remedies down the years. Swann used urine to toughen the skin; Jim Laker preferred friars' balsam, Richie Benaud calamine lotion; others swear by olive oil. Moeen was at a loss. These days, cricket teams are provided with the best medical care money can buy. But it was an email from an England fan in Norfolk, Susan Thompson-Craig, who worked with the NHS, that changed his series. She suggested Medihoney, a gel used for soothing burns and cuts. He tried it and felt almost instant relief. The finger did not bother him again. He even passed it on to other spinners in the county game, including Middlesex's Josh De Caires, the son of Mike Atherton.

'After the first Test this lady sent me a letter,' says Moeen. 'She said: "I'm a big fan of yours. I saw the wound and cut on the finger, and I want to send you some stuff to help." It was a healing anti-bacterial gel made of Manuka honey. It worked wonders and started healing extremely fast. I find it an amazing thing. I am playing cricket and somebody who has never met me is generous enough to do that. That is why England is an amazing place because of things like that.'

The Medihoney allowed him to bowl two crucial Ashes spells: that one at Headingley, when Labuschagne and Smith might have taken the Test away from England, then on the last day at The Oval. He walked off with Broad, getting the send-off his popularity deserved, and was grateful he answered that message from Stokes. 'I would have regretted it later in life,' he says. 'It was quite daunting, because I'd never done well against Australia. I still don't believe I did that well, but it was great to finish like that.'

Unlike the other spinners who played for Stokes, Moeen was part of Morgan's white-ball resurgence, and in a position to reflect on their similarities. 'The biggest thing is sticking to your plan,' he says. 'We were losing 2–0 before Headingley. That was when Bazball was really tested. It is how you come out as captain and coach. Nothing changed. In fact, it was more evident after we won in Leeds that we stuck to what we do. We were exactly the same. That is the evidence to me it is working. Morgs was the same when he was captain.'

Will Jacks was a different kind of gamble – an unknown quantity handed a debut in Pakistan. A youngster will generally do whatever the captain asks, but Stokes tries not to be too top-down: he wanted Jacks to take responsibility as well. Jacks played in Rawalpindi only because his Surrey teammate Ben Foakes failed to recover from sickness, and was given ten minutes' notice, which probably helped the nerves. But, with England racking up 657, he had more than a day to think about his bowling. It might have been daunting: this was England's first Test in Pakistan since 2005–06, against batsmen reared on turning pitches. And in four years since his Surrey debut until the start of the 2022 season, he had sent down just 86 first-class overs. He bowled in T20, but Gareth Batty, the new Surrey coach and a former England off-spinner himself, saw something he could work with. Jacks's 17 wickets at 47 in the 2022 championship hardly screamed 'take me to Pakistan'. But county statistics rarely come into the equation at selection meetings these days, and England picked him on a hunch.

'Ben chucked me in after 11 overs,' says Jacks. 'He said "you're bowling the next one", which took me by surprise.

It was very flat, and we were going to have to work hard. So getting in there early, getting the cobwebs off and getting my first over in, was a nice relief. I bowled a ten-over spell, and I was none for 50 overnight, but I was just happy I landed a few, and felt I was part of the team.

'Going into day three, we spoke about working hard – grind it out. If we're going to win the Test, we're going to have to be bowling for the next three days. We expected that. They were 220 for none. I accidentally chucked one really wide into the footholes – well, there weren't any footholes, but it gripped on something and did a little bit, so I went over to Stokesy and said: "Why don't we just try chucking it wide for two or three overs?" And that's how I claimed my first wicket – Abdullah Shafique edging a cut. So I'll claim all the captaincy for that. And we just went from there. I picked up a few fortunate wickets. I wasn't overly thinking it too much.

'Everything was just about taking wickets. Baz, Stokesy and Jeetan were not bothered about how many runs I went for. If I bowled four wide balls, of which three were overpitched, but I got the fourth one right and got a nick – they didn't care about that. It is liberating. The way we play at Surrey, we back our skills over four days, so we take it slow. We're very happy to grind other people out. When I bowl, it's often on green wickets: can I bowl eight overs for 14 runs, something like that? It's different. It is nice knowing as a bowler that if you do bowl a bad ball and get whacked for four, the captain's five metres away saying "nice mate", or "don't worry".'

Batty compared him to Moeen, because spin bowling was a secondary skill that had to be honed for the highest level. Jacks, taller and more upright, did find turn in Rawalpindi, and finished with six for 161 in the first innings, bowling 40.3 overs, more than he had ever got through in an entire first-class match. A couple of wickets were chancy, but it was a debut of promise, even if three more innings on tour did not produce another wicket.

Jacks is likely to get another chance. Moeen's Test career is over. He retired with the same fourth-innings average (23) as Shane Warne. And he joked he would delete any more messages from Stokes asking him to play Test cricket again. But who knows – perhaps it will be the coach's turn to get in touch. 'It's hard to say no to Baz,' says Moeen. 'He has this amazing way of convincing you. It is a great skill to have as a coach.'

12

Won't work against us

The thing about blazing a trail is that others are waiting
– no, praying – for you to combust. Throughout the
first year of Bazball, Ben Stokes was at pains to stress he
was not trying to tell other teams how to play. He said
it again, for the umpteenth time, after the Ashes. Other
sides were welcome to do it their way. If they wanted to
follow England's lead, then great. If not, no hard feelings.
This was sensible: English cricket has never shaken off the
perception that it knows best, that it has some kind of
moral claim on the right way of playing the game. The
Spirit of Cricket is a cherished concept at MCC, who
dreamed it up: witness the scenes at Lord's after Alex
Carey stumped Jonny Bairstow, unleashing the righteous
indignation of middle-aged men in jackets and ties. But
the notion has been less well-received abroad – proof,
if needed, that England were still speaking a different
language in the third decade of the twenty-first century.
Stokes, then, had to proceed carefully, for fear of being
accused of sermonising. On the one hand, he really did
want to help save Test cricket. On the other, he didn't

want to do it from a pulpit. His message would be strictly secular; others could ignore it, or take heed, as they wished.

Most opponents did neither. England's 3–0 win against New Zealand had been a friendly affair between teams who enjoyed each other's company, and regarded sledging as a tactic used mainly by Australia, their mutual foe. If there were any doubts that England could go on the attack in seam-friendly conditions against Trent Boult, Tim Southee, Kyle Jamieson and Neil Wagner, they were aired mainly on social media, where England fans had been honing their gallows humour during the tours of Australia and the West Indies. Besides, New Zealand now had another reason to be affable: a shared history with Brendon McCullum. If Baz had a plan, theirs was the last dressing-room likely to mock it.

Instead, the first sign of dissent came when India returned for the long-delayed fifth and final Test at Edgbaston in July 2022. They carried over a 2–1 lead from the previous summer, which ended prematurely when they opted out of the series finale at Old Trafford amid worries that Covid was taking hold in their camp. Others suspected their main concern was ensuring their safe and healthy arrival in the Gulf for the resumption of the IPL, which had been interrupted by the pandemic and was due to restart only five days after the final day in Manchester. A year on, India were about to encounter a different beast from the England side who had rolled over and had their tummies tickled. Had the Indians stayed on in 2021, they might already have been celebrating a 3–1 victory. But a rejuvenated England team had breezed past targets of 277, 299 and 296 against New Zealand, and suddenly believed they could chase anything.

For the first three days in Birmingham, India were on course for a handsome win. Their first innings had been resurrected from 98 for five by a stand of 222 between Rishabh Pant – a natural Bazball cricketer himself, who later that year was lucky to survive a night-time car crash after apparently falling asleep at the wheel – and Ravindra Jadeja. India's bowlers then reduced England to 84 for five on the second evening. After the close, India's most combative seamer, Mohammed Siraj, was in confident mood. 'When we saw the New Zealand series,' he said, 'we realised that our every bowler is 140kmh-plus [87mph], and they didn't have that. We had that ability, and we also played against England last year. So that was our plus point, as we're aware of their weak points, and that is why we got success.' It was hardly an outlandish claim and, even though a century next day from Jonny Bairstow dragged England to 284, India still led by 132. When they closed the third day on 125 for three, 257 ahead, the game looked over.

The New Zealand series, though, had thrown up an intriguing possibility. In each of the three Tests, England's aggression had left their opponents increasingly unsure how to approach the third innings, since no advantage seemed safe. It was as if they were the unwitting subjects of a mad experiment. The erosion of their confidence had begun when they blew a strong position at Lord's: 242 ahead, with six wickets in hand and their two batting stars of the summer, Daryl Mitchell and Tom Blundell, at the crease. Then, at Trent Bridge, they made 553, only for England to reply with 539 at 4.20 an over. In their second innings, New Zealand slipped from 104 for one to 284 all out. Finally, at Headingley, they found themselves 274 for five in their second innings, a lead of 243. Their last five fell for 52, opening the door once again; England barged through, as Bairstow followed his first-innings 162 from 157 balls with 71 not out from 44.

To squander one such position in a series would be galling. Three out of three suggested England were messing with their minds.

Asked whether he had thought it possible to bat in Test cricket as Bairstow had done, New Zealand captain Kane Williamson replied: 'It's not meant to be possible, but it certainly was. He had the courage to do it. It goes slightly against the grain of what we've seen in Test cricket, although not with Baz.'

Three of England's 12 highest fourth-innings chases had now taken place inside a month. Another entry was about to join the list – straight in at No 1. At Edgbaston, it was as if India hadn't been watching the New Zealand series, despite what Siraj said. On a careless fourth day, they declined from 153 for three to 245 all out, with Stokes collecting four cheap wickets. It meant England needed 378, which was 19 more than Australia had set them at Headingley three summers earlier – until now, the best chase in their history. Stokes, the hero that day in 2019, wasn't required at all this time, as Alex Lees and Zak Crawley began with what was then England's fastest century opening stand. Joe Root and Bairstow, who finished the game with 220 runs for once out, added an undefeated 269 – England's largest partnership in a successful fourth-innings chase. Records were coming as thick and fast as fours and sixes.

By the time South Africa arrived for the second full series of the summer, the mood had changed. Having pulled off four big chases in a row, England had backed word with deed, making the leap from theory to practice. Journalists were hardly going to pass up the chance to ask opposing captains what they made of it all – and South Africa's Dean Elgar was happy to oblige. A rugged left-hander from the down-at-heel mining town of Welkom in Orange Free State, part of the Afrikaner heartland, he had built his career on one of Test cricket's most unyielding principles: give the bowlers nothing, and only then think about a run or two. For him, Bazball wasn't simply an alien concept: it was an affront to all he held dear. During a pre-series interview with *Wisden Cricket Monthly*, Elgar voiced his distaste.

'The new England style is quite interesting,' he said, his first and final stab at diplomacy. 'But I don't see that there's longevity in brave cricket, because I see things evening out over time in Test cricket... I've got absolutely no interest in the style they've played. I think it can go one of two ways for them, and it can go south very quickly. There was often parity between England and New Zealand, and had New Zealand taken their opportunities and their catches, then things could have been very different. England would have come away with egg on their faces.'

He echoed Siraj, saying he would like to see England 'do it against our seamers'. The implication was clear: their recklessness would catch up with them sooner or later. Both the weight of history and the law of averages said so. The stage was set for a clash of philosophies.

Not long after South Africa arrived, Elgar's nose was tweaked once more – this time by the Lions, England's second-string team, during a four-day game at Canterbury. The Lions received two pep talks – the first from Brendon McCullum. Ben Duckett, still trying to fight his way back into the Test team after an absence of almost six years, recalls its gist: 'It was just Baz-style: you're here for a reason – go out and play that way. I feel they picked that squad around how they wanted us to play. Dan Lawrence at three, Brooky four, me five – we're the kind who play that aggressive brand anyway. It was probably a bit of a surprise to him how well we did play in that game. But we were basically a group who had already been doing it for our counties.'

The second pep talk came from Craig Overton, the Somerset seamer whose twin brother, Jamie, had played his part with the bat against New Zealand at Headingley. Craig's message was simple, urging his colleagues to 'do what the England boys are doing'. The Lions did just that. In reply to South Africa's 433 (made at a respectable 3.48 an over), they thrashed 672 at 5.74, with Lawrence hitting 97 from 97 balls, Brook 140 from 170, and Duckett 145 from 168; Sam Billings added 92 from 96. The Lions won by an innings and 56. To McCullum's delight, Bazball was seeping through the English system: by the end of the year, both Brook and Duckett had enjoyed superb Test tours of Pakistan.

The Lions' sense of adventure lent even more piquancy to the Test series, which began at Lord's five days later. Elgar remained punchy. 'The warm-up was a good exercise,' he said, glossing over the significance of events at Canterbury. 'And if they come out playing like that in an official Test match and it goes pear-shaped, that will not look very good for England.' He seemed to take even the mention of Bazball as a personal slight: 'I am really not going to entertain that phrase any more. I just want to crack on with the cricket. The game deserves that respect. Mudslinging is a thing of the past for me, and we are not going to go back and forth around that.'

Elgar was not the only bemused South African. Coach Mark Boucher, once part of a highly successful Test side that had played uncompromising cricket under Graeme Smith, told the media, only half in jest: 'If you mention Bazball, you've got to have a tequila. I'll bring the bottle.' Had South Africa lost at Lord's, it might have been Elgar and Boucher with egg on their face. Instead, their outstanding pace attack, led by Kagiso Rabada and Anrich Nortje, brushed England aside for 165 and 149 in a total of 82.4 overs.

For the naysayers, Elgar included, this was confirmation that England's approach could backfire, though their conservative method under Chris Silverwood and Root had fared just as badly, more often. And instead of berating his players for their first defeat under his watch, McCullum urged them to 'go harder' at Old Trafford and The Oval. It was a typically cute piece of psychology, borne out when England came from behind to take the series. No matter that the win in Manchester included a pair of almost old-fashioned centuries from Stokes and Ben Foakes: the thrust of McCullum's message was that the team had done nothing wrong. As per his promise at the start of it all, he would be backing them in times of trouble.

After South Africa subsided to their first series defeat in five, a run that had taken them to the top of the World Test Championship, Elgar interrupted a reporter who was asking him what he made of England's approach: 'I said I am not speaking about that.' And when he did speak about it, he might as well have been holding his nose: 'I actually thought they played relatively good Test cricket. I don't think they played extraordinary cricket. I thought they played the correct tempo. I didn't see that B-word coming through at all.'

He was about one-third right. At Old Trafford, England had scored at 3.89 an over in their only innings, with the match-defining partnership of 173 between Stokes and Foakes coming at 3.22. But they had continually emphasised that clever cricket was their aim, not recklessness. Events at The Oval, meanwhile, fitted Elgar's hypothesis less snugly:

England scored at 4.34 in their first innings, even if they were bowled out for just 158 in reply to South Africa's 118, and at 5.77 in their second, as they sped to a nine-wicket win. Five months later, Elgar was sacked as Test captain, after his side's repeated failure to put together serviceable totals.

This didn't dissuade South African batsman Rassie van der Dussen from making an interesting comment later in the year. 'To an extent, they tried it against us and it didn't really work, even though we lost the series,' he said. 'As soon as the bowlers are a bit more into it, like we saw at Lord's, it's a very fine line between going out and playing aggressively and then getting out, as opposed to being more disciplined. People like seeing that – a lot of shots and a lot of runs – but the purist and the real Test fan likes it when the balance is even between bat and ball, and the bowlers are in the game as much as the batters.'

It was not an uncommon view. England were upsetting an ancient apple cart and had to expect resentment. Yet van der Dussen's critique seemed to stem from a high-church view of the game – the kind of view, in fact, for which England had often been pilloried. England was supposed to be the spiritual home of cricketing orthodoxy: to dispense with 145 years of Test wisdom was to mess with a cherished narrative.

A theme was emerging, as each new series became Bazball's latest acid test. And so off they headed to Pakistan, where they had won only two matches out of 24 dating back to 1961–62, when Ted Dexter's team won 1–0. Australia had made the same trip earlier in 2022, grinding out a 1–0 victory in a three-match series on lifeless surfaces that left observers talking about a '15-day Test'. The only route to success, they argued, was to hang on in there until an opportunity arose at the very end. This wasn't entirely unreasonable, since Nasser Hussain's side had won in Pakistan in precisely that manner in 2000–01, pinching victory in the dark at Karachi. But when the 15-day Test theory was put to Stokes after the Oval victory against South Africa, his response was lukewarm. England were not going back to what they regarded as the grim old days.

Hints of respect threatened to emerge. Asked whether all-out aggression might work on Pakistani pitches, Shan Masood – one of their top-order batsmen – began with a friendly warning during an interview with the *Mail on Sunday*: 'It's risky. As a batsman, one bad shot here, and you get everyone on your back.' But he also admired what England were doing. 'They played quality teams in New Zealand, India and South Africa: they're not lesser teams. And it's just exciting watching them play. What's good is that they continue to play that way, don't change and stay true to their blueprint. They've made people watch Test cricket and see what they're doing differently. They've made it more entertaining and put the spark back in it.' Later, Pakistan would become the first team to adapt England's approach.

Australia remained largely aloof, though Steve Smith and David Warner had been unable to resist a couple of friendly digs when Bazball got going in 2022. 'Guys just keep joking about it,' said Smith, before resorting to a familiar line: 'If you come on a wicket that's got some grass, and Josh Hazlewood, Pat Cummins and Mitchell Starc are rolling in at you, is it going to be the same? We'll see what happens.' The following summer, all three would disappear at between four and five an over – in each instance the most expensive Test series of their long careers.

Warner, meanwhile, pounced on England's defeat by South Africa at Lord's: 'Bazball didn't work that Test.' Not that he actually cared: 'I haven't really taken much notice of it.' But he was in mischievous mood: 'I don't know if you guys know. We've got Ronball' – a reference to Australia's head coach Andrew 'Ron' McDonald. On 10 December, with the second Test between Pakistan and England under way at Multan, Australia's players showed how little they had been thinking about Bazball by placing a handwritten note reading 'RON BALL' in the window of their dressing-room during a Test against West Indies at Adelaide.

As the Ashes approached, the talk grew louder. Some Australians, it seemed, believed Bazball meant slogging. 'If they are five for 50, are they still coming out and swinging?' asked Starc. Others wondered about the wisdom of Stokes's pre-series demand for 'fast, flat' pitches, not least because Australia's failure to win a series in England since 2001 had been based on their batsmen's dislike of lateral movement. But Marnus Labuschagne, who would start the Ashes as Test cricket's top-ranked batsman, was trying to rise above it all. 'I don't care what wickets are rolled out,' he told the *Daily Mail*. 'But if they feel that's their best way to beat us, we'll certainly take it on. We have one of, if not *the* best, bowling attacks in the world, so if you want to take us on at our own game, then I commend them if they can get on top of a high-quality attack.'

Fundamental to Australian scepticism was the idea that, because their own attack had yet to put Bazball through its paces, England's strategy lacked legitimacy. At the end of May, Mitchell Johnson – the former left-arm quick who had run riot during the 2013–14 Ashes – announced in the *West Australian* newspaper that it was 'time to call bullshit on Bazball'. For Johnson, it was a con trick, a transparent act of desperation ahead of a meeting with a superior foe.

'Gamesmanship and getting into opponents' heads is definitely a key ingredient here,' he wrote. 'But all the bluff and bluster surrounding Bazball won't intimidate Pat Cummins and his team. England's new obsession with attacking at all costs could actually play right into Australia's hands and backfire spectacularly during the Ashes. Call it what you like, but Bazball is nothing new. England are hardly the first team in Test cricket to use attack and aggression to try to overwhelm their rivals. McCullum and Stokes are being too clever by half if they follow through on a request to their groundsmen for flat pitches and shorter boundaries to assist with their Bazball approach.'

So much for the phoney war. Once the cricket started, it was clear Australia were changing their plans because of England, not the other way round. At the end of the first day at Edgbaston, when Stokes declared on 393 for eight to allow himself a few overs – fruitless, as it turned out – against Australia's openers, Hazlewood suggested their attack had done well to limit England to five an over, and not allow them to go at seven or eight. Elsewhere, a piece in the *Guardian* was headlined: 'Lyon works magic as Australia blunt Bazball and keep England in check.' This was after a day in which England had scored more quickly – at 5.03 an over – in the first innings of any Ashes Test with the exception of Edgbaston 2005, when they hit 407 runs on the opening day at 5.13. The times they really were a-changin'.

But Australians remained unconvinced by England's new approach, especially when Cummins steered them to a two-wicket victory in that game, allowing touring reporters to ask him whether he, like Stokes, would have declared his side's first innings with only eight wickets down and their star batsman well into three figures (Root was 118 not out). Cummins is no gloater, and offered a straight bat: 'Probably not, no.' It fed into the narrative of reckless England against ruthless Australia.

The second Test at Lord's provided more fodder, as England's batsmen took turns getting out to the short ball on the second evening, throwing away a promising position. In this instance, the strongest criticism came from the British press, who despaired at the prospect of going 2–0 down. 'It was not Bazball, it was not Benball,' wrote Scyld Berry in the *Daily Telegraph*. 'It was simply brainless. This was English cricket's remake of the Charge of the Light Brigade.' The *Mail*'s back page screamed: 'You suckers!' In *The Times*, Mike Atherton observed: 'Even for Stokes, things had got a little out of kilter. That's how mad things were for a while.' Michael Vaughan took up the baton in the *Telegraph*. 'All England needed to do was duck under a few,' he wrote. 'Australia would have soon gone to another tactic because that is properly back-bending work. That is actually the brave option, to get under a few, wear a few, try to see off a spell.' Everyone was having their say, especially those who had been wary of Bazball in the first place.

'A few of us former players were just a touch sceptical,' wrote Geoffrey Boycott, also in the *Telegraph*. 'Why? Well, the bowling they had faced was good, but not great, and the pitches had been flat with no pace and very batsman-friendly. Us old hands thought: "Surely you cannot bat like that against top-class bowling without coming a cropper somewhere. It is risky." Until this series, the England batting has been refreshing, exciting and injected new life into Test cricket. Suddenly in these past two Tests they have lost their focus and their brains. Talk of winning has been replaced by talk of entertaining and that it does not matter if they lose. Batsmen were running down the pitch swiping and swishing. Their batting was gung-ho. It would appear the players started to believe their own publicity that they were so good they were unbeatable and untouchable. Whenever you think you are better than you are, or get too big for your boots, sport will bite you on the backside.'

After that, it was perhaps inevitable that England should win the third Test at Headingley. At Old Trafford, their batsmen provided an answer to Smith's pre-series question about Hazlewood (who went for 126 in 27 overs), Cummins (129 in 23) and Starc (137 in 25). 'Has Bazball spooked Australia?' wondered the former Australian fast bowler Jason Gillespie in the *Mail on Sunday*. 'A number of Australian players in interviews have insisted that they will play their way and they will focus on what they can do. But what we have seen is reactive plans to England's style of play. We wouldn't be seeing all these defensive fields and raucous bouncer plans if Australia simply focused on what they do well.'

Even now, not everyone was convinced. Back in Australia, the former leg-spinner Kerry O'Keeffe was reflecting on Australia's 2–1 lead going into the final Test. 'Bazball was smashed,' he told Fox Sports. 'It's a manufactured thing, Bazball. It depends totally on a flat pitch, which Ben Stokes ordered and were produced by the curators. You've got to take risks when you bat. They've been able to get away with it a couple of times because of the nature of the pitch.'

But for those who had been watching more closely, England's raucous batting in Manchester felt like the moment to take Bazball seriously. In the *Telegraph*, Justin Langer – the former Australia coach whose intensity had ruled out any chance of his replacing Silverwood in the England job – enthused with the zeal of a convert.

'I get it now, this Bazball thing,' he wrote. 'We had heard about it, even been threatened by it. Now we have seen it with our own eyes, and I have to say, it was spectacular to watch. England might not have won the Ashes this time but, on the second afternoon of the fourth Test, I finally understood what they were doing and why they were doing it. That was some of the most awe-inspiring cricket I have seen for a very long time. It was absolutely breathtaking to watch, and proved to me that this style of play could work against the best bowling attack in the world.'

England, felt Langer, had found a formula that could work against 'the very best teams'.

Warner, though, was sticking to his guns. Speaking ahead of the Oval Test, he sniffed: 'I haven't really seen Bazball yet, to be honest.' Of Ronball, there was no mention. Langer, on the other hand, finished the series as a paid-up advocate: 'Australia were limping at the end, just holding on. They will be happy to have retained the urn, but they were in the contest of their lives. When the players board their flight home, I have no doubt there will be a sense of relief. They will take a deep breath out and say: "Thank goodness I am going home." Playing Ashes cricket in England is exhausting, especially when you are getting beaten. There is nowhere to hide.'

And Boycott? He hadn't quite forgotten England's excesses at Edgbaston and Lord's, but in the *Telegraph* he was in a more forgiving mood: 'England could have won all five Tests – certainly they were good enough to win 4–0. They were winning at Edgbaston for 90 per cent of the time and it was even at Lord's until brainless batting cost them their wickets. The Aussies go home with the Ashes, but their series was just a remake of the 1963 Steve McQueen film, *The Great Escape*. They were totally outplayed in three Tests, and in the other two England gave it away. That is the sadness of it all, because England were excellent.'

Never in doubt, Geoffrey. Never in doubt.

The 2023 Ashes

Fifth Test, The Oval

When play resumed at 4.20 p.m. on the final afternoon of the fifth Test, the 2023 Ashes got the rousing send-off to which it felt entitled. A couple of hours earlier, Australia – chasing 384 for an improbable 3–1 win – had gone into lunch on 238 for three, moments after Steve Smith had benefited from a freakish lapse by Ben Stokes. On 39, Smith propped forward and gloved Moeen Ali high to leg slip, where Stokes plucked the ball from the skies. But on the downswing of his right arm – either an attempt to regain his balance, or the start of a celebration – he brushed his hand against his thigh. The ball fell to earth. The expression on Stokes's face was unequivocal: he knew he had blown it. In desperation, England asked for a review, hoping the umpires might somehow rule he had retained control. Plainly, he had not, though Stokes harangued the officials as the players trooped off, arguing England should not have lost a review. Blackening skies matched his mood.

Up in the commentary box, Nasser Hussain recalled the World Cup match at Headingley in 1999, when South Africa's Herschelle Gibbs put down Australian captain Steve Waugh while celebrating a simple catch. After all the work England had put into their fightback, was this how the series would be remembered – with a Stokes drop at the start, to reprieve Lyon in the last half hour at Edgbaston, and a Stokes drop at the end? Although Waugh never really told Gibbs he had 'just dropped the World Cup', the Twitterati were now preparing all manner of merciless memes for England's captain.

Certainly, when the rain returned just as play was about to restart after lunch, it felt as if England had missed their chance. And when, after the resumption, Smith and Travis Head took Australia to 264 for three, the pendulum – exhausted after spending the previous half-dozen weeks swinging back and forth – was inching in their direction. We should have known better. The next four overs, from Chris Woakes and Moeen Ali, each brought a wicket, as Australia collapsed in sight of the line: Moeen had Head caught at slip, removing him for the third time in the series, and Mitchell Marsh caught behind, the rejuvenated Bairstow athletically anticipating a bat-pad catch to his right; Woakes had both Smith, for 54, and Mitchell Starc, for a duck, caught at second slip by Crawley, who had become England's safest pair of hands. When Pat Cummins, unable to replicate his Edgbaston heroics, was caught by Stokes, making swift ground to his left at short leg after a pull ballooned off the batsman's pads, Australia were 294 for eight. The sun was shining now, and they knew their fate at a venue where it had often been sealed: an 18th defeat, to set against eight wins (including one against India only weeks earlier), was looming.

Alex Carey and Todd Murphy gave it a good go, and Stokes later admitted: 'I'm not going to lie. In the back of my mind when we got them eight down it would have taken...' He paused, seeking an adjective without an expletive... 'an almighty train wreck if we didn't win the game.' But for once the demands of the narrative were not disappointed by reality.

Two days earlier, Stuart Broad had announced he would be retiring at the end of the game, bringing down the curtain on a career that had started nearly 16 years earlier on possibly the world's flattest pitch, Colombo's SSC, but had since reaped more than 600 wickets in all manner of conditions. Next morning, he received a guard of honour from the Australians as he resumed his innings. Here was his chance to wrap things up with one more Ashes vignette for the memoirs. In Australia's first innings, he had cheekily switched the bails at the striker's end the ball before Marnus Labuschagne was brilliantly caught at first slip by Joe Root off Mark Wood. Now, having been told by Stokes he was about to be taken off, he repeated the trick at the other end. With Australia 329 for eight, he charged in to bowl to Murphy, thinking it might be his last ball as a Test cricketer.

Repeatedly in the previous few overs, Broad had passed the bat of the two left-handers, angling the ball in from round the wicket, then swinging or seaming it away. Finally, in the nick of time, Murphy edged an away-swinger to Bairstow, sending The Oval into raptures, and persuading Stokes not to bring on Wood after all. Soon, Carey fell the same way: Broad wheeled away in the South London sunshine as the crowd rose in unison. 'I thought it was another play and miss, because Broady carries on like he's nicked everyone off,' said Stokes. 'But seeing him run off, and the slips go up and celebrate, was one of those moments. It was just always going to happen when we got to that stage of the game.'

In the stands, a box full of Broads and other friends and family jumped around just as heartily. Having earlier hit the final ball he faced in Test cricket for six, their man had signed off with a wicket with the last ball he had bowled. Graham Gooch had once asked Ian Botham: 'Who writes your scripts?' Whoever it was had evidently been redeployed. England had won by 49 runs and squared the series, dramatically and deservedly, prolonging Australia's long wait for an away Ashes win: by the time they return in 2027, it will have been 26 years, longer than England have ever had to suffer between victories in Australia. 'Once we got a couple we really began to believe,' said Broad. 'The crowd was so loud, we jumped on the back of it.'

As had been the case four years earlier, Australia were invited to celebrate their retention of the urn moments after failing to win the series. Almost the whole of July had passed without them winning a Test, but Edgbaston and Lord's had given them a buffer for which they were grateful.

'I think 2–2 was fair,' said Cummins. 'It's been a wonderful series to be part of. Of course we wanted to come over here and win the Ashes. Unfortunately it was not to be, but we can be hugely proud of retaining them.' Since their arrival, Australia had won the World Test Championship final against India, then the first two in the Ashes. They had extended their custody of the urn by at least another two-and-a-half years. And yet the introduction of Cummins by Australia's media manager as the 'Ashes-retaining captain' rang hollow. His team had won none of the last three Tests, and might have lost them all. They had limped towards the line, happy to cross it in lockstep with their opponents.

Stokes was contending with an opposing set of emotions, the pleasure of victory offset by the disappointment of seeing Australia still in possession of the Ashes. A draw, he said generously, was 'a fair reflection. Australia are the world Test champions and a quality team. I don't think many teams would have responded the way we did. I'm standing here pretty content with what we've achieved.' Pushed by an Australian reporter to explain how he felt when he watched Cummins lift the urn, he replied: 'Not a lot. We won the game, so I'm pretty happy.' The swirl of sentiment captured the chaos of the cricket. If spectators seemed tired and emotional, so did the players.

The fourth nailbiter of the series had got off to an unusual start, when Cummins finally won a toss. In overcast conditions, on a pitch tinged with green, he chose to bowl. Murphy came in for Cameron Green, having been curiously omitted at Old Trafford, while England resisted the chance to replace Jimmy Anderson after a subdued series, and named an unchanged team. At 62 without loss in the 12th over, they had responded well to their insertion, aided by sloppiness in the field; at 73 for three, less so. But Carey, diving to his right, dropped Harry Brook off Cummins on 5, and Australia suffered the consequences. The last six overs of the session brought 54, and Brook's fourth-wicket stand with Moeen was worth 111 in just 18 overs when Moeen – hampered by a groin strain – missed a heave at Murphy.

England grew careless. Stokes was bowled by a beauty from Starc, Bairstow via the edge by Hazlewood. When Brook drove Starc to second slip for 85, his best score of the summer, it was 212 for seven. In advance, Brook had agreed with a journalist's suggestion that 2–2 would represent a 'moral victory' for England because of the Manchester rain; 3–1 to Australia would have been a harder square to circle. But Wood hit out for 28, Woakes for a skilful 36: a total of 283 wasn't riches, but it was something to play with.

England took their turn to chip away with the ball. Woakes removed David Warner on the first evening, but on the second morning Usman Khawaja and Labuschagne produced the most anti-Bazball partnership of the series, consuming 26 overs while adding 42. At one point, either side of stumps, England sent down 18 maidens out of 27. Were their bowlers impossible to get away? Or were Australia making an exaggerated point about the virtue of patience? Whatever was going on, the absence of quick singles meant the batsmen got stuck. And after Broad switched the bails, Labuschagne was on his way for 9 off 82 balls, chuntering to the umpires about the gloom, and perhaps inwardly chiding himself for his passivity.

After lunch, Broad became the first England bowler to reach 150 Ashes wickets when he trapped Khawaja in front for 47, and quickly added Head, fiddling to Bairstow. Anderson bowled Marsh, before Root did Carey in the flight. When Wood bounced out Starc, Australia were 185 for seven and in danger of conceding a damaging lead.

Moments after tea England were convinced Smith had been run out for 43. After pushing Woakes towards midwicket, he had turned for a second, only to be surprised by the speed of sub fielder George Ealham, son of former England all-rounder Mark. His pick-up and throw were immaculate but, as Smith dived headlong for safety, and before the ball arrived, Bairstow nudged the off stump with his left glove. After countless slo-mos, and painstaking analysis of which spigot of which bail had left which stump at precisely which moment, TV umpire Nitin Menon concluded that Bairstow's gaffe had cost England their breakthrough. It was such a borderline decision, though, that the opposite verdict would have made equal sense.

Woakes eventually induced a loose shot from Smith on 71, but Murphy hooked Wood for three sixes, and Australia drew level – having taken 98.4 overs to reach a score England had ticked off in 54.4. Cummins was last out for 36 to end the second day, Stokes making a tricky boundary catch look simple, and Australia led by 12. The Ashes were boiling down to a one-innings shootout.

England immediately knocked off the deficit in a Starc over costing 13 – Australia's most expensive at the start of an Ashes innings – and Duckett had reached his second rapid 40 of the match when he edged Starc. With Ali still injured, Stokes walked out at No 3 to a reception that felt like a show of thanks for all he had done in his first year as captain. England's lunchtime score of 130 for one in 25 overs was another statement of intent. Crawley soon fell for 73 off 76 balls, Stokes for 42, Brook for 7. But Root and Bairstow, emitting the same furious energy that had fuelled him in Manchester, reasserted control with a century stand. As at Old Trafford, Root was denied a hundred by a grubber, this time from Murphy, before Starc removed Bairstow for 78, then picked up a couple more as England faltered. But their lead, once Anderson fell next morning, was not far off 400. Only once had Australia chased down more to win a Test – at Headingley in 1948, when Don Bradman's Invincibles made light work of a target of 404. At the end of their sixth Test in seven-and-a-half weeks, a new entry in the record books was asking a lot.

Even so, the rest of a truncated fourth day belonged to the Australians, with Warner and Khawaja comfortably knocking 135 off the balance. Shortly before rain ended play in mid-afternoon, the umpires changed the ball, which had become misshapen by a blow to Khawaja's helmet. And when Australia resumed the final day needing another 249, its replacement began to deviate. Woakes removed Warner – for the fourth innings in a row – and Khawaja, while Wood took care of Labuschagne: 140 without loss had become 169 for three. And it was true that the replacement ball looked rather newer than its 36-overs-old predecessor. The story would run for several days back in Australia, even if Smith and Head added 95 either side of Stokes's lapse at leg slip.

Then came the final twist, as a fit-again Ali and Woakes – two of the series' gentlest souls – obliterated Australia's middle order. After bringing on Broad at the Pavilion End on the last afternoon, with Australia suddenly eight down, Stokes told Woakes: 'You're a massive reason we're in this position right now.' Later, Stokes captured Woakes's modesty after a series in which he had picked up 19 wickets at 18 in three Tests, and the Compton–Miller Medal, awarded to the Player of the Series: 'He wasn't having a bar of it. He just said: "Let's finish the job and get it done." He's been awesome for us – just a quality cricketer.'

Ali, meanwhile, had re-retired, slipping away with none of Broad's fanfare, but with his captain's gratitude. 'Mo got picked for what he could do on his best days,' said Stokes, 'and today was his best day in the Ashes. What a day to produce that.'

What a day. And what a series.

ENGLAND v AUSTRALIA (5th Test)

At The Oval, London, on 27, 28, 29, 30, 31 July 2023.
Toss: Australia. Result: **ENGLAND** won by 49 runs.
Debuts: None.

ENGLAND

Z.Crawley	c Smith b Cummins	22		c Smith b Cummins	73
B.M.Duckett	c Carey b Marsh	41		c Carey b Starc	42
M.M.Ali	b Murphy	34	(7)	c Hazlewood b Starc	29
J.E.Root	b Hazlewood	5		b Murphy	91
H.C.Brook	c Smith b Starc	85		c Carey b Hazlewood	7
* B.A.Stokes	b Starc	3	(3)	c Cummins b Murphy	42
† J.M.Bairstow	b Hazlewood	4	(6)	c Carey b Starc	78
C.R.Woakes	c Head b Starc	36		c Khawaja b Starc	1
M.A.Wood	b Murphy	28		c Marsh b Murphy	9
S.C.J.Broad	c Head b Starc	7		not out	8
J.M.Anderson	not out	0		lbw b Murphy	8
Extras	(B 9, LB 7, NB 2)	18		(LB 4, NB 3)	7
Total	**(54.4 overs)**	**283**		**(81.5 overs)**	**395**

AUSTRALIA

U.T.Khawaja	lbw b Broad	47	(2)	lbw b Woakes	72
D.A.Warner	c Crawley b Woakes	24	(1)	c Bairstow b Woakes	60
M.Labuschagne	c Root b Wood	9		c Crawley b Wood	13
S.P.D.Smith	c Bairstow b Woakes	71		c Crawley b Woakes	54
T.M.Head	c Bairstow b Broad	4		c Root b Ali	43
M.R.Marsh	b Anderson	16		c Bairstow b Ali	6
† A.T.Carey	c Stokes b Root	10		c Bairstow b Broad	28
M.A.Starc	c Duckett b Wood	7		c Crawley b Woakes	0
* P.J.Cummins	c Stokes b Root	36		c Stokes b Ali	9
T.R.Murphy	lbw b Woakes	34		c Bairstow b Broad	18
J.R.Hazlewood	not out	6		not out	4
Extras	(B 17, LB 12, NB 1, W 1)	31		(B 10, LB 10, NB 2, W 5)	27
Total	**(103.1 overs)**	**295**		**(94.4 overs)**	**334**

AUSTRALIA	O	M	R	W	O	M	R	W
Starc	14.4	1	82	4	20	2	100	4
Hazlewood	13	0	54	2	15	0	67	1
Cummins	13	2	66	1	16	0	79	1
Marsh	8	0	43	1	8	0	35	0
Murphy	6	0	22	2	22.5	0	110	4

ENGLAND	O	M	R	W	O	M	R	W
Broad	20	5	49	2	20.4	4	62	2
Anderson	26	9	67	1	14	4	53	0
Wood	22	4	62	2 (6)	9	0	34	1
Woakes	25	8	61	3 (3)	19	4	50	4
Root	7.1	1	20	2	9	0	39	0
Brook	3	1	7	0				
Ali				(4)	23	2	76	3

FALL OF WICKETS

Wkt	E 1st	A 1st	E 2nd	A 2nd
1st	62	49	79	140
2nd	66	91	140	141
3rd	73	115	213	169
4th	184	127	222	264
5th	193	151	332	274
6th	208	170	360	274
7th	212	185	364	275
8th	261	239	375	294
9th	270	288	379	329
10th	283	295	395	334

Umpires: H.D.P.K.Dharmasena (*Sri Lanka*) and J.S.Wilson (*West Indies*).
Referee: R.S.Madugalle (*Sri Lanka*).　　　　　　Player of the Match: C.R.Woakes.
Close of Play – Day 1: A(1) 61-1; Day 2: A(1) 295; Day 3: E(2) 389-9; Day 4: A(2) 135-0.

13

No going back

The Oval was almost empty. As the cleaners descended on the stands to clear up half-eaten bags of crisps and pour away glasses of Pimm's, television crews and journalists gathered around Stuart Broad. He was explaining why this Test – his 167th – would be his last. It had not been an easy decision. Bazball had been such fun, and his unexpected Indian summer had left him wistful; it would be a wrench to leave it all behind. Broad might have declared the 2021–22 Ashes 'void', but he was not cancelling this one. 'The last 14 months have been out of this world,' he said. He wished he was ten years younger.

Back in the early summer of 2022, when Brendon McCullum declared that one of his main goals as England coach would be to reinvigorate Test cricket, it made for a good soundbite. But many feared it lacked substance. How could a team that had just lost in the West Indies become trailblazers? Subsequent events, culminating in an unforgettable drawn Ashes series, felt like vindication. Stay off the front page, McCullum had warned his team. Now, both front and back were full of their deeds, in the most-watched series of the social-media age.

Next morning, even BBC Radio 4's *Today* programme, that most august of news shows, was talking Bazball. In the *i* newspaper, under the headline 'How Bazball Can Change Your Life', Simon Kelner reckoned it could be adapted for business and politics. The *Times of India* asked if Bazball could work in their country. A piece in the *Sydney Morning Herald* trumpeted: 'A salute to Bazball: it works, damn it.' Australia's ABC News ran a feature asking how it would change world cricket. Doubters remained, naturally: many, especially outside England, had invested too much hope in Bazball's failure to change tack. But it was increasingly hard to argue that Test cricket's landscape hadn't been fundamentally altered.

'The history of Test-match batting has been ripped up by the Bazballers,' says the former Ashes-winning captain Michael Vaughan, sitting in the JM Finn Stand at The Oval in the final moments of England's second innings. 'They say: "We are here to save Test cricket." And I think they are well on their way to doing that, if other teams buy into it.'

McCullum had recognised the untapped talent washing around English cricket, with its 18 first-class counties, centres of excellence and Sky money. It just needed a new direction: to harness the players' white-ball skills in the Test arena, and give them the freedom to fail by constantly having their backs. He also sensed it would not be long before Test teams were packed with players who had been born in the Twenty20 era. Harry Brook had not long turned four when T20 first hit county grounds in June 2003. Zak Crawley was five, so too Ollie Pope. 'We just don't have players these days who are born to play forward defensives and leaves,' says Vaughan. 'Their natural way is this way, and when you combine that with the management saying "failing is fine", then it can succeed.'

By running the world's best Test team so close, England proved they were on to something. McCullum had won 13 out of 18 Tests with largely the same team who had won one out of 17 under Chris Silverwood. They had lost two close Ashes Tests, having dictated terms in the first, before becoming the first side to prevent Australia turning a 2–0 lead into a series win. And they had got inside Australian heads. Several days after England had levelled it at 2–2, Nathan Lyon – the off-spinner whose series was ruined by a calf injury – was still playing down the transformative effects of their cricket. 'I think there's a lot of smoke and mirrors with Bazball,' he said. 'I know everyone keeps talking about Bazball, but to be honest I didn't really see Bazball throughout my two Tests against them.'

In fairness to Lyon, it had been a long series, and its opening day – when he picked up four wickets but went at 5.13 an over – seemed an age ago. Twenty-four hours earlier, Ben Stokes had vowed to entertain: except on the rain-ruined last two days in Manchester, no one who bought a ticket for any of the five Tests could grumble they did not get value for money, especially when England were batting.

If Test cricket is to be saved, players of all nationalities will have to be bolder, and coaches and boards more willing to accept failure. In most countries, the game too easily accepts empty stadiums. But why shouldn't the cricketers have a go at filling them up again? After the Second World War, following the end of the often turgid timeless Tests, the sport became about not losing first, winning second. In the 1960s, as the western world underwent social change, the Ashes went the other way: 15 of the 25 Tests that decade were drawn, with England scoring at 2.40 an over, Australia 2.45. Even when Andrew Strauss's team won Down Under in 2010–11, they scored at only 3.50. And until 2023, when England sped along at 4.74, their fastest-scoring Ashes had been 2005, at 3.87. Stokes's England, then, scored at almost a run an over faster than in the series which, until now, had been considered the acme of abandon. Smoke and mirrors indeed.

McCullum and Stokes had joined forces at the right time. They are well off compared with their predecessors, bringing a level of security when taking risky decisions. Their cricketing legacies, too, were already assured: even without Bazball, Stokes would have been remembered as one of England's greats, McCullum as one of New Zealand's. Because their England jobs will not define their careers, they have a latitude not granted to previous incumbents.

Where they proved their strength of character, however, was in not blinking when they went 2–0 down in the Ashes. They knew they were on to something, having seen Australia sit back and adapt to their tactics, not vice versa, which was the usual pecking order. As McCullum stood on the Lord's outfield after the second Test, the adrenaline still at work following the stumping of Jonny Bairstow and Stokes's six-filled retaliation, he insisted England could win the series. And, as it wore on, the teams moved further apart. England were still racing along, scoring 283 at 5.17 in the first innings at The Oval, but Australia's 295 in reply came at 2.85 – their second-slowest innings of the series.

England's relaxed approach was summed up by McCullum's posture for most of the fifth Test – almost horizontal on a reclining chair at the front of the dressing-room, feet on the metal handrail, eyes hidden behind shades. If the coach tells the players they should not fear failure, it's best he gives off the same vibes.

'We took Test cricket so seriously,' says Mike Atherton, reflecting on his own 115-Test career in the Sky studio overlooking The Oval, with England creaming it around in the second innings down below. 'If you lost, it was almost like the end. You got so depressed after a bad day or a bad defeat. You look back and you think: *why?* Why did we take it so seriously? Why were we so affected by it? I remember clearly when I made my Test debut, our coach Micky Stewart said to me that 230 for three was an average day of Test cricket. Well, 230 runs in a day for three down now would be scorned, I think.'

Scorned in England, yes, and the Australians reacted badly when one fan called them 'boring' as they walked up the steps to the Oval dressing-room. Would it be scorned in the rest of the world? Not necessarily. Attitudes will be slow to change, partly because of an anti-English bias that has deep and complicated roots in colonialism, partly because not many captains have the vision of Stokes, or his freedom to fail. So is Bazball a new philosophy for Test cricket, or the final twitch of a terminally ill patient? 'I think there is no going back for England,' says Atherton. 'They will always play like this under Stokes, but I also think his legacy will live on here. Other countries will play according to the talent available to them. If you don't have the players to do it, it will be foolhardy to try.'

In an interview with *Wisden Cricket Monthly* soon after the Ashes, the former Sri Lanka captain Kumar Sangakkara argued that 'even though the urn was retained by Australia and the series drawn, England came out on top by far. They played much more attractive cricket, more attacking cricket and, barring the weather they would have taken the Ashes back.' He added: 'I wish that I had played my cricket in the Test arena with the freedom that this team exhibits.' This from a player who scored 12,400 Test runs at an average of 57.

Former Australian players, too, were starting to give Bazball credit. 'I think it has been awesome for the game,' said Mike

Hussey. 'I was intrigued to see if England would have the courage to play that way, because it's not easy to smack high-quality bowlers out of the park on pitches doing a bit. But they did.'

Brad Hogg felt Australia would need to 'change the way they play' if they were to hold on to the urn in 2025–26, while Ricky Ponting told Tasmanian radio show SEN Tassie: 'There was a lot of talk about Bazball and how England would approach it, and would that style stand up against the quality of the Australian attack. Looking back, it probably did. It probably had some of the Australian players, coaches and the captain at different times scratching their head as to how they were going to combat it. I think even the Australian boys might be sitting back and looking at the way they played, [and asking] what can we do a little bit better to combat that in the future? I think a lot of other countries around the world might be looking at it as well and saying if we want to compete with Australia maybe this is the way we have to go.'

The Pakistan–New Zealand series that followed England's 3–0 win in Pakistan in December 2022 had clearly been influenced by Bazball. Babar Azam, Pakistan's captain, set New Zealand 138 in 15 overs, which was taking it to the extreme. In the second Test, Tim Southee, who was heavily influenced by McCullum, responded with a declaration setting 319 in a day and a bit. The carrot was dangled, almost perfectly: Pakistan finished on 304 for nine.

But while England and Australia were playing to packed houses, India and West Indies completed a turgid two-Test series at deserted grounds in the Caribbean. West Indies never batted faster than 2.57 an over, and India were not much quicker, with Rohit Sharma and Virat Kohli – two of the world's great white-ball players – chugging along in the first Test at strike-rates of 46 and 41. India are a very good team, and will say 'we are doing fine, thank you,' but they have lost two World Test Championship finals in a row. Something is missing.

Ravichandran Ashwin, their world-class off-spinner and most thoughtful cricketer, doubts there is enough acceptance of failure in the subcontinent – though Ramiz Raja, the former chief executive of the Pakistan Cricket Board, believed his country wasn't ready for Bazball either, and was proved wrong. Ashwin said on his YouTube channel: 'We are playing Test cricket very well. But we will go through a transition soon. And things won't be easy during that phase. There will be a few issues here and there. But let's assume India adopts Bazball during this phase. Let us assume a player throws his bat at everything, like Harry Brook, and gets out and we lose two Test matches. What will we do? Will we back Bazball and the players? We will drop at least four players from our playing XI. That's how our culture has always been. We can't copy others' style of play just because it worked for them. It works for them because their management is fully in with this style of play, their selectors back the players to play this way. In fact, even their crowd and Test-match-watching public are backing the team in this process. But we can't do this.'

With England due to tour India for five Tests in early 2024, the inevitable question will be asked: can Bazball succeed there? Stokes rolled his eyes when it was put to him in his post-Ashes press conference at The Oval, and simply pointed out that a similar question had been asked of him before almost every series in the previous year. 'Time will tell,' he added. He might also have pointed out that taking the game to India in their home conditions had to be worth a try. Since Alastair Cook's team triumphed 2–1 in 2012–13 – the last time India failed to win a home series – England had lost seven of their nine Tests there, all thumpings.

But while India may be resistant to change, West Indies are surely ripe for it. Some of their white-ball talent, such as Nicholas Pooran and Shimron Hetmyer, would have nothing to lose – except the occasional franchise contract – by applying their gifts to the Test arena. It may even coax more supporters into the stands. But that needs the management to be fully on board, and Kraigg Brathwaite, the West Indies captain, is a blocker who would not be out of place in the 1950s. South Africa, too, are losing their way in Test cricket, with their board pouring resources into a new Twenty20 League. But since their batting was so badly exposed in England and Australia in 2022, why not pick their latest T20 star, Tristan Stubbs, in the Test side, and see how he gets on? The fight to save Test cricket requires more than just one team remembering that their primary role is to entertain.

The South Africans sneered at Bazball a year ago, but lost 2–1. Pakistan had their fingers burned at home, but subsequently played a more expansive game. Shan Masood, who also captained Yorkshire in 2023, admitted they had learned from England, and a batting camp in Lahore before a series against Sri Lanka focused on aggression. One rule of thumb was that batsmen should not play out more than two dot balls in a row: during practice sessions, this would cost them their wicket. Sure enough, in the second Test in Colombo, Pakistan applied their new approach, and amassed 576 for five at 4.29 an over, the fastest they had scored in an innings of longer than 30 overs since 2014.

The Sri Lankans were less sure. Silverwood, who had advocated a more attritional game during his time as England coach, had quickly taken the Sri Lankan job after his sacking, and was asked after the Pakistan series if his team should embrace Bazball. The suggestion must have stuck in the craw.

'We don't want to be anyone else, we want to be Sri Lanka,' he said. 'I don't want to go far away from how we do things. The dressing-room is Sri Lankan, so let's be Sri Lankan.'

No other board is as invested in the longer form as the ECB; they even announced the venues for the 2027 home Ashes before the 2023 series had finished. The Hundred is designed to attract new audiences, but it is the existing fans who flock to Test matches that help provide the income propping up the English game. Around the world, two-Test series are becoming the norm, as boards who lose money staging the longer format turn to Twenty20. Priorities have changed. Before the one-off Test at Lord's last summer, Ireland's high performance director Richard Holdsworth said the game, for his side, was not a 'pinnacle event': World Cup qualification was higher up the Irish agenda. Commercially, his argument made sense; emotionally, it was hard to take.

'We can make Test cricket work if we make it more of an event,' Manoj Badale, part-owner of the Rajasthan Royals IPL franchise, told the BBC's 'Tailenders' podcast. He seemed to be predicting a horrifying future for lovers of Test cricket. 'We should have it at the same time every year, played between a small set of nations that can actually afford it, and Lord's becomes like Wimbledon, an event that is in the diary. The amount of times I hear arguments like "Ben Stokes wants to play Test cricket" – that is important, but what is really important is what the fans of the future want to watch, and where are they going to spend their hard-earned money. We are going to have to think creatively about Test cricket if we want it to work.'

Badale is invested in the IPL, so his viewpoint is understandable. But vast, multi-year contracts from franchises who own teams across the globe will soon be tempting even England's well-paid centrally contracted cricketers. 'I've got a little bit of scaredness about what's going to happen in the next five to ten years, where cricket is actually heading,' said Australian opener David Warner before the Ashes. FICA, the global players' union, surveys its members on a regular basis. Its 2021 employment survey discovered that 74 per cent still ranked Test cricket as the most important format, which was down from 82 per cent in 2018. Back in 2007, Twenty20 had made up 14 per cent of international fixtures; in 2021, it was 71 per cent, though that includes the Associate nations, who were granted full T20 international status in January 2019. If the rise felt artificially inflated, it also reflected the direction of travel.

England played six Tests in eight weeks in the summer of 2023, a total that will have risen to 43 by 2027. In the Future Tours Programme, the fixture list agreed by the international boards, Australia are second with 40, India third on 38, with those three scheduling five-match series against each other. South Africa (28 Tests), West Indies (26) and Sri Lanka (25) will play less Test cricket than before. In total, 12 of South Africa's 14 series will comprise two matches. The ICC scheduled a global tournament every year, and the money those generate prop up cricket outside the Big Three, who keep the lion's share of ICC income anyway. The Board of Control for Cricket in India will take nearly 40 per cent of the ICC's net earnings between 2024 and 2027 (around $230 million annually) after the latest funding model was waved through with the support of England and Australia.

A more equitable model is needed, but there isn't the appetite or power bloc to take on the Big Three. All boards received an increase from the ICC's latest rights deal, which calmed the situation, and the BCCI argue that, because they bring in the most money, they deserve the greatest percentage. Their team also play a lot of cricket worldwide, boosting their hosts' coffers. Despite that, other Test nations must turn to Twenty20 to survive.

'It's been proved time and time again there's still a place for Test cricket,' Simon Harmer, the South African spinner, told the *i* newspaper early in 2023. 'But then you have a situation where some countries are playing close to 50 Test matches in a four-year cycle and other countries are in the mid-20s. I'll ask you the question: those countries that are only picking up 20 to 25 Tests in a four-year cycle, what is motivating their players to pursue Test match cricket when there is so much T20 cricket and so much money on offer around the world?'

An unintended consequence of so many two-Test series is that embracing risk becomes, well, riskier: lose the first match, and you can't win the series. A safety-first mentality can kick in. In their only two-match series so far, in New Zealand, England's Bazballers attacked regardless, but after the Ashes Australia's coach Andrew McDonald suggested another solution: 'The two-Test-match series should be put on the back burner. It would show the importance of Test cricket to every nation if it was a minimum of three Test matches.'

England are rare in awarding their head coaches long contracts: McCullum's four-year deal meant he had more time to bed in and survive early results had his plans taken longer to succeed. But not all his peers are granted such luxury. England's greater financial muscle also allows them to appoint the best coach, who can concentrate on one format: McCullum would not have been interested in a job that also involved the white-ball teams.

Bazball has offered a liberating challenge to the game's basics. England's run-rate against Australia of 4.74 posed constant problems for Pat Cummins, who had to think about his fields every ball. It is partly why the over-rate, around 12 an hour, was so abysmal (England were just as bad). Australia responded by becoming more entrenched, but the only time England were rattled was when Travis Head or Mitchell Marsh went after them – the two Australians in whom they see something of themselves. Perhaps Bazball will spread naturally: the best way to beat England, at least in their own conditions, is to take them on at their own game. Out-Bazballing the Bazballers would make for blockbuster viewing.

'What Bazball has done is pose the question of what is the riskiest way of batting in Test cricket?' says Vaughan. 'Is it riskier to play the Bazball way, which is aggressive, flamboyant and always looking to put pressure on the bowlers and create theatre? Or is it riskier to bat attritionally, for long periods of time and score at 2.5–2.7 an over but then lose a few wickets?

'Australia's old-school method puts more pressure on their team than England's aggression does on England. Australia might be stubborn and say they retained the urn, but at times ex-Australian players told me they were embarrassed by their team's approach, compared with England's hybrid model. This team will be talked about for years because they entertained, even though they have not won the Ashes. Bucket hats, Mark Wood playing Barbie songs at press conferences… They were the new cool. Kids want to be these players.'

As we wrote this book and spoke to the England players, one theme constantly popped up: they were having fun. Today's players have so many other options. While the Ashes were taking place, the first Major League Cricket Twenty20 competition was playing out in the United States. Jason Roy, once an England Test cricketer, had signed up, forfeiting an ECB incremental contract. Joe Root had played in the IPL for the first time in 2023, having taken part in the first ILT20 competition in the UAE. Brook landed a £1.35 million

IPL deal with Sunrisers Hyderabad, when he was not even centrally contracted by England.

'There are so many options these days that you've got to make Test cricket enjoyable, not just on the field but off it too,' said McCullum, who organised golf trips and hosted the team in New Zealand as he sought to create an environment that players miss when they are not together. 'We want to try to get those guys to know that, when they board the plane to head overseas, or jump into the car to head down to Lord's, it is to join up with a team they know they're going to have a great time with.' For the entire Ashes, the England players drank out of silver tankards given to them by McCullum – a club-cricket gesture in an international set-up.

In early 2023, the 18 county directors of cricket held their annual summit at the Hilton Hotel at St George's Park, Burton upon Trent, the FA's training academy. They were joined for an hour on Zoom by McCullum, who dialled in from New Zealand, and by Stokes, from home. What followed was, essentially, an idiot's guide to Bazball, which they hoped the counties who produce their players would adopt in the four-day championship, in theory easing the transition to Test cricket. The directors of cricket also held in-person meetings with Rob Key and Mo Bobat, the ECB's performance director. They chatted about soaking up pressure, choosing the right moments to attack, losing the fear of chasing – Bazball basics. The hope was the message would be absorbed, and spread around the shires, allowing them to shake off old constraints, and foster adventure.

Some will do it better than others, with Durham leading the way, possibly because Alex Lees, who holds hopes of a recall, is their captain; meanwhile, their new head coach, Ryan Campbell, was an expansive player himself for Western

Australia. He had also survived a serious heart attack while coaching the Netherlands. For Campbell, cricket exists to be enjoyed. 'There are a few teams who have taken it on, but not everywhere,' says Lees. 'Some people are still playing quite traditionally. Others are desperate to play Test cricket, and they are trying to deliver on what Ben and Brendon want, but then there are guys who know they are never going to play for England and are just going about their business.'

England are suspicious of county cricket: the longer a player remains in the system, the less likely he is to be picked by Key and McCullum. It is why they plucked Josh Tongue and Rehan Ahmed out of the county game so early, despite modest championship returns. Crawley, too, remained in the team, even with a first-class average of 30.

Liam Livingstone, who turned down a gig in Australia's Big Bash League to join the Test tour of Pakistan, only to suffer a knee injury at Rawalpindi, agrees far-reaching change will take time. 'It's very difficult for county cricket, because of the way it's run,' he says. 'It's all so negative. It would be great to see it, but I've seen at first hand how people are clinging on for a contract for another year. The mentality's just so different. It was just refreshing to be involved with England. It was exactly the way I wanted to play. It's unfortunate that not everyone can experience it. Sometimes I'm around a county dressing-room, and all you're doing is training and travelling. There's more to life than that.'

As Lees points out, if you are a county player with England ambitions, you have no choice but to try to fit into the Bazball template. For most county cricketers, however, the priority is remaining in gainful employment. Perhaps with more and more making better livings in franchise tournaments overseas than in their own domestic game, it will not be long before that attitude changes. 'The way the game is going,' says Atherton, 'every young player coming in now wants to play multi-format, and two of those formats are white-ball, so you will see players like Harry Brook naturally wanting to play the longer format in this style.'

In 2023, the counties trialled the use of the Australian Kookaburra ball, with its less pronounced seam, for two rounds of the championship: totals rose, and spinners bowled more overs. Atherton again: 'My lad [Middlesex's Josh De Caires] bowled 48 overs of spin at the Ageas Bowl. You would probably not get that chance with a Dukes. County cricket does not necessarily encourage some of the skills that are essential to Test cricket: pace, spin and the ability to manufacture wickets on flat pitches. You can still make the argument that county cricket, if it is only seen as a nursery ground for the Test arena, still has a lot of work to do.'

McCullum created a club atmosphere in the England dressing-room. Free thinking was encouraged, and top-down management abandoned, at least when dealing with the players, if not with all the non-playing staff. Other sports have taken note. Gareth Southgate, the England football manager, is a big cricket fan and was interviewed by *Test Match Special* at Lord's. 'In the end you are looking at what is going to help you to win,' he said. 'They have an alignment with the captain and coach. They are all on the same page, which in any sport is absolutely crucial.'

Richard Wigglesworth, the England rugby union attack coach, also believes his sport can learn from Bazball, which will please McCullum, who still plays a bit of rugby himself. 'I'm really interested in the environment they look like they've got there, where players can go out and express themselves and be happy,' said Wigglesworth. 'That is certainly something we want to do. We want players to enjoy being part of this England squad. We are really conscious of that. Maybe with this rose on my chest now, I might be able to visit a few places and pick their brains.'

England's hockey team took on board lessons from cricket as they prepared for the 2023 World Cup in India. 'We have gone down the Bazball mentality, really, and it's great our coaches are encouraging that,' England forward Sam Ward told *The Times* in January. 'It's not just the style on the pitch, it's also the philosophy – removing the fear of failure, just like Ben and Brendon have done. We feel the same as Stokes does about cricket: we want to excite people, we want to entertain people. We want them to think England are great to watch.' But Bazball can't achieve miracles: soon after Ward was interviewed, England lost in the quarter-finals after a penalty shoot-out – against Germany.

Steve Wilson, the UK vice-chair of EY, one of the country's largest consultancy firms, believes industry leaders can learn something too. 'The Stokes captaincy will be a leadership case study for the years to come,' he told the *Daily Telegraph*. 'It looks like he has provided clarity about his expectations, is derisking the outcomes from the team, and giving them the psychological safety to perform at their best.' If they wish, Bazball's high command will one day be able to make a good living from advising businessmen over corporate breakfasts.

At The Oval, as he stood on the outfield at the end of the series, Stokes supped a beer from the inscribed silver pint tankard given to every player who went on the pre-Ashes golf trip to Loch Lomond. A few hours later, a slightly dishevelled Harry Brook, standing in his socks, took delivery of three carrier bags of food from a Deliveroo rider at the Hobbs Gate. The England players held presentations in the changing-rooms to those who were retiring. They went on so long they did not have the traditional post-series drinks with the Aussies, giving some of the more blinkered Australian media one last chance to lash out at the Poms. It was a storm in a beer bottle, but also a small insight into Bazball: England shut out everyone else and enjoyed their own company.

The Oval has been the scene of a few triumphant England Ashes moments this century. Vaughan, Strauss and Cook all hoisted the urn in front of an emotional packed house. But those teams all shared one thing: they ran out of steam. Vaughan's side never played together again. Strauss won in Australia and went to No 1 in the world, before it all came crashing down three years later. Cook's 2013 team were whitewashed by Australia a few months after beating them 3–0. His 2015 team suffered a similar fate, winning at home, then losing the return series 4–0 in 2017–18. Like Stokes and Brook, those England players enjoyed their Oval moments, but none threatened to change the game like Stokes's team, urn or no urn.

As night drew in, and the dressing-room lights beamed across the empty ground, some fundamental questions occurred. Will the Bazballers shine brightly, then fizzle out? Or will they update the oldest format so it can appeal to modern tastes?

One fully paid-up member of the Seen It All Before Club was Broad, the man who stole the headlines that day at The Oval. 'I've learned so much about leadership, about how to go about managing people off those two, and I just feel in a fantastic place, as a player, as a person,' he said. 'Seeing what Baz and Ben have done for the mindset of a team – I'll love cricket for ever for that.' A career in the Sky commentary box awaits. Audiences around the world may be hearing about Bazball for a while yet.

England Test teams rarely enjoy prolonged success, and this one – full of 30-somethings – will need refreshing before the 2025–26 Ashes in Australia. There are countless reports gathering dust in filing cabinets at the ECB offices, commissioned in the wake of another Ashes beating. There are still problems with the county system, and they will take years to address. But by appointing an outsider in McCullum and a captain with a taste for adventure in Stokes, England found two visionary leaders who dared to be different, shaking English cricket out of its conservatism and caution. Together, in barely a year, they have changed it. It has been a phenomenal achievement.

McCullum never says 'Bazball', of course, and rarely gives interviews, but when he sat down with the ECB in-house video crew before the Ashes, he reminded everyone of his ideology. 'Take wickets. We need 20 to win a Test match. With the bat absorb pressure, identify when the time has come to put pressure back on the opposition, be brave enough to pull the trigger. In the field, it is about chasing the ball hard to the boundaries. Three simple philosophies.'

It sounds easy, but Test cricket is devilishly complicated, with multiple ingredients and infinite outcomes. The beauty of Bazball is that it has distilled the sport to its basics. 'For some people, their ledger is runs and wickets, wins and losses,' said McCullum. 'The skipper's and mine is not that. It is heart, soul and commitment. This game has been around for a hundred years. Some people want it to be around for another hundred, but it needs a real shot in the arm.'

From no-hopers to pioneers, the Bazballers' shock treatment has breathed new life into an old game. It has been a true Test cricket revolution.

Scorecards

ENGLAND v NEW ZEALAND (1st Test)

At Lord's London, on 2, 3, 4, 5 June 2022.
Toss: New Zealand. Result: **ENGLAND** won by five wickets.
Debuts: England – M.W.Parkinson, M.J.Potts.

NEW ZEALAND

Batsman	1st innings		2nd innings	
T.W.M.Latham	c Bairstow b Anderson	1	c Foakes b Potts	14
W.A.Young	c Bairstow b Anderson	1	c Foakes b Anderson	1
* K.S.Williamson	c Foakes b Potts	2	c Bairstow b Potts	15
D.P.Conway	c Bairstow b Broad	3	c Foakes b Broad	13
D.J.Mitchell	b Potts	13	c Foakes b Broad	108
† T.A.Blundell	b Potts	14	lbw b Anderson	96
C.de Grandhomme	not out	42	run out	0
K.A.Jamieson	c Potts b Anderson	6	b Broad	0
T.G.Southee	c Potts b Anderson	26	c Root b Parkinson	21
A.Y.Patel	lbw b Potts	7	lbw b Potts	4
T.A.Boult	c Pope b Stokes	14	not out	4
Extras	(LB 3)	3	(B 1, LB 4, NB 3, W 1)	9
Total	**(40 overs)**	**132**	**(91.3 overs)**	**285**

ENGLAND

Batsman	1st innings		2nd innings	
A.Z.Lees	lbw b Southee	25	b Jamieson	20
Z.Crawley	c Blundell b Jamieson	43	c Southee b Jamieson	9
O.J.D.Pope	c Blundell b Jamieson	7	b Boult	10
J.E.Root	c Southee b de Grandhomme	11	not out	115
J.M.Bairstow	b Boult	1	b Jamieson	16
* B.A.Stokes	c Blundell b Southee	1	c Blundell b Jamieson	54
† B.T.Foakes	c Mitchell b Southee	7	not out	32
M.J.Potts	c Mitchell b Boult	0		
S.C.J.Broad	b Southee	9		
J.M.Anderson	not out	7		
M.W.Parkinson	c Mitchell b Boult	8		
M.J.Leach				
Extras	(B 14, LB 7, NB 1)	22	(B 6, LB 9, NB 2, W 6)	23
Total	**(42.5 overs)**	**141**	**(5 wkts; 78.5 overs)**	**279**

ENGLAND	O	M	R	W		O	M	R	W
Anderson	16	6	66	4		21	7	57	2
Broad	13	0	45	1		26	7	76	3
Potts	9.2	4	13	4		20	3	55	3
Stokes	1.4	0	5	1		8	1	43	0
Parkinson						15.3	0	47	1
Root						1	0	2	0

NEW ZEALAND	O	M	R	W		O	M	R	W
Southee	14	3	55	4		23.5	5	87	0
Boult	13.5	4	21	3		24	3	73	1
De Grandhomme	8	2	24	1	(4)	3.5	1	3	0
Jamieson	7	3	20	2	(3)	25	4	79	4
Mitchell						0.1	0	0	0
Patel						2	0	22	0

FALL OF WICKETS

Wkt	NZ 1st	E 1st	NZ 2nd	E 2nd
1st	1	59	5	31
2nd	2	75	30	32
3rd	7	92	35	46
4th	12	96	56	69
5th	27	98	251	159
6th	36	100	251	-
7th	45	100	251	-
8th	86	125	265	-
9th	102	130	281	-
10th	132	141	285	-

Umpires: M.A.Gough (*England*) and R.J.Tucker (*Australia*).
Referee: Sir R.B.Richardson (*West Indies*). Player of the Match: J.E.Root.
Close of Play – Day 1: E(1) 116-7; Day 2: NZ(2) 236-4; Day 3: E(2) 216-5.
M.W.Parkinson replaced M.J.Leach after 23 overs NZ(1) (concussion).

ENGLAND v NEW ZEALAND (2nd Test)

At Trent Bridge, Nottingham, on 10, 11, 12, 13, 14 June 2022.
Toss: England. Result: **ENGLAND** won by five wickets.
Debut: New Zealand – M.G.Bracewell.

NEW ZEALAND

* T.W.M.Latham	c Potts b Anderson	26		b Anderson		4
W.A.Young	c Crawley b Stokes	47		run out		56
D.P.Conway	c Foakes b Anderson	46		c Bairstow b Leach		52
H.M.Nicholls	c Foakes b Stokes	30		c Lees b Potts		3
D.J.Mitchell	c Foakes b Potts	190		not out		62
† T.A.Blundell	c Stokes b Leach	106		c Stokes b Broad		24
M.G.Bracewell	c Root b Anderson	49		c Broad b Potts		25
K.A.Jamieson	c Foakes b Broad	14	(10)	c Foakes b Broad		1
T.G.Southee	c Root b Broad	4	(8)	run out		0
M.J.Henry	c Crawley b Leach	0	(9)	c Foakes b Broad		18
T.A.Boult	not out	16		c Stokes b Anderson		17
Extras	(B 1, LB 16, NB 8)	25		(B 9, LB 5, NB 6, W 2)		22
Total	**(145.3 overs)**	**553**		**(84.4 overs)**		**284**

ENGLAND

A.Z.Lees	c Mitchell b Henry	67	c Blundell b Southee		44
Z.Crawley	c Blundell b Boult	4	c Southee b Boult		0
O.J.D.Pope	c Henry b Boult	145	c Blundell b Henry		18
J.E.Root	c Southee b Boult	176	c and b Boult		3
J.M.Bairstow	c Blundell b Boult	8	c Blundell b Boult		136
* B.A.Stokes	c Boult b Bracewell	46	not out		75
† B.T.Foakes	run out	56	not out		12
S.C.J.Broad	c Mitchell b Bracewell	9			
M.J.Potts	b Boult	3			
M.J.Leach	not out	0			
J.M.Anderson	st Blundell b Bracewell	9			
Extras	(B 12, LB 3, W 1)	16	(B 5, LB 6)		11
Total	**(128.2 overs)**	**539**	**(5 wkts; 50 overs)**		**299**

ENGLAND	O	M	R	W		O	M	R	W
Anderson	27	9	62	3		8.4	1	20	2
Broad	26	4	107	2		20	4	70	3
Potts	30.3	6	126	1		15	6	32	2
Stokes	23	2	85	2	(5)	17	3	62	0
Leach	35	6	140	2	(4)	24	5	86	1
Root	4	0	16	0					

NEW ZEALAND	O	M	R	W		O	M	R	W
Southee	32	1	154	0		11	0	67	1
Boult	33.3	8	106	5		16	1	94	3
Henry	27	5	128	1		15	3	67	1
Jamieson	16.3	3	66	0					
Bracewell	17.2	2	62	3	(4)	8	0	60	0
Mitchell	2	0	8	0					

FALL OF WICKETS

Wkt	NZ 1st	E 1st	NZ 2nd	E 2nd
1st	84	6	4	12
2nd	84	147	104	53
3rd	161	334	115	56
4th	169	344	131	93
5th	405	405	176	272
6th	496	516	204	-
7th	513	527	213	-
8th	517	527	245	-
9th	520	530	249	-
10th	553	539	284	-

Umpires: M.A.Gough (*England*) and P.R.Reiffel (*Australia*).
Referee: Sir R.B.Richardson (*West Indies*).   Player of the Match: J.M.Bairstow.
Close of Play – Day 1: NZ(1) 318-4; Day 2: E(1) 90-1; Day 3: E(1) 473-5; Day 4: NZ(2) 224-7.

ENGLAND v NEW ZEALAND (3rd Test)

At Headingley, Leeds, on 23, 24, 25, 26, 27 June 2022.
Toss: New Zealand. Result: **ENGLAND** won by seven wickets.
Debut: England – J.Overton.

NEW ZEALAND

T.W.M.Latham	c Root b Broad	0	c Bairstow b Overton	76
W.A.Young	lbw b Leach	20	c Pope b Potts	8
* K.S.Williamson	c Foakes b Broad	31	c Bairstow b Potts	48
D.P.Conway	b Overton	26	c Pope b Root	11
H.M.Nicholls	c Lees b Leach	19	c and b Leach	7
D.J.Mitchell	c Stokes b Leach	109	lbw b Potts	56
† T.A.Blundell	lbw b Potts	55	not out	88
M.G.Bracewell	c Crawley b Broad	13	c Crawley b Leach	9
T.G.Southee	c Stokes b Leach	33	b Leach	2
N.Wagner	c Bairstow b Leach	4	c Billings b Leach	0
T.A.Boult	not out	0	b Leach	4
Extras	(B 4, LB 14, NB 1)	19	(B 9, LB 2, NB 2, W 4)	17
Total	**(117.3 overs)**	**329**	**(105.2 overs)**	**326**

ENGLAND

A.Z.Lees	b Boult	4	run out	9
Z.Crawley	b Boult	6	c Williamson b Bracewell	25
O.J.D.Pope	b Boult	5	b Southee	82
J.E.Root	c Blundell b Southee	5	not out	86
J.M.Bairstow	c Boult b Bracewell	162	not out	71
* B.A.Stokes	c Williamson b Wagner	18		
† B.T.Foakes	lbw b Wagner	0		
J.Overton	c Mitchell b Boult	97		
S.C.J.Broad	b Southee	42		
M.J.Potts	not out	1		
M.J.Leach	lbw b Southee	8		
S.W.Billings				
Extras	(LB 11, W 1)	12	(B 9, LB 12, NB 2)	23
Total	**(67 overs)**	**360**	**(3 wkts; 54.2 overs)**	**296**

ENGLAND	O	M	R	W		O	M	R	W
Broad	23	8	62	3		24	7	63	0
Potts	26	11	34	1	(3)	25	5	66	3
Overton	23	2	85	1	(4)	14	2	61	1
Leach	38.3	8	100	5	(2)	32.2	12	66	5
Root	7	0	30	0	(6)	6	0	29	1
Stokes					(5)	4	0	30	0
NEW ZEALAND									
Boult	22	4	104	4		12	2	65	0
Southee	23	2	100	3		19	5	68	1
Wagner	12	1	75	2	(4)	8	2	33	0
Bracewell	7	0	54	1	(3)	15.2	0	109	1
Mitchell	3	0	16	0					

FALL OF WICKETS

	NZ	E	NZ	E
Wkt	*1st*	*1st*	*2nd*	*2nd*
1st	0	4	28	17
2nd	35	14	125	51
3rd	62	17	152	185
4th	83	21	153	-
5th	123	55	161	-
6th	243	55	274	-
7th	265	296	291	-
8th	325	351	305	-
9th	329	351	305	-
10th	329	360	326	-

Umpires: M.Erasmus (*South Africa*) and R.A.Kettleborough (*England*).
Referee: D.C.Boon (*Australia*).   Player of the Match: M.J.Leach.
Close of Play – Day 1: NZ(1) 225-5; Day 2: E(1) 264-6; Day 3: NZ(2) 168-5; Day 4: E(2) 183-2.
S.W.Billings replaced B.T.Foakes at the start of Day Four (Covid replacement).

ENGLAND v INDIA (5th Test)

At Edgbaston, Birmingham, on 1, 2, 3, 4, 5 July 2022.
Toss: England. Result: **ENGLAND** won by seven wickets.
Debuts: None.

INDIA

S.Gill	c Crawley b Anderson	17	c Crawley b Anderson		4
C.A.Pujara	c Crawley b Anderson	13	c Lees b Broad		66
G.H.Vihari	lbw b Potts	20	c Bairstow b Broad		11
V.Kohli	b Potts	11	c Root b Stokes		20
† R.R.Pant	c Crawley b Root	146	c Root b Leach		57
S.S.Iyer	c Billings b Anderson	15	c Anderson b Potts		19
R.A.Jadeja	b Anderson	104	b Stokes		23
S.N.Thakur	c Billings b Stokes	1	c Crawley b Potts		4
Mohammed Shami	c Leach b Broad	16	c Lees b Stokes		13
* J.J.Bumrah	not out	31	c Crawley b Stokes		7
M.Siraj	c Broad b Anderson	2	not out		2
Extras	(B 4, LB 17, NB 14, W 5)	40	(B 6, LB 7, NB 3, W 3)		19
Total	**(84.5 overs)**	**416**	**(81.5 overs)**		**245**

ENGLAND

A.Z.Lees	b Bumrah	6	run out	56
Z.Crawley	c Gill b Bumrah	9	b Bumrah	46
O.J.D.Pope	c Iyer b Bumrah	10	c Pant b Bumrah	0
J.E.Root	c Pant b Siraj	31	not out	142
J.M.Bairstow	c Kohli b Shami	106	not out	114
M.J.Leach	c Pant b Shami	0		
* B.A.Stokes	c Bumrah b Thakur	25		
† S.W.Billings	b Siraj	36		
S.C.J.Broad	c Pant b Siraj	1		
M.J.Potts	c Iyer b Siraj	19		
J.M.Anderson	not out	6		
Extras	(B 16, LB 5, NB 13, W 1)	35	(B 8, LB 7, NB 2, W 3)	20
Total	**(61.3 overs)**	**284**	**(3 wkts; 76.4 overs)**	**378**

ENGLAND	O	M	R	W	O	M	R	W
Anderson	21.5	4	60	5	19	5	46	1
Broad	18	3	89	1	16	1	58	2
Potts	20	1	105	2	17	3	50	2
Leach	9	0	71	0	12	1	28	1
Stokes	13	0	47	1	11.5	0	33	4
Root	3	0	23	1	6	1	17	0

INDIA	O	M	R	W	O	M	R	W
Bumrah	19	3	68	3	17	1	74	2
Mohammed Shami	22	4	78	2	15	2	64	0
Siraj	11.3	2	66	4	(4) 15	0	98	0
Thakur	7	0	48	1	(5) 11	0	65	0
Jadeja	2	0	3	0	(3) 18.4	3	62	0

FALL OF WICKETS

	I	E	I	E
Wkt	1st	1st	2nd	2nd
1st	27	16	4	107
2nd	46	27	43	107
3rd	64	44	75	109
4th	71	78	153	-
5th	98	83	190	-
6th	320	149	198	-
7th	323	241	207	-
8th	371	248	230	-
9th	375	267	236	-
10th	416	284	245	-

Umpires: Aleem Dar (*Pakistan*) and R.A.Kettleborough (*England*).
Referee: D.C.Boon (*Australia*).   Player of the Match: J.M.Bairstow.
Close of Play – Day 1: I(1) 338-7; Day 2: E(1) 84-5; Day 3: I(2) 125-3; Day 4: E(2) 259-3.
This Test concluded the interrupted 2021 series.

ENGLAND v SOUTH AFRICA (1st Test)

At Lord's, London, on 17, 18, 19 August 2022.
Toss: South Africa. Result: **SOUTH AFRICA** won by an innings and 12 runs.
Debuts: None.

ENGLAND

A.Z.Lees	c Verreynne b Rabada	5	c Verreynne b Nortje	35
Z.Crawley	c Markram b Rabada	9	lbw b Maharaj	13
O.J.D.Pope	b Rabada	73	lbw b Maharaj	5
J.E.Root	lbw b Jansen	8	c Markram b Ngidi	6
J.M.Bairstow	b Nortje	0	c Verreynne b Nortje	18
* B.A.Stokes	c Petersen b Nortje	20	c Maharaj b Rabada	20
† B.T.Foakes	b Nortje	6	c Verreynne b Nortje	0
S.C.J.Broad	c Elgar b Rabada	15	c Elgar b Rabada	35
M.J.Potts	not out	6	b Jansen	1
M.J.Leach	b Jansen	15	not out	0
J.M.Anderson	lbw b Rabada	0	b Jansen	1
Extras	(B 1, LB 7)	8	(B 5, LB 7, NB 3)	15
Total	**(45 overs)**	**165**	**(37.4 overs)**	**149**

SOUTH AFRICA

* D.Elgar	b Anderson	47
S.J.Erwee	c Foakes b Stokes	73
K.D.Petersen	c Bairstow b Potts	24
A.K.Markram	c Foakes b Leach	16
H.E.van der Dussen	lbw b Stokes	19
M.Jansen	c Crawley b Broad	48
† K.Verreynne	c Foakes b Broad	11
K.A.Maharaj	c Potts b Stokes	41
K.Rabada	c Broad b Potts	3
A.A.Nortje	not out	28
L.T.Ngidi	c Bairstow b Broad	0
Extras	(B 1, LB 11, NB 3, W 1)	16
Total	**(89.1 overs)**	**326**

SOUTH AFRICA	O	M	R	W		O	M	R	W
Rabada	19	3	52	5		8	2	27	2
Ngidi	5	1	12	0		7	2	15	1
Jansen	8	1	30	2	(5)	3.4	0	13	2
Nortje	13	2	63	3		7	1	47	3
Maharaj					(3)	12	0	35	2

ENGLAND	O	M	R	W
Anderson	18	3	51	1
Broad	19.1	3	71	3
Potts	20	2	79	2
Stokes	18	3	71	3
Leach	14	3	42	1

FALL OF WICKETS

Wkt	E 1st	SA 1st	E 2nd
1st	6	85	20
2nd	25	138	38
3rd	42	160	57
4th	55	187	81
5th	100	192	86
6th	116	210	86
7th	134	282	141
8th	145	289	146
9th	164	318	146
10th	165	326	149

Umpires: R.K.Illingworth (*England*) and N.N.Menon (*India*).
Referee: R.S.Madugalle (*Sri Lanka*).   Player of the Match: K.Rabada.
Close of Play – Day 1: E(1) 116-6; Day 2: SA(1) 289-7.

ENGLAND v SOUTH AFRICA (2nd Test)

At Old Trafford, Manchester, on 25, 26, 27 August 2022.
Toss: South Africa. Result: **ENGLAND** won by an innings and 85 runs.
Debuts: None.

SOUTH AFRICA

* D.Elgar	c Bairstow b Broad	12	(2)	b Anderson		11
S.J.Erwee	c Foakes b Anderson	3	(1)	c Foakes b Robinson		25
K.D.Petersen	c Root b Broad	21		c Foakes b Stokes		42
A.K.Markram	c Foakes b Stokes	14		c Crawley b Broad		6
H.E.van der Dussen	lbw b Stokes	16		c Foakes b Stokes		41
† K.Verreynne	c Foakes b Broad	21		not out		17
S.R.Harmer	lbw b Anderson	2		b Anderson		16
K.A.Maharaj	lbw b Anderson	0		c Pope b Robinson		2
K.Rabada	c Root b Leach	36		c Root b Anderson		2
A.A.Nortje	lbw b Robinson	10		c Foakes b Robinson		0
L.T.Ngidi	not out	4		b Robinson		0
Extras	(B 2, LB 4, NB 6)	12		(B 8, LB 2, NB 7)		17
Total	**(53.2 overs)**	**151**		**(85.1 overs)**		**179**

ENGLAND

A.Z.Lees	c Verreynne b Ngidi	4
Z.Crawley	c Verreynne b Nortje	38
O.J.D.Pope	b Nortje	23
J.E.Root	c Erwee b Rabada	9
J.M.Bairstow	c Erwee b Nortje	49
* B.A.Stokes	c Elgar b Rabada	103
† B.T.Foakes	not out	113
S.C.J.Broad	st Verreynne b Harmer	21
O.E.Robinson	c Markram b Maharaj	17
M.J.Leach	b Maharaj	11
J.M.Anderson		
Extras	(B 5, LB 6, NB 6, W 10)	27
Total	**(9 wkts dec; 106.4 overs)**	**415**

ENGLAND	O	M	R	W	O	M	R	W
Anderson	15	4	32	3	15	4	30	3
Robinson	14	0	48	1	15.1	3	43	4
Broad	11	1	37	3	(5) 13	5	24	1
Stokes	7	0	17	2	(6) 14	3	30	2
Leach	6.2	1	11	1	(3) 23	13	26	0
Root					(4) 5	2	16	0

SOUTH AFRICA	O	M	R	W
Rabada	23	2	110	2
Ngidi	18	3	61	1
Nortje	20	1	82	3
Maharaj	22.4	4	78	2
Harmer	23	4	73	1

FALL OF WICKETS

Wkt	SA 1st	E 1st	SA 2nd
1st	3	5	33
2nd	35	34	39
3rd	41	43	54
4th	68	134	141
5th	76	147	151
6th	92	320	172
7th	92	361	175
8th	108	395	178
9th	143	415	179
10th	151	-	179

Umpires: C.B.Gaffaney (*New Zealand*) and R.K.Illingworth (*England*).
Referee: R.S.Madugalle (*Sri Lanka*).　　　　Player of the Match: B.A.Stokes.
Close of Play – Day 1: E(1) 111-3; Day 2: SA(2) 23-0.

ENGLAND v SOUTH AFRICA (3rd Test)

At The Oval, London, on 8 (*no play*), 9 (*no play*), 10, 11, 12 September 2022.
Toss: England. Result: **ENGLAND** won by nine wickets.
Debut: England – H.C.Brook.

SOUTH AFRICA

* D.Elgar	b Robinson	1	(2)	lbw b Broad		36
S.J.Erwee	c Foakes b Anderson	0	(1)	c Root b Stokes		26
K.D.Petersen	b Robinson	12		c Pope b Anderson		23
R.D.Rickelton	c Foakes b Broad	11		lbw b Broad		8
K.Zondo	c Lees b Broad	23		lbw b Robinson		16
† K.Verreynne	c Foakes b Robinson	0	(7)	c and b Anderson		12
P.W.A.Mulder	c Foakes b Robinson	3	(6)	b Robinson		14
M.Jansen	c Root b Robinson	30		b Stokes		4
K.A.Maharaj	b Broad	18	(10)	b Broad		18
K.Rabada	not out	7	(9)	c Brook b Stokes		0
A.A.Nortje	c Stokes b Broad	7		not out		0
Extras	(LB 2, NB 4)	6		(B 4, LB 4, NB 4)		12
Total	**(36.2 overs)**	**118**		**(56.2 overs)**		**169**

ENGLAND

A.Z.Lees	b Jansen	13	lbw b Rabada		39
Z.Crawley	lbw b Jansen	5	not out		69
O.J.D.Pope	c Verreynne b Rabada	67	not out		11
J.E.Root	c Petersen b Jansen	23			
H.C.Brook	c Rabada b Jansen	12			
* B.A.Stokes	c Erwee b Nortje	6			
† B.T.Foakes	c Petersen b Jansen	14			
S.C.J.Broad	c Verreynne b Rabada	6			
O.E.Robinson	c Elgar b Rabada	3			
M.J.Leach	b Rabada	0			
J.M.Anderson	not out	0			
Extras	(B 1, LB 1, NB 7)	9	(LB 6, NB 5)		11
Total	**(36.2 overs)**	**158**	**(1 wkt; 22.3 overs)**		**130**

ENGLAND	O	M	R	W		O	M	R	W		FALL OF WICKETS			
											SA	E	SA	E
Anderson	8	2	16	1		15.2	4	37	2	*Wkt*	*1st*	*1st*	*2nd*	*2nd*
Robinson	14	3	49	5		15	5	40	2	1st	2	17	58	108
Broad	12.2	1	41	4		13	2	45	3	2nd	7	43	83	–
Leach	2	1	10	0						3rd	21	84	91	–
Stokes					(4)	13	2	39	3	4th	31	107	95	–
										5th	32	129	120	–
SOUTH AFRICA										6th	36	133	133	–
Rabada	13	1	81	4		11	1	57	1	7th	72	151	146	–
Jansen	12.2	2	35	5		7.3	0	40	0	8th	99	155	146	–
Mulder	2	0	11	0						9th	110	158	169	–
Nortje	9	0	29	1	(3)	4	0	27	0	10th	118	158	169	–

Umpires: R.A.Kettleborough (*England*) and N.N.Menon (*India*).
Referee: R.S.Madugalle (*Sri Lanka*).   Player of the Match: O.E.Robinson.
Close of Play – Day 1: No play (rain); Day 2: No play following the death of HM The Queen; Day 3: E(1) 154-7; Day 4: E(2) 97-0.

PAKISTAN v ENGLAND (1st Test)

At Rawalpindi Cricket Stadium, on 1, 2, 3, 4, 5 December 2022.
Toss: England. Result: **ENGLAND** won by 74 runs.
Debuts: Pakistan – Haris Rauf, Mohammad Ali, Saud Shakeel, Zahid Mahmood; England – W.G.Jacks, L.S.Livingstone.

ENGLAND

Z.Crawley	b Rauf	122		c Rizwan b Mohammad Ali	50
B.M.Duckett	lbw b Mahmood	107		c Salman b Shah	0
† O.J.D.Pope	lbw b Mohammad Ali	108		c Shah b Mohammad Ali	15
J.E.Root	lbw b Mahmood	23		c Imam b Mahmood	73
H.C.Brook	c Shakeel b Shah	153		b Shah	87
* B.A.Stokes	b Shah	41		c Shakeel b Mahmood	0
L.S.Livingstone	c Shakeel b Shah	9	(8)	not out	7
W.G.Jacks	c Shah b Mohammad Ali	30	(7)	c Imam b Salman	24
O.E.Robinson	lbw b Mahmood	37			
M.J.Leach	not out	6			
J.M.Anderson	c Imam b Mahmood	6			
Extras	(B 2, LB 10, NB 2, W 1)	15		(LB 3, NB 5)	8
Total	**(101 overs)**	**657**		**(7 wkts dec; 35.5 overs)**	**264**

PAKISTAN

Abdullah Shafique	c Pope b Jacks	114		c Brook b Robinson	6
Imam-ul-Haq	c Robinson b Leach	121		c Pope b Anderson	48
Azhar Ali	lbw b Leach	27		c Root b Robinson	40
* Babar Azam	c Leach b Jacks	136		c Pope b Stokes	4
Saud Shakeel	c Pope b Robinson	37		c sub (K.K.Jennings) b Robinson	76
† Mohammad Rizwan	c Stokes b Anderson	29		c Pope b Anderson	46
Agha Salman	c Crawley b Jacks	53		lbw b Robinson	30
Naseem Shah	c Leach b Jacks	15		lbw b Leach	6
Zahid Mahmood	st Pope b Jacks	17		c Pope b Anderson	1
Haris Rauf	c Root b Jacks	12		lbw b Anderson	0
Mohammad Ali	not out	0		not out	0
Extras	(B 15, NB 3)	18		(LB 3, NB 8)	11
Total	**(155.3 overs)**	**579**		**(96.3 overs)**	**268**

PAKISTAN	O	M	R	W	O	M	R	W
Naseem Shah	24	0	140	3	9.5	0	66	2
Mohammad Ali	24	1	124	2	10	0	64	2
Haris Rauf	13	1	78	1				
Zahid Mahmood	33	1	235	4	(3) 11	1	84	2
Agha Salman	5	0	38	0	(4) 5	0	47	1
Saud Shakeel	2	0	30	0				
ENGLAND								
Anderson	22	4	52	1	(3) 24	12	36	4
Robinson	21	2	72	1	(1) 22	6	50	4
Leach	49	7	190	2	(4) 18.3	6	56	1
Jacks	40.3	5	161	6	(5) 6	0	38	0
Root	16	3	54	0	(6) 6	0	16	0
Stokes	7	0	35	0	(2) 20	4	69	1

FALL OF WICKETS

Wkt	E 1st	P 1st	E 2nd	P 2nd
1st	233	225	1	20
2nd	235	245	36	25
3rd	286	290	96	89
4th	462	413	192	176
5th	515	473	192	198
6th	539	475	248	259
7th	576	497	264	260
8th	641	554	-	264
9th	649	576	-	264
10th	657	579	-	268

Umpires: Ahsan Raza (*Pakistan*) and J.S.Wilson (*West Indies*).
Referee: A.J.Pycroft (*Zimbabwe*). Player of the Match: O.E.Robinson.
Close of Play – Day 1: E(1) 506-4; Day 2: P(1) 181-0; Day 3: P(1) 499-7; Day 4: P(2) 80-2.
Azhar Ali retired hurt at 20-1 P(2) and resumed at 176-4.

PAKISTAN v ENGLAND (2nd Test)

At Multan Cricket Stadium, on 9, 10, 11, 12 December 2022.
Toss: England. Result: **ENGLAND** won by 26 runs.
Debut: Pakistan – Abrar Ahmed.

ENGLAND

Z.Crawley	b Ahmed	19		run out	3
B.M.Duckett	lbw b Ahmed	63		b Ahmed	79
† O.J.D.Pope	c Shafique b Ahmed	60	(6)	run out	4
J.E.Root	lbw b Ahmed	8		c Shafique b Ahmed	21
H.C.Brook	c Nawaz b Ahmed	9		c Shakeel b Mahmood	108
* B.A.Stokes	b Ahmed	30	(7)	c Mohammad Ali b Nawaz	41
W.G.Jacks	lbw b Ahmed	31	(3)	b Ahmed	4
O.E.Robinson	c Nawaz b Mahmood	5		b Ahmed	3
M.A.Wood	not out	36		c Azam b Mahmood	6
M.J.Leach	b Mahmood	0		not out	0
J.M.Anderson	b Mahmood	7		lbw b Mahmood	4
Extras	(B 1, LB 12)	13		(NB 2)	2
Total	**(51.4 overs)**	**281**		**(64.5 overs)**	**275**

PAKISTAN

Abdullah Shafique	c Pope b Leach	14		b Wood	45
Imam-ul-Haq	c Pope b Anderson	0	(5)	c Root b Leach	60
* Babar Azam	b Robinson	75		b Robinson	1
Saud Shakeel	c Anderson b Leach	63		c Pope b Wood	94
† Mohammad Rizwan	b Leach	10	(2)	b Anderson	30
Agha Salman	c Stokes b Root	4	(8)	not out	20
Mohammad Nawaz	c Robinson b Leach	1		c Pope b Wood	45
Faheem Ashraf	c Duckett b Wood	22	(6)	c Crawley b Root	10
Mohammad Ali	c Crawley b Root	0	(11)	c Pope b Robinson	0
Zahid Mahmood	lbw b Wood	0		b Wood	0
Abrar Ahmed	not out	7	(9)	c Duckett b Anderson	17
Extras	(B 4, LB 1, NB 1)	6		(LB 3, NB 3)	6
Total	**(62.5 overs)**	**202**		**(102.1 overs)**	**328**

PAKISTAN	O	M	R	W		O	M	R	W
Faheem Ashraf	4	1	16	0	(2)	5	2	12	0
Mohammad Ali	6	1	29	0	(1)	9	0	44	0
Abrar Ahmed	22	1	114	7		29	3	120	4
Zahid Mahmood	7.4	0	63	3	(5)	10.5	1	52	3
Mohammad Nawaz	12	0	46	0	(4)	10	0	42	1
Agha Salman						1	0	5	0
ENGLAND									
Anderson	5	0	16	1	(5)	16	1	44	2
Leach	27	7	98	4		26	0	113	1
Wood	11.5	1	40	2	(4)	21	2	65	4
Root	10	3	23	2	(3)	21	3	65	1
Jacks	4	0	18	0	(6)	4	0	15	0
Robinson	5	3	2	1	(1)	14.1	3	23	2

FALL OF WICKETS

Wkt	E 1st	P 1st	E 2nd	P 2nd
1st	38	5	11	66
2nd	117	25	25	67
3rd	145	142	79	83
4th	164	158	147	191
5th	167	165	155	210
6th	228	169	256	290
7th	231	169	259	291
8th	245	169	270	310
9th	245	179	271	319
10th	281	202	275	328

Umpires: Aleem Dar (*Pakistan*) and M.Erasmus (*South Africa*).
Referee: A.J.Pycroft (*Zimbabwe*).　　　　Player of the Match: H.C.Brook.
Close of Play – Day 1: P(1) 107-2; Day 2: E(2) 202-5; Day 3: P(2) 198-4.

PAKISTAN v ENGLAND (3rd Test)

At National Stadium, Karachi, on 17, 18, 19, 20 December 2022.
Toss: Pakistan. Result: **ENGLAND** won by eight wickets.
Debuts: Pakistan – Mohammad Wasim; England – R.Ahmed.

PAKISTAN

Abdullah Shafique	lbw b Leach	8	lbw b Leach		26
Shan Masood	c Leach b Wood	30	b Leach		24
Azhar Ali	c Foakes b Robinson	45	b Leach		0
* Babar Azam	run out	78	c Pope b Ahmed		54
Saud Shakeel	c Pope b Ahmed	23	c Leach b Ahmed		53
† Mohammad Rizwan	c Stokes b Root	19	c Foakes b Ahmed		7
Agha Salman	st Foakes b Leach	56	c Brook b Ahmed		21
Faheem Ashraf	lbw b Ahmed	4	c Foakes b Root		1
Nauman Ali	c Stokes b Leach	20	lbw b Wood		15
Mohammad Wasim	not out	8	c Robinson b Ahmed		2
Abrar Ahmed	b Leach	4	not out		1
Extras	(B 2, LB 2, NB 4, W 1)	9	(B 4, LB 3, NB 5)		12
Total	**(79 overs)**	**304**	**(74.5 overs)**		**216**

ENGLAND

Z.Crawley	lbw b Ahmed	0	lbw b Ahmed		41
B.M.Duckett	lbw b Nauman	26	not out		82
O.J.D.Pope	b Ahmed	51			
J.E.Root	c Salman b Nauman	0			
H.C.Brook	lbw b Wasim	111			
* B.A.Stokes	run out	26	(4) not out		35
† B.T.Foakes	c Shafique b Nauman	64			
R.Ahmed	c Shakeel b Nauman	1	(3) b Ahmed		10
M.A.Wood	c Shafique b Ahmed	35			
O.E.Robinson	b Ahmed	29			
M.J.Leach	not out	9			
Extras	(NB 1, W 1)	2	(LB 1, NB 1)		2
Total	**(81.4 overs)**	**354**	**(2 wkts; 28.1 overs)**		**170**

ENGLAND	O	M	R	W		O	M	R	W
Robinson	8	1	31	1	(5)	7	1	13	0
Leach	31	2	140	4	(1)	26	6	72	3
Wood	15	2	33	1	(4)	12	3	25	1
Ahmed	22	2	89	2	(3)	14.5	1	48	5
Root	3	0	7	1	(2)	7	1	31	1
Stokes						8	3	20	0

PAKISTAN	O	M	R	W	O	M	R	W
Abrar Ahmed	34.4	5	150	4	12	0	78	2
Nauman Ali	30	1	126	4	5	0	38	0
Mohammad Wasim	15	1	71	1	9.1	1	40	0
Faheem Ashraf	1	0	2	0	2	0	13	0
Agha Salman	1	0	5	0				

FALL OF WICKETS

Wkt	P 1st	E 1st	P 2nd	E 2nd
1st	18	0	53	87
2nd	46	58	53	97
3rd	117	58	54	–
4th	162	98	164	–
5th	196	145	176	–
6th	219	262	177	–
7th	237	265	178	–
8th	285	316	208	–
9th	300	324	211	–
10th	304	354	216	–

Umpires: Ahsan Raza (*Pakistan*) and J.S.Wilson (*West Indies*).
Referee: A.J.Pycroft (*Zimbabwe*). Player of the Match: H.C.Brook.
Close of Play – Day 1: E(1) 7-1; Day 2: P(2) 21-0; Day 3: E(2) 112-2.

NEW ZEALAND v ENGLAND (1st Test)

At Bay Oval, Mount Maunganui, on 16, 17, 18, 19 February 2023 (day/night).
Toss: New Zealand. Result: **ENGLAND** won by 267 runs.
Debuts: New Zealand – S.C.Kuggeleijn, B.M.Tickner.

ENGLAND

Z.Crawley	c Bracewell b Southee	4		c Blundell b Kuggeleijn	28
B.M.Duckett	c Bracewell b Tickner	84		c Latham b Tickner	25
O.J.D.Pope	c Latham b Southee	42		c Blundell b Wagner	49
J.E.Root	c Mitchell b Wagner	14	(5)	c Mitchell b Bracewell	57
H.C.Brook	b Wagner	89	(6)	c Mitchell b Tickner	54
* B.A.Stokes	c Latham b Kuggeleijn	19	(8)	st Blundell b Bracewell	31
† B.T.Foakes	c Williamson b Wagner	38		c Blundell b Tickner	51
S.C.J.Broad	c Conway b Kuggeleijn	2	(4)	c Nicholls b Wagner	7
O.E.Robinson	not out	15		c Nicholls b Kuggeleijn	39
M.J.Leach	c Latham b Wagner	1		st Blundell b Bracewell	12
J.M.Anderson				not out	6
Extras	(LB 7, NB 6, W 4)	17		(B 5, LB 6, NB 2, W 2)	15
Total	**(9 wkts dec; 58.2 overs)**	**325**		**(73.5 overs)**	**374**

NEW ZEALAND

T.W.M.Latham	c Pope b Robinson	1		b Broad	15
D.P.Conway	c Pope b Stokes	77		b Broad	2
K.S.Williamson	lbw b Anderson	6		b Broad	0
H.M.Nicholls	c Crawley b Anderson	4		c Foakes b Robinson	7
N.Wagner	c Robinson b Broad	27	(10)	c Foakes b Anderson	9
D.J.Mitchell	lbw b Robinson	0	(5)	not out	57
† T.A.Blundell	c and b Anderson	138	(6)	b Broad	1
M.G.Bracewell	c Stokes b Leach	7	(7)	c Brook b Leach	25
S.C.Kuggeleijn	b Robinson	20	(8)	lbw b Anderson	2
* T.G.Southee	c Duckett b Robinson	10	(9)	c Root b Anderson	0
B.M.Tickner	not out	3		b Anderson	8
Extras	(B 4, LB 3, NB 5, W 1)	13			–
Total	**(82.5 overs)**	**306**		**(45.3 overs)**	**126**

NEW ZEALAND	O	M	R	W	O	M	R	W
Southee	13	1	71	2	15	2	49	0
Wagner	16.2	0	82	4	13	0	110	2
Tickner	13	0	72	1	12	0	55	3
Kuggeleijn	13	0	80	2	14	1	81	2
Bracewell	3	0	13	0	19.5	2	68	3
ENGLAND								
Anderson	16.5	5	36	3	10.3	3	18	4
Broad	17	2	72	1	15	5	49	4
Robinson	19	2	54	4	8	0	34	1
Leach	18	3	84	1	11	4	25	1
Root	5	2	15	0	1	1	0	0
Stokes	7	0	38	1				

FALL OF WICKETS

	E	NZ	E	NZ
Wkt	*1st*	*1st*	*2nd*	*2nd*
1st	18	10	52	14
2nd	117	23	68	14
3rd	152	31	82	19
4th	154	82	144	27
5th	209	83	225	28
6th	298	158	237	68
7th	305	182	293	71
8th	319	235	335	71
9th	325	247	358	91
10th	–	306	374	126

Umpires: Aleem Dar (*Pakistan*) and C.B.Gaffaney (*New Zealand*).
Referee: D.C.Boon (*Australia*).   Player of the Match: H.C.Brook.
Close of Play – Day 1: NZ(1) 37-3; Day 2: E(2) 79-2; Day 3: NZ(2) 63-5.

NEW ZEALAND v ENGLAND (2nd Test)

At Basin Reserve, Wellington, on 24, 25, 26, 27, 28 February 2023.
Toss: New Zealand. Result: **NEW ZEALAND** won by 1 run.
Debuts: None.

‡ (S.C.Kuggeleijn)

ENGLAND

Z.Crawley	c Blundell b Henry	2		b Southee	24
B.M.Duckett	c Bracewell b Southee	9		c Blundell b Henry	33
O.J.D.Pope	c Bracewell b Henry	10	(4)	c Latham b Wagner	14
J.E.Root	not out	153	(5)	c Bracewell b Wagner	95
H.C.Brook	c and b Henry	186	(6)	run out	0
* B.A.Stokes	c sub‡ b Wagner	27	(7)	c Latham b Wagner	33
† B.T.Foakes	st Blundell b Bracewell	0	(8)	c Wagner b Southee	35
S.C.J.Broad	lbw b Bracewell	14	(9)	c Wagner b Henry	11
O.E.Robinson	c Southee b Henry	18	(3)	c Bracewell b Southee	2
M.J.Leach	not out	6		not out	1
J.M.Anderson				c Blundell b Wagner	4
Extras	(LB 8, W 2)	10		(LB 1, NB 1, W 2)	4
Total	**(8 wkts dec; 87.1 overs)**	**435**		**(74.2 overs)**	**256**

NEW ZEALAND

T.W.M.Latham	c Root b Leach	35	lbw b Root	83
D.P.Conway	c Foakes b Anderson	0	c Pope b Leach	61
K.S.Williamson	c Foakes b Anderson	4	c Foakes b Brook	132
W.A.Young	c Foakes b Anderson	2	b Leach	8
H.M.Nicholls	c Pope b Leach	30	c Brook b Robinson	29
D.J.Mitchell	c Pope b Leach	13	c Root b Broad	54
† T.A.Blundell	c Leach b Broad	38	c Root b Leach	90
M.G.Bracewell	c and b Broad	6	run out	8
* T.G.Southee	c Crawley b Broad	73	c sub (M.J.Potts) b Leach	2
M.J.Henry	c Anderson b Broad	6	c Root b Leach	0
N.Wagner	not out	0	not out	0
Extras	(NB 2)	2	(B 1, LB 5, NB 8, W 2)	16
Total	**(53.2 overs)**	**209**	**(162.3 overs)**	**483**

NEW ZEALAND	O	M	R	W		O	M	R	W
Southee	24	5	93	1		20.1	5	45	3
Henry	22.1	3	100	4		21.5	3	75	2
Mitchell	9	1	61	0					
Wagner	21	1	119	1		15.2	0	62	4
Bracewell	11	0	54	2	(3)	17	2	73	0
ENGLAND									
Anderson	10	1	37	3		27	7	77	0
Broad	14.2	2	61	4	(3)	24	3	79	1
Robinson	12	4	31	0	(2)	28	6	84	1
Leach	17	1	80	3		61.3	12	157	5
Root						12	0	39	1
Stokes						2	0	16	0
Brook						8	0	25	1

FALL OF WICKETS

	E	NZ	NZ	E
Wkt	*1st*	*1st*	*2nd*	*2nd*
1st	5	1	149	39
2nd	21	7	155	53
3rd	21	21	167	59
4th	323	60	222	80
5th	362	77	297	80
6th	363	96	455	202
7th	389	103	478	202
8th	424	201	482	215
9th	-	208	482	251
10th	-	209	483	256

Umpires: C.B.Gaffaney (*New Zealand*) and R.J.Tucker (*Australia*).
Referee: D.C.Boon (*Australia*).   Player of the Match: K.S.Williamson.
Close of Play – Day 1: E(1) 315-3; Day 2: NZ(1) 138-7; Day 3: NZ(2) 202-3; Day 4: E(2) 48-1.

ENGLAND v IRELAND (Only Test)

At Lord's, London, on 1, 2, 3, June 2023.
Toss: England. Result: **ENGLAND** won by ten wickets.
Debuts: England – J.C.Tongue; Ireland – F.P.Hand.

IRELAND

J.A.McCollum	c Root b Broad	36	(2)	retired hurt	12
P.J.Moor	lbw b Broad	10	(1)	lbw b Tongue	11
* A.Balbirnie	c Crawley b Broad	0		c Bairstow b Tongue	2
H.T.Tector	c Potts b Broad	0		c Brook b Tongue	51
P.R.Stirling	c Bairstow b Leach	30		c Bairstow b Tongue	15
† L.J.Tucker	lbw b Leach	18		b Leach	44
C.Campher	b Leach	33		c Stokes b Root	19
A.R.McBrine	c Bairstow b Potts	19		not out	86
M.R.Adair	b Broad	14		c Bairstow b Potts	88
F.P.Hand	c Bairstow b Potts	1		c Crawley b Tongue	7
G.I.Hume	not out	0		b Broad	14
Extras	(B 1, LB 9, NB 1)	11		(LB 8, NB 5)	13
Total	**(56.2 overs)**	**172**		**(86.2 overs)**	**362**

ENGLAND

Z.Crawley	c and b Hand	56	not out	12
B.M.Duckett	b Hume	182	not out	0
O.J.D.Pope	st Tucker b McBrine	205		
J.E.Root	b McBrine	56		
H.C.Brook	not out	9		
* B.A.Stokes				
† J.M.Bairstow				
S.C.J.Broad				
M.J.Potts				
J.C.Tongue				
M.J.Leach				
Extras	(B 7, LB 5, NB 1, W 3)	16		–
Total	**(4 wkts dec; 82.4 overs)**	**524**	**(0 wkts; 0.4 overs)**	**12**

ENGLAND	O	M	R	W	O	M	R	W
Broad	17	5	51	5	14.2	2	62	1
Potts	12.2	4	36	2	21	3	77	1
Tongue	13	4	40	0	21	2	66	5
Leach	14	2	35	3	20	4	90	1
Root					10	0	59	1

IRELAND	O	M	R	W	O	M	R	W
Adair	20	2	127	0	0.4	0	12	0
Hume	17	0	85	1				
Hand	19	2	113	1				
Campher	13	0	88	0				
McBrine	13.4	0	99	2				

FALL OF WICKETS

Wkt	Ire 1st	E 1st	Ire 2nd	E 2nd
1st	15	109	16	–
2nd	19	361	18	–
3rd	19	507	63	–
4th	64	524	126	–
5th	98	–	162	–
6th	104	–	162	–
7th	142	–	325	–
8th	169	–	340	–
9th	172	–	362	–
10th	172	–	–	–

Umpires: A.T.Holdstock (*South Africa*) and P.Wilson (*Australia*).
Referee: Sir R.B.Richardson (*West Indies*).   Player of the Match: O.J.D.Pope.
Close of Play – Day 1: E(1) 152-1; Day 2: Ire(2) 97-3.
J.A.McCollum retired hurt at 25-2 Ire(2).

Statistics

BAZBALL IN NUMBERS

by Andrew Samson

Bazball denoted in **bold**.

Fastest Test Hundreds for England

Balls	Name	Score	Against	Venue	Match Date
76	G.L.Jessop	104	Australia	The Oval	11-08-1902
77	**J.M.Bairstow**	**136**	**New Zealand**	**Nottingham**	**10-06-2022**
80	**H.C.Brook**	**153**	**Pakistan**	**Rawalpindi**	**01-12-2022**
85	B.A.Stokes	101	New Zealand	Lord's	21-05-2015
86	**Z.Crawley**	**122**	**Pakistan**	**Rawalpindi**	**01-12-2022**
86	I.T.Botham	118	Australia	Manchester	13-08-1981
87	I.T.Botham	149*	Australia	Leeds	16-07-1981
88	K.P.Pietersen	102	West Indies	Port-of-Spain	06-03-2009
90	**O.J.D.Pope**	**108**	**Pakistan**	**Rawalpindi**	**01-12-2022**
93	**Z.Crawley**	**189**	**Australia**	**Manchester**	**19-07-2023**
95	G.A.Gooch	123	India	Lord's	26-07-1990
95	**J.M.Bairstow**	**162**	**New Zealand**	**Leeds**	**23-06-2022**
99	I.T.Botham	103	New Zealand	Nottingham	25-08-1983

All hundreds in fewer than 100 balls are listed.

Fewest Balls to Reach 1000 Test Runs

Balls	Name	Team	M	Inns	NO	Date Achieved
1058	**H.C.Brook**	**England**	**10**	**17**	**1**	**06-07-2023**
1140	C.de Grandhomme	New Zealand	20	30	4	12-12-2019
1167	T.G.Southee	New Zealand	37	61	6	26-11-2014
1168	**B.M.Duckett**	**England**	**12**	**23**	**2**	**28-06-2023**
1200*	Kapil Dev	India	25	34	3	29-01-1980
1265	G.P.Swann	England	45	53	7	19-07-2012
1310*	M.W.Tate	England	33	44	3	01-01-1931
1330	A.C.Gilchrist	Australia	18	26	4	05-07-2001
1331	Sarfraz Ahmed	Pakistan	16	28	7	17-06-2015
1341	Shahid Afridi	Pakistan	18	32	1	26-05-2005

*Details of balls faced are not completely available.

Runs Rates per Test

Against	Venue	Match Date	Result	England				Opponent				Diff
				Runs	*Wkts*	*Overs*	*RPO*	*Runs*	*Wkts*	*Overs*	*RPO*	
New Zealand	Lord's	02-06-2022	Won	420	15	121.4	3.45	417	20	131.3	3.17	0.28
New Zealand	Nottingham	10-06-2022	Won	838	15	178.2	4.69	837	20	230.1	3.63	1.06
New Zealand	Leeds	23-06-2022	Won	656	13	121.2	5.40	655	20	222.5	2.93	2.47
India	Birmingham	01-07-2022	Won	662	13	138.1	4.79	661	20	166.4	3.96	0.83
South Africa	Lord's	17-08-2022	Lost	314	20	82.4	3.79	326	10	89.1	3.65	0.14
South Africa	Manchester	25-08-2022	Won	415	9	106.4	3.89	330	20	138.3	2.38	1.51
South Africa	The Oval	08-09-2022	Won	288	11	58.5	4.89	287	20	92.4	3.09	1.80
Pakistan	Rawalpindi	01-12-2022	Won	921	17	136.5	6.73	847	20	252	3.36	3.37
Pakistan	Multan	09-12-2022	Won	556	20	116.3	4.77	530	20	165	3.21	1.56
Pakistan	Karachi	17-12-2022	Won	524	12	109.5	4.77	520	20	153.5	3.38	1.39
New Zealand	Mount Maunganui	16-02-2023	Won	699	19	132.1	5.28	432	20	128.2	3.36	1.92
New Zealand	Wellington	24-02-2023	Lost	691	18	161.3	4.27	692	20	215.5	3.20	1.07
Ireland	Lord's	01-06-2023	Won	536	4	83.2	6.43	534	19	142.4	3.74	2.69
Australia	Birmingham	16-06-2023	Lost	666	18	144.2	4.61	668	18	208.4	3.20	1.41
Australia	Lord's	28-06-2023	Lost	652	20	157.5	4.13	695	20	202.3	3.43	0.70
Australia	Leeds	06-07-2023	Won	491	17	102.3	4.79	487	20	127.5	3.80	0.99
Australia	Manchester	19-07-2023	Drawn	592	10	107.4	5.49	531	15	161.2	3.29	2.20
Australia	The Oval	27-07-2023	Won	678	20	136.3	4.96	629	20	197.5	3.17	1.79
Totals				10599	271	2196.4	4.83	10078	342	3027.2	3.33	1.50

England have scored faster than their opponents in all 18 Bazball Tests

Test Series Wins in Pakistan by Touring Teams

Team	Season	M	Won	Lost	Drawn
West Indies	1980–81	4	1	0	3
Sri Lanka	1995–96	3	2	1	0
South Africa	1997–98	3	1	0	2
Australia	1998–99	3	1	0	2
Sri Lanka	1999–00	3	2	1	0
England	2000–01	3	1	0	2
India	2003–04	3	2	1	0
Australia	2021–22	3	1	0	2
England	**2022–23**	**3**	**3**	**0**	**0**

Minimum 3 matches

Teams Winning or Drawing a Test Series After Losing the First Two Matches

Team	Against	Venue	Season	M	Won	Lost	Drawn
South Africa	England	South Africa	1927–28	5	2	2	1
Australia	England	Australia	1936–37	5	3	2	0
England	West Indies	West Indies	1953–54	5	2	2	1
South Africa	England	South Africa	1956–57	5	2	2	1
England	**Australia**	**England**	**2023**	**5**	**2**	**2**	**1**

Fastest Test Innings Over 300

RPO	Total	Overs	Team	Against	Venue	Match Date
6.80	340-3	50	South Africa	Zimbabwe	Cape Town	04-03-2005
6.50	**657**	**101**	**England**	**Pakistan**	**Rawalpindi**	**01-12-2022**
6.33	**524-4**	**82.4**	**England**	**Ireland**	**Lord's**	**01-06-2023**
5.73	447-3	78	England	Bangladesh	Chester-le-Street	03-06-2005
5.63	370	65.4	New Zealand	Australia	Christchurch	20-02-2016
5.57	**325-9**	**58.2**	**England**	**New Zealand**	**Mount Maunganui**	**16-02-2023**
5.49	**592**	**107.4**	**England**	**Australia**	**Manchester**	**19-07-2023**
5.37	**360**	**67**	**England**	**New Zealand**	**Leeds**	**23-06-2022**
5.36	555-5	103.3	Sri Lanka	Bangladesh	Colombo-SSC	06-09-2001
5.32	301-3	56.3	West Indies	India	Mohali	10-12-1994

Fastest Test Innings Over 300 by England

RPO	Total	Overs	Team	Against	Venue	Match Date
6.50	**657**	**101**	**England**	**Pakistan**	**Rawalpindi**	**01-12-2022**
6.33	**524-4**	**82.4**	**England**	**Ireland**	**Lord's**	**01-06-2023**
5.73	447-3	78	England	Bangladesh	Chester-le-Street	03-06-2005
5.57	**325-9**	**58.2**	**England**	**New Zealand**	**Mount Maunganui (1st inns)**	**16-02-2023**
5.49	**592**	**107.4**	**England**	**Australia**	**Manchester**	**19-07-2023**
5.37	**360**	**67**	**England**	**New Zealand**	**Leeds**	**23-06-2022**
5.13	407	79.2	England	Australia	Birmingham	04-08-2005
5.06	**374**	**73.5**	**England**	**New Zealand**	**Mount Maunganui (2nd inns)**	**16-02-2023**
5.03	**393-8**	**78**	**England**	**Australia**	**Birmingham**	**16-06-2023**
4.99	**435-8**	**87.1**	**England**	**New Zealand**	**Wellington**	**24-02-2023**

Fewest Overs to Reach 300 in a Test Innings

Overs	Team	Against	Venue	Match Date
43.4	South Africa	Zimbabwe	Cape Town	04-03-2005
49.2	**England**	**Pakistan**	**Rawalpindi**	**01-12-2022**
50	**England**	**Ireland**	**Lord's**	**01-06-2023**
50.3	West Indies	England	Leeds	22-07-1976
51.5	**England**	**Australia**	**Manchester**	**19-07-2023**
52.5	New Zealand	Pakistan	Sharjah	26-11-2014
53	**England**	**New Zealand**	**Mount Maunganui (2nd inns)**	**16-02-2023**
54	India	Sri Lanka	Mumbai-B	02-12-2009
54.2	**England**	**New Zealand**	**Mount Maunganui (1st inns)**	**16-02-2023**

Highest Winning Fourth Innings Totals
for England

Total	Overs	Against	Venue	Match Date
378-3	**76.4**	**India**	**Birmingham**	**01-07-2022**
362-9	125.4	Australia	Leeds	22-08-2019
332-7	159.5	Australia	Melbourne	29-12-1928
315-4	73.2	Australia	Leeds	16-08-2001
307-6	146.4	New Zealand	Christchurch	14-02-1997
299-5	**50**	**New Zealand**	**Nottingham**	**10-06-2022**
298-4	88.1	Australia	Melbourne	01-03-1895
296-3	**54.2**	**New Zealand**	**Leeds**	**23-06-2022**
294-4	88	New Zealand	Manchester	23-05-2008
284-6	71.3	New Zealand	Nottingham	10-06-2004

England Success Rate Chasing Targets Over 250

Era	Targets	Chased	Success %
1877–1939	39	4	10.25
1946–1959	11	0	0.00
1960–1979	37	0	0.00
1980–1999	33	1	3.03
2000–May 2022	61	6	9.83
Bazball	**7**	**5**	**71.42**
Totals	188	16	8.51

Most Sixes in a Test Career*

Name	Team	6s	Runs	Inns	6/Inns
B.A.Stokes	**England**	**124**	**6117**	**175**	**0.70**
B.B.McCullum	New Zealand	107	6453	176	0.60
A.C.Gilchrist	Australia	100	5570	137	0.72
C.H.Gayle	West Indies	98	7214	182	0.53
J.H.Kallis	South Africa	97	13289	280	0.34
V.Sehwag	India	91	8586	180	0.50
B.C.Lara	West Indies	88	11953	232	0.37
C.L.Cairns	New Zealand	87	3320	104	0.83
I.V.A.Richards	West Indies	85	8540	182	0.46
T.G.Southee	New Zealand	83	1976	134	0.61
A.D.Mathews	Sri Lanka	83	7361	188	0.44

*To 1 October 2023.

Most Sixes in a Test Series for England

Sixes	Matches	Against	Venue	Season
43	**5**	**Australia**	**England**	**2023**
36	5	Australia	England	2005
31	4	South Africa	South Africa	2019–20
30	**3**	**New Zealand**	**England**	**2022**
29	5	South Africa	South Africa	2004–05
27	3	Sri Lanka	Sri Lanka	2018–19
25	**3**	**Pakistan**	**Pakistan**	**2022–23**
25	5	Australia	Australia	2013–14
24	4	South Africa	South Africa	2015–16
24	5	Australia	England	2019
21	**2**	**New Zealand**	**New Zealand**	**2022–23**

Most Declarations of a First Innings in Under 110 Overs

Captain	Team	Tests	Declarations	Drawn
B.A.Stokes	**England**	**19**	**5**	**0**
S.P.Fleming	New Zealand	80	5	2
P.B.H.May	England	41	3	2
A.Ranatunga	Sri Lanka	56	3	3
G.C.Smith	South Africa	109	3	0
Intikhab Alam	Pakistan	17	2	2
W.R.Hammond	England	20	2	2
L.Hutton	England	23	2	1
M.J.Clarke	Australia	47	2	0
J.E.Root	England	64	2	1
V.Kohli	India	68	2	1
A.R.Border	Australia	93	2	1

'Drawn' is included as many of these declarations were in rain-affected matches.

Test Captaincy Record

Captain	Team	From	To	Played	Won	Lost	Tied	Drawn	%Won
S.R.Waugh	Australia	05-03-1999	02-01-2004	57	41	9	0	7	71.92
B.A.Stokes	**England**	**08-07-2020**	**27-07-2023**	**19**	**13**	**5**	**0**	**1**	**68.42**
D.G.Bradman	Australia	04-12-1936	14-08-1948	24	15	3	0	6	62.50
R.T.Ponting	Australia	08-03-2004	26-12-2010	77	48	16	0	13	62.33
D.R.Jardine	England	27-06-1931	10-02-1934	15	9	1	0	5	60.00
F.M.M.Worrell	West Indies	09-12-1960	22-08-1963	15	9	3	1	2	60.00
Waqar Younis	Pakistan	01-12-1993	02-01-2003	17	10	7	0	0	58.82
V.Kohli	India	09-12-2014	11-01-2022	68	40	17	0	11	58.82
A.L.Hassett	Australia	24-12-1949	15-08-1953	24	14	4	0	6	58.33
J.M.Brearley	England	16-06-1977	27-08-1981	31	18	4	0	9	58.06

Minimum 15 Tests

Team Bowling Strike-rate by Captain

Captain	Team	Balls	Wkts	Balls/Wkt
F.du Plessis	South Africa	29406	610	48.20
V.Kohli	India	60856	1205	50.50
P.J.Cummins	Australia	18379	351	52.36
B.A.Stokes	**England**	**19162**	**358**	**53.52**
S.R.Waugh	Australia	55733	1031	54.05
I.V.A.Richards	West Indies	47548	862	55.16
Wasim Akram	Pakistan	23096	418	55.25
S.P.D.Smith	Australia	37753	669	56.43
R.T.Ponting	Australia	78786	1392	56.59
L.Hutton	England	22682	399	56.84

Team Bowling Strike-rate by Captain for England

Captain	Balls	Wkts	Balls/Wkt
B.A.Stokes	**19162**	**358**	**53.52**
L.Hutton	22682	399	56.84
A.C.MacLaren	20343	352	57.79
J.E.Root	61079	1052	58.05
M.P.Vaughan	51176	872	58.68
A.J.Strauss	48568	817	59.44
A.N.Cook	59750	991	60.29
J.M.Brearley	33016	543	60.80
P.B.H.May	44219	702	62.99
N.Hussain	41683	640	65.12

Minimum 350 wickets

% of Wins where Team Batted Fewer than 140 Overs in the Match

Years	Wins	<140 overs	%
1877–1939	198	68	34.34
1946–1959	136	25	18.38
1960–1979	211	26	12.32
1980–1999	366	103	28.14
2000–2022	699	196	28.04
Bazball	**13**	**12**	**92.30**

% of Wins as Captain where Team Batted Fewer than 140 Overs in the Match

Name	Team	Wins	<140 overs	%
B.A.Stokes	**England**	**13**	**12**	**92.30**
R.B.Richardson	West Indies	11	7	63.63
N.Hussain	England	17	8	47.05
P.J.Cummins	Australia	11	5	45.45
Imran Khan	Pakistan	14	6	42.85
Javed Miandad	Pakistan	14	6	42.85
I.V.A.Richards	West Indies	27	11	40.74
Babar Azam	Pakistan	10	4	40.00
S.P.Fleming	New Zealand	28	11	39.28
F.du Plessis	South Africa	18	7	38.88

Individual Player Strike Rates Before and During Bazball

Batting		Before Bazball				Bazball			
Name	M	Runs	Avg	SR	M	Runs	Avg	SR	SR diff
J.M.Anderson	18	77	5.92	34.22	14	78	7.80	46.98	12.76
J.M.Bairstow	13	771	33.52	51.46	12	1003	59.00	89.31	37.85
S.C.J.Broad	14	201	15.46	64.01	15	250	13.88	75.30	11.29
Z.Crawley	17	923	28.84	55.77	18	1117	34.90	78.49	22.72
M.J.Leach	12	157	11.21	29.84	13	69	8.62	37.91	8.07
O.J.D.Pope	16	602	22.29	50.63	15	1104	42.46	77.04	26.41
O.E.Robinson	9	125	8.92	38.94	10	227	18.91	72.06	33.12
J.E.Root	25	2290	52.04	55.00	18	1527	58.73	75.63	20.63
B.A.Stokes	16	1005	33.50	52.56	18	1056	39.11	69.56	17.00
M.A.Wood	11	172	10.11	54.60	5	160	26.66	107.38	52.78

Before is 1 August 2020 to 31 May 2022

Bowling		Before Bazball						Bazball						
Name	M	Balls	Runs	Wkts	Avg	RPO	SR	M	Balls	Runs	Wkts	Avg	RPO	SR	SR diff
J.M.Anderson	18	3617	1344	56	24.00	2.22	64.58	14	2821	1220	50	24.40	2.59	56.42	8.16
S.C.J.Broad	14	2496	1105	52	21.25	2.65	48.00	15	3123	1787	67	26.67	3.43	46.61	1.39
M.J.Leach	12	3211	1532	45	34.04	2.86	71.35	13	3091	1720	45	38.22	3.33	68.68	2.67
O.E.Robinson	9	1888	830	39	21.28	2.63	48.41	10	1830	858	37	23.18	2.81	49.45	-1.04
J.E.Root	25	1196	644	17	37.88	3.23	70.35	18	1057	614	15	40.93	3.48	70.46	-0.11
B.A.Stokes	16	1567	785	27	29.07	3.00	58.03	18	1221	729	23	31.69	3.58	53.08	4.95
M.A.Wood	11	1975	1109	34	32.61	3.36	58.08	5	885	446	22	20.27	3.02	40.22	17.86

Batting differential is shown as Bazball strike-rate minus pre-Bazball strike-rate.
Bowling differential is shown as pre-Bazball strike-rate minus Bazball strike-rate.

England Averages Under Bazball

BATTING AND FIELDING

S/Rate		M	I	NO	HS	Runs	Avge	100	50	Ct/St
91.76	H.C.Brook	12	20	1	186	1181	62.15	4	7	9
89.31	J.M.Bairstow	12	20	3	162	1003	59.00	4	4	41/1
75.63	J.E.Root	18	31	5	176	1527	58.73	5	7	31
89.23	B.M.Duckett	11	21	2	182	1011	53.21	2	6	12
77.04	O.J.D.Pope	15	27	1	205	1104	42.46	3	5	24/1
69.56	B.A.Stokes	18	29	2	155	1056	39.11	2	4	18
51.81	B.T.Foakes	9	14	3	113*	428	38.90	1	3	35/1
78.49	Z.Crawley	18	34	2	189	1117	34.90	2	5	28
107.38	M.A.Wood	5	8	2	36*	160	26.66	-	-	-
65.21	M.M.Ali	4	7	-	54	180	25.71	-	1	-
55.23	A.Z.Lees	7	13	-	67	327	25.15	-	2	5
98.88	W.G.Jacks	2	4	-	31	89	22.25	-	-	-
79.79	C.R.Woakes	3	5	1	36	79	19.75	-	-	1
72.06	O.E.Robinson	10	15	3	39	227	18.91	-	-	4
75.30	S.C.J.Broad	15	20	2	42	250	13.88	-	-	4
37.91	M.J.Leach	13	15	7	15	69	8.62	-	-	7
46.98	J.M.Anderson	14	17	7	12	78	7.80	-	-	6
46.87	M.J.Potts	6	6	2	19	30	7.50	-	-	5

Also batted: R.Ahmed (1 Test) 1, 10; S.W.Billings (2) 36 (3 ct); L.S.Livingstone (1) 9, 7*; J.Overton (1) 97; M.W.Parkinson (1) 8; J.C.Tongue (2) 1, 19 (1 ct).

BOWLING

	O	M	R	W	Avge	Best	5wI	S/Rate
C.R.Woakes	113.2	22	345	19	18.16	5-62	1	35.78
M.A.Wood	147.3	23	446	22	20.27	5-34	1	40.22
O.E.Robinson	305	67	858	37	23.18	5-49	1	49.45
J.M.Anderson	470.1	119	1220	50	24.40	5-60	1	56.42
J.C.Tongue	76	13	257	10	25.70	5-66	1	45.60
S.C.J.Broad	520.3	98	1787	67	26.67	5-51	1	46.61
M.J.Potts	216.1	48	673	23	29.26	4-13	-	56.39
B.A.Stokes	203.3	25	729	23	31.69	4-33	-	53.08
M.J.Leach	515.1	104	1720	45	38.22	5-66	3	68.68
J.E.Root	176.1	24	614	15	40.93	2-19	-	70.46
Also bowled:								
R.Ahmed	36.5	3	137	7	19.57	5-48	1	31.57
W.G.Jacks	54.3	5	232	6	38.66	6-161	1	54.50
M.M.Ali	126	15	463	9	51.44	3-76	-	84.00

H.C.Brook 14-2-37-1; J.Overton 37-4-146-2; M.W.Parkinson 15.3-0-47-1.

Acknowledgements

International cricketers lead busy lives and face countless demands. None of them was obliged to speak to us for this book but, almost to a man, they agreed. We are grateful they gave so generously of their time to help us tell the Bazball story, even if we weren't supposed to call it that. Thank you to those who helped set up interviews: Tim Bostock, John Curtis, James Price, Adam Sofrionou. At Bloomsbury, Ian Marshall was the best kind of editor, encouraging, enthusiastic and with unerring eye for the better adjective. Thanks, too, to his colleague Fabrice Wilmann, and everyone else in the Bloomsbury team. Andrew Samson provided some typically illuminating stats. Our agent, David Luxton, was a constant source of wisdom and optimism, even when it was raining on the last day of the Ashes at The Oval.

Nick Hoult writes: My thanks go firstly to Catriona, my wife, and daughters Abigail and Sophia for putting up with a lot of cricket chat and my long absences on the road. Catriona's first response to the book idea was a blank look and the question: 'What is Bazball?' Hopefully we have answered that, both for cricket fans and, like her, non-cricket fans. My *Daily Telegraph* cricket-writing colleagues are a constant source of knowledge, and my thanks go to Scyld Berry,

Will Macpherson and Tim Wigmore. I would also like to thank Gary Payne, the former *Telegraph* head of sport, as well as colleagues Jake Goodwill, Julian Bennetts and Jack De Menezes for their direction and support during the Ashes.

Lawrence Booth writes: My colleagues at the *Daily Mail* were as supportive as I knew they would be – thanks in particular to Lee Clayton, Marc Padgett, Paul Newman and Richard Gibson. Above all, thank you to my wife, Anjali, who is the best mum to our girls, Aleya and Anoushka, and bears a lot of the family's mental load, especially while I'm away watching cricket. I'm lucky both that she's so understanding, and to be able to call it work.

Note on the authors

Lawrence Booth has edited the last twelve editions of *Wisden Cricketers' Almanack*, and has won awards for his work with the *Daily Mail*, including the SJA's coveted Scoop of the Year prize.

@BoothCricket

Nick Hoult is chief cricket correspondent of the *Daily Telegraph* and was voted Cricket Journalist of the Year by the SJA in 2020.

@NHoultCricket